Accomplished Teaching

The Key to National Board Certification

• Revised Second Edition •

Bess A. Jennings, M.Ed., NBCT
MaryAnn D. Joseph, M.Ed., NBCT
with Frank J. Orlando, Ed.D.

KENDALL/HUNT PUBLISHING COMPANY
4050 Westmark Drive   Dubuque, Iowa 52002

Cover image:
Wave image (c) CoKo, 2007
Book image (c) Kmitu, 2007
Used under license from Shutterstock, Inc.

Printed in the United States of America
10 9 8 7 6 5 4 3

CONTENTS

List of Figures

Preface

The great promise of the National Board is that it clearly delineates standards for accomplished teaching and creates the prospect for a career continuum from entry to expert practice.

-The National Commission on Teaching and America's Future. 1996.
What Matters Most: Teaching for America's Future. New York: Author

As the Director of the National University Support and Leadership Center and the President of the California Association of NBCTs, I celebrate and applaud the National Board for Professional Teaching Standards organization, all that it represents and all that it charges us to do as professional educators and on behalf of the children we serve.

While teachers and school districts wrestle with the challenge of producing, employing and keeping high quality teachers, the NBPTS provides solutions to the problems and frustrations we face: teacher effectiveness, recruitment and retention issues, unacceptable achievement levels, ineffective professional development and lack of collaborative leadership opportunities.

The National Board provides all educators with a common language around what highly accomplished teachers should know and be able to do in the subjects that they teach and in alignment with the developmental levels of the students they serve. These standards are consistent with NCATE and INTASC accreditation criteria.

Simply by being exposed to these standards, at the very least, a teacher begins to transform his/her way of thinking and responding to teaching and learning. As teachers engage in the development of the NBCT portfolio entries, they are challenged to take greater responsibility for their own learning. To demonstrate accomplished teaching, they seek out resources to address their strengths and areas in need of improvement identified in their own performances as measured against the high and rigorous standards described in their certificate area of expertise.

At National University, our Chancellor and Faculty have embraced the mission, vision and goals of the NBPTS in multiple ways. Our overarching goal is to support teachers, administrators and school districts in their efforts to increase student achievement by utilizing the tools that the NBPTS provides through a collaborative model. Our NU-NBCT Support and Leadership Center serves communities across California and offers opportunities for professional development, support for candidates, graduate degrees and adjunct faculty positions for NBCTs. Most impressive are our two Master's Degree programs that require students to develop the NBCT portfolio, either as an active or pre-candidate. Certified Support Providers serve as NBCT adjunct faculty who teach in the NBCT master's programs online, on ground or in hybrid delivery modes in states across the nation. Our goal is not to count the number of teachers who certify as a result of participation in our program, but rather, the number of students who provide evidence that their teaching and student learning improved as a result of engaging in the development of the portfolio exercises and aligned assignments.

The California Association of NBCTs (CaNBCT) is dedicated to providing all children with learning environments that enhance their full potential to achieve and succeed. We believe that National Board Certified Teachers and candidates are the key to creating schools that foster the academic excellence our children need to become successful, both in school and as members of our society. As with many other state NBCT organizations, the CaNBCT provides NBC Teacher Leaders with a platform for mobilizing so that their collective energy, expertise and knowledge is utilized in ways that penetrate and strengthen the educational system at the local, state and national levels.

This book, *Accomplished Teaching: The Key to National Board Certification*, effectively aligns with the NBPTS code of ethics and provides teachers with a resource that will support them as they analyze and reflect on the judgments and decisions they make about their practices and professional contributions, the achievement of their students and the steps they will take to continuously learn and develop in their professional careers. It is the best resource I have found to accompany instructors in our five NBCT university courses, as an aid for support providers and for teachers who choose to travel the NBCT journey alone.

Don't wait for someone else to encourage you — explore the NBCT assessment through the pages of this well organized book, start your Master's Degree with a NBCT focus, or go to the nbpts.org website and apply to be an active candidate!

So many choices, so many demands, so little time, but no excuses for not offering your most accomplished teaching to the students you serve.

Enjoy!

Ronarae Adams, NBCT
President, CA Association of NBCTs
Director, NBCT Support and Leadership Center and Lead Faculty
National University
San Diego Headquarters
radams@nu.edu

Acknowledgements

The National Board for Professional Teaching Standards (NBPTS)

As with the first edition, this text would not be possible without public access to the materials provided by the National Board for Professional Teaching Standards. Throughout this book, you will find numerous references to key documents and phrases used in these materials, which are available at the NBPTS website: www.nbpts.org. We thank the NBPTS for living the model of Core Proposition 5; *Teachers Are Members of Learning Communities*, in making the National Board Certification materials widely available for discussions about accomplished teaching.

NBPTS documents and terms are intrinsic to the use of this book, and it is our intent that the book be used in tandem with the source material. We acknowledge these original sources as the work of the National Board for Professional Teaching Standards. In lieu of footnoting each and every time these documents and phrases are referenced, the following information is provided to help the reader locate the source material:

Key Documents:
The following documents are available as editions specific to each area of National Board Certification. All editions are found at www.nbpts.org, under headings for individual certificate areas:

- Standards
- Portfolio Instructions, including The Five Core Propositions
- Scoring Guide, including the Level 4, 3, 2, and 1 rubrics

Key Terms and Phrases:
Used throughout the text to focus the reader's attention on accomplished teaching as defined by the NBPTS, the following terms and phrases have their origin in materials developed and provided by the National Board for Professional Teaching Standards:

- The Five Core Propositions (Portfolio Instructions: Introduction)
  1. *Teachers are committed to students and their learning.*
  2. *Teachers know the subjects they teach and how to teach those subjects to students.*
  3. *Teachers are responsible for managing and monitoring student learning.*
  4. *Teachers think systematically about their practice and learn from experience.*

5. *Teachers are members of learning communities.*

- *Clear, convincing and consistent evidence*
  (Portfolio Instructions, Level 4 rubric)
- *These students, at this time, in this setting*
- *The architecture of accomplished teaching*
  (NBPTS Facilitator Training I material, 2001)

Individuals

We would also like to thank the following outstanding teachers whose words of wisdom are found throughout this book. They are all part of a growing community of NBCTs and supporters, some of them new friends, NBCTs or candidates that we have met since our last edition. We thank all, new and old, for continuing to give us inspiration and insight.

- Shirley Allen
      NBCT, Early Adolescence/English Language Arts
- Loren Ayersman
      High School Mathematics, Hawaii State Dept. of Education
- Merry Blechta
      Elementary Generalist, Hawaii State Dept. of Education
- Michael Breslow
      NBCT, EA Science
- Colleen Collins
      NBCT, Early Childhood Through Young Adult/
      Exceptional Needs Specialist
- Pascale Creek Pinner
      NBCT, Early Adolescence/Science
- Nina Garcia
      Elementary Generalist, Hawaii State Dept. of Education
- Sue Hovey
      Founding Member National Board for Professional
      Teaching Standards, 1987-1993;
      NBPTS Support Program Facilitator, University of Idaho
- Ben Joseph
      Student Teacher, St. Joseph's University, PA
- AbbyMarie Joseph
      Physical Therapist, Philadelphia, PA
- Judy Locke
      NBCT, Middle Childhood Generalist
- Dr. Robert O'Boyle,
      NBCT, Early Adolescence through Young Adulthood/Art
- Kathy Prisbell
      NBCT, Early Adolescence/English Language Arts

- Christine Rodek
    NBCT, Early Childhood/Generalist
- Ruth Ann Santos
    NBCT, Early and Middle Childhood Literacy: Reading-
    Language Arts
- Wendy Smith
    NBCT, Early Childhood/Generalist
- Tonya Uibel
    NBCT, Middle Childhood Generalist
- Ingrid Williams
    NBCT, Early Adolescence through Young
    Adult/Mathematics

We thankfully acknowledge Matthew Morehouse and Sara Morehouse whose illustrations from the first edition, drawn when they were age 12 and 10, continue to brighten these pages.

Gregory Joseph deserves special thanks for the formatting and editing the text and CD.   Christopher Joseph deserves recognition for his support and time spent reading the manuscript.

Many friends and colleagues have contributed in spirit to this second edition of *Accomplished Teaching, The Key to National Board Certification.* In person, by phone, and on-line, they have effectively erased issues of time and distance as members of a nationwide teaching community dedicated to continued improvement of the teaching profession. These on-going conversations keep us firmly grounded in the cycle of reflection and renewal as we seek to deepen our own understanding through new perspectives on candidate support. We are particularly grateful for input and clarification from individuals associated with the National Board for Professional Teaching Standards through Candidate Support Provider trainings as well as informal conversations.

Finally, we thank our families and friends for their patience and support as we covered all available surfaces with various resources and piles of papers, poured over numerous drafts, and worked long hours at our computers and telephones to bring this new edition to completion.

If you are returning to these pages as an old friend, we are pleased that you have found our work helpful, and hope that the new material in this second edition will continue to support your efforts. If you are a new reader, welcome! We are pleased to have you join us in the rewarding dialogue about the National Board Teaching Standards and wish you success in your own journey of accomplished teaching.

About the Authors

MaryAnn Joseph and Bess Jennings

Since their first edition of ***Accomplished Teaching, the Key to National Board Certification***, Bess Jennings and MaryAnn Joseph have had the privilege of presenting their work nationally, including presentations at NBPTS Conferences. Across the country, they continue to work with colleagues as teacher leaders. For both MaryAnn and Bess, being an NBCT means an opportunity to continue learning from candidates and other colleagues the real meaning of accomplished teaching. They share the fruits of their continued collaboration within these new pages.

Bess lives in a rural area on the island of Hawaii. As a Complex Area Resource Teacher for the Hawaii State Department of Education, she works as a member of the leadership team for local area schools to promote standards-based teaching practices and assist with the implementation of various state initiatives. She is also an adjunct faculty member and Hawaii program liaison for an online NBC Master's Degree developed by National University in La Jolla, California.

In New Jersey, MaryAnn is the program coordinator for the Educational Information and Resource Center NBPTS statewide support classes. She is a member of CAPP – the Committee to Advance Professional Practice, a group of professional and business persons who are working to promote the professional development of teachers through the National Board Teaching Standards in New Jersey.

Introduction

"The best thing about my teacher is her way of understanding and explaining things." (Student, Age 15)
- Judy Gordon Morrow[1]

It has been our pleasure to revisit, reflect on and revise the first edition of *Accomplished Teaching: The Key to National Board Certification.* It is our goal to explain this subject well, so that other teachers will understand and feel successful in their own journey of accomplished teaching.

We hope that this second edition will more effectively guide teachers—both candidates and non-candidates—who engage in a study of the National Board Teaching Standards. The importance of the Teaching Standards and the assessment process is increasingly evident in the profession, as the National Board for Professional Teaching Standards (NBPTS) has given the profession a common language for discussions of accomplished teaching and the tools to help teachers review and improve their practices. While many fine teachers will choose not to engage in the National Board Certification process, our intent is to encourage all educators to know and use the Standards to guide their practices.

Since the first edition was published, we have continued our work with candidates and other support providers and are most thankful to the ever-growing professional learning community that surrounds the National Board Certification process. It is through our conversations and work with you that we continue to develop and deepen our own understanding of accomplished teaching. For those of you who join us after finding our first edition helpful, we welcome you back. For those of you who are with us for a first read, we look forward to working with you in the chapters that follow. We hope that, through these pages, we have contributed to the dialogue on accomplished teaching and to the strength of our profession.

Big Ideas

Our work on the first edition of the book was largely shaped by our own experiences in working with candidates, as well as through conversations with other candidate support providers. From all over the country, it was apparent that those involved in the certification process shared common feelings and concerns. There was, and still is, great appreciation for the value of the process and its potential to improve the teaching profession.

At the same time, most support providers describe similar issues and challenges in working with candidates. Time is often limited, and support opportunities vary considerably from one area to another. As a result, we chose three big ideas to frame our discussion of accomplished teaching. They are:

1. As professional educators, all teachers should know and embrace the NBPTS Standards.

2. The National Board Certification process is a powerful professional development experience requiring the acquisition of new skills for most teachers; therefore,

3. Candidates are entitled to quality support as they engage in the National Board Certification process.

All teachers should know and embrace the NBPTS Standards:

...if we want to improve the quality of teaching and learning for all students, we have to be able to go beyond merely identifying accomplished teachers. We need to know how to make teachers into accomplished teachers.

- Jill Harrison Berg, NBCT[2]

Regardless of National Board Certification, The Five Core Propositions and the Standards developed by NBPTS have provided our profession with a common foundation and vision for discussions of accomplished teaching.   Just as state-developed standards define what well-prepared students should know and be able to do, the NBPTS Standards describe what accomplished teachers should know and be able to do.

In the public arena, the teaching profession is buffeted by outside forces like no other, and educators are pressured to achieve outstanding results no matter what learning challenges their students bring to the classroom. The National Board Teaching Standards help define the body of knowledge that is specific to the work of the profession; and provide an anchor for its members in the core propositions of accomplished teaching.

The Standards encourage teachers to share their insights, to seek improvement in the profession, and to keep student learning at the heart of the discussion. Potentially, they will define an identity for the profession that includes advocacy based on knowledge of human development and learning as a counterpoint to policies based on political expediency.

We believe all teachers can, and should be, encouraged to use the Standards as a guide for improvement, either as an individual endeavor or within the context of professional development sessions offered by school districts, universities, or other organizations. The text is purposefully written to include and support teachers who may choose to measure their teaching practices against the Standards without seeking National Board Certification.

The National Board Certification process is a powerful professional development experience requiring the acquisition of new skills for most teachers:

> *As a candidate and veteran (27 years) teacher, I was overwhelmed by the entire process.... Candidates need a well-paved road map... and user-friendly materials to guide the veteran teacher through a truly novice educational experience.*
>
> *-Shirley Allen, NBCT*

No matter how experienced in the classroom, few teachers are accustomed to the deep, conscious analysis and reflection called for in a NBPTS portfolio entry. Most have never thought about the core structure of their instruction nor have they been asked to provide "evidence" of good practice by writing about their teaching. These skills are intrinsic to successful National Board Certification, and are a common focus of candidate support sessions.

Teachers who have hesitated in the past now have a new opportunity to test their practices against the Standards. They may complete, submit, and receive a score on a single portfolio entry through the *Take One* materials developed by NBPTS, then decide if they want to complete the remainder of the assessment process. Whether teachers complete one or four entries, they need support for developing new skills and practice in applying them as they construct evidence of teaching to the Standards in portfolio entries.

The National Board Certification process is consistent with national trends, providing a powerful tool for documenting, improving, and articulating one's teaching. Most teachers want and deserve assistance to develop and practice these skills until they are imbedded in pedagogy. Throughout the text, teachers are encouraged to read their Standards, provide evidence, and maintain habits of reflection on their teaching— activities that appear in the mainstream of current literature on professional improvement practices.

Candidates need to be supported through the National Board Certification process:

> *We experienced the inspiration of collaborative efforts, both on the part of the National Board and from each other. We also discovered the vitality of alternative and authentic assessments, gained confidence in our professional skills and learned what it means to be an excellent educator.*
>
> *- Rick Wormeli, NBCT[3]*

Candidates should be encouraged to participate in support programs, especially those designed as professional learning communities. Many teachers feel overwhelmed at their first encounter with the National Board Certification materials and requirements. Support programs help candidates understand the relationship between the documents and other resources, provide a systematic approach to the National Board assessment task, and help candidates develop the thinking and writing skills needed to submit an accomplished portfolio entry.

Support systems also play a critical role in sustaining teachers through the rigor of the process over extended periods of time. Although candidates can and do earn National Board Certification in the course of a single year, many teachers will need more time to achieve success. After the first year as a candidate, a teacher is given two additional years as an "advanced candidate" to achieve National Board Certification. New skills and perspectives grow through the candidates' consistent use of analytical, reflective practice in writing their entries. As they think more deeply about specific aspects of teaching and learning, their discourse becomes more deliberate and focused. Some teachers simply need additional time to develop these skills and may achieve a deeper understanding of accomplished teaching as a result of their prolonged engagement in the process.

We know that curriculum for students must "spiral" to revisit previously learned concepts at new levels, and adult learners also need to revisit material as they proceed through different stages in the learning process. The book is intended to serve as a resource for this purpose, leading teachers to ever-deeper layers of analysis, reflection, and understanding as teaching practice is examined and re-examined against the Standards.

A New Vision for Studying the NBPTS Standards

In an effort to address the issues above, this book was written with the intent to provide teachers a key to understanding and developing the skills of accomplished teaching needed for successful National Board Certification. Based on our work with candidates over the past several years, our goal is to give new candidates and prospective candidates a quality support experience. Identifiable elements of the National Board Certification process are provided in a form that allows teachers to proceed at their own pace through the process and revisit the material many times over. This book is not meant to supplant candidate support sessions, but to supplement and enhance them.

One of the persistent dilemmas in support sessions is the use of time. In any group, the needs of individuals are different. Some candidates move forward rapidly, while others need more time to process and absorb information. It is challenging to find the balance between providing enough information to ensure value for everyone, while not overwhelming individuals with too much in a single session. There are always candidates who lag far behind the rest and ask questions covered in previous sessions when others are ready to move forward. There is often little time for one-to-one conversations with candidates who need feedback on their individual entries. Learners have different needs, understandings, and areas of concern in regard to their portfolio work. Advanced candidates in their second or third year are not well served by support sessions for new candidates, as their questions are different.

In the past, we found ourselves doing much of the talking in group support sessions, as we provided necessary information and guidance to candidates. Now, with the book as a resource for candidates, we can provide more time for teachers to converse with their peers, hear new perspectives, and re-examine many aspects of their teaching through the lens of the National Board Standards.

Success in the National Board Certification process is more likely when teachers have been well prepared for the experience and understand what is expected of them. Interested teachers should know what they need to do before they decide to enter the process. Both candidates and facilitators of teacher learning communities will find this book a useful tool for this purpose. It serves as a reference for understanding the National Board Certification process and for developing the skills of accomplished teaching.

On the Second Edition

We are grateful to all the teachers and candidate support providers who praised the first edition of the book and found it useful in their work. We hoped that it would be well-received and it has surpassed our expectations, as it has become the text of choice for both individual candidates and for numerous candidate support programs based in higher education settings. As with any aspect of teaching, however, one's work is never done, and we have been eager to add new dimensions to the original text.

As we embarked on this revision, we knew there were areas in need of improvement, but we did not want to disappoint our readers by editing out material that they have found useful. While much of the original material has been reorganized, nearly all of it is still in this revised edition. We have added new sections, including chapters on student-centered teaching, reflective practice, and working with advanced candidates; and reordered information to incorporate these chapters and to improve overall fluency.

We have expanded the discussion of evidence for accomplished teaching, and have added new figures and exercises to support candidates' growth in the process. The information on candidate support has been divided between two chapters: One for candidates at the beginning of the book, and the other for candidate support providers at the end of the book. Finally, Entry 4 has been given a much-deserved chapter of its own.

The result, we think, is a much richer edition that is well-synthesized with current trends in education and well-positioned to support the professional growth of teachers at all stages of their careers. As with the first edition, candidates can work independently between support sessions, reading and re-reading sections of interest as they grow through or toward National Board Certification. They can pace themselves through the process and gain additional value from group sessions. We believe it will help them develop the deep, personal reflection of accomplished teaching, and the confidence to participate fully in a variety of professional learning communities.

In the best of circumstances, it will prompt discussions between educators who see improvement of practice as a career-long commitment. We hope it will be the key that opens the door for deeper conversations about accomplished teaching among teachers, candidates, and support providers who choose to journey the path of the National Board Teaching Standards.

We both start and end where the practice of accomplished teaching ultimately takes us…improved student learning.

Bess A. Jennings, NBCT Early Childhood Generalist, Hawaii
MaryAnn D. Joseph, NBCT Middle Childhood Generalist, New Jersey

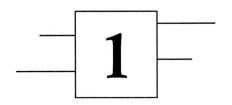

Accomplished Teaching

Congratulations on taking the first steps on a challenging and exciting professional journey! In the months ahead, you will examine your teaching practice in detail. You will be able to articulate the strengths of your work, and may find areas in need of improvement. You will discover a path that leads to greater effectiveness in boosting student learning and greater satisfaction through the focus and clarity it brings to your work in the classroom.

This book is intended to help good teachers become better by guiding them through a self-study via the National Board Certification process. It may be used by individual teachers, participants of formal or informal study groups, and teachers in advanced college courses studying the National Board Standards with or without National Board Certification.

If you are a National Board candidate, it will be your guide to reaching the Standards for accomplished teaching as defined by the National Board for Professional Teaching Standards (NBPTS). If you are a new candidate support provider (CSP), or a teacher learning about the process, it will help you understand what candidates need to do.

Many accomplished teachers may want to measure their teaching against the NBPTS Standards without the formal recognition of National Board Certification. Whether or not you are ready to seek National Board Certification is a personal decision and may depend on your level of experience, current teaching situation, and personal circumstances.

Meeting the Teaching Standards

Becoming a National Board Certified Teacher (NBCT) is a rigorous process. While no one can guarantee your success, as NBCTs and candidate support providers, we believe that any teacher with sufficient experience and motivation can and will achieve National Board Certification. We will acquaint you with the process and expectations for National Board Certification, provide you with a selection of tools to help you meet those expectations, and systematically guide you through a reflective and analytic study of your personal teaching practices.

"I know what I'm doing in the classroom. Why should I study standards for teachers?"

Why should you study the National Board Teaching Standards if you are not ready to seek National Board Certification? Because at some point you will be required to show that your work as a teacher is knowledgeable and purposeful, and that you can produce positive results for student learning.

Our profession is at a crossroads, and we believe that it is important for all educators to study and internalize the National Board Teaching Standards and demonstrate the qualities of accomplished teaching for reasons including the following:

School Reform: At no other time in history has the field of education been subjected to greater scrutiny than it is today. Despite the hard work and dedication of caring teachers nationwide, taxpayers and policymakers alike justifiably ask why student achievement is not higher.

In response to federal demands to improve student test scores, a variety of school reforms are sweeping the country. States are required to have standards for student achievement that establish high expectations, clear targets, and accountability for student learning in a progressively more challenging curriculum. Education is political fodder for well-intentioned but often ill-informed policy makers at local, state, and national levels. The message is clear: If teachers do not take charge of their profession, someone else will.

It is time for teachers to come together under professional standards based on essential principles of good practice: an appreciation for and focus on the strengths of each student and their learning; thorough knowledge and responsibility for teaching to the subject area; responsive instruction based on frequent monitoring; continual improvement of practice; and utilization of resources including current research in education.

...in many states and school districts, the work of teaching is regarded as following procedures or instructional plans designed by others and under the close direction of a supervisor. ...such characteristics define teaching as semi-skilled work in which teachers, at the lowest level of the bureaucratic hierarchy, take direction from their superiors. In recognition of this situation, the educational literature is replete with pleas for teaching to become a true profession.

-Charlotte Danielson [4]

Teachers as Leaders: There is growing consensus that principals alone cannot effect needed changes and that school reform at its best is a collaborative effort. References to teachers as leaders in school reform efforts are on the increase in professional literature.

Never before has the need been so great for classroom teachers to assume leadership roles that position them as problem solvers and change agents in their local schools.

-NBPTS Director of Teacher Outreach [5]

Research cited by NBPTS has linked the National Board Certification process with the development of teacher leadership in school reform efforts. NBCTs demonstrate a desire to serve in leadership roles that include being professional development leaders, supervising student teachers, and serving as team leaders and mentors, and virtually all are engaged in at least one such leadership activity in their schools. [6]

Accomplished teachers are key figures on school faculties, contributing to curriculum decisions, modeling professional behavior and attitudes, and often mentoring newcomers to the profession. Most importantly, teacher leaders have a profound influence on the fundamental culture of a school, helping to shape how people think and act on their campuses. By helping to create a climate of collegiality, open communication, and support, teacher leaders promote learning in both adults and students at their schools.

Accountability: "Accountability" is a key issue in school reform, and there are high expectations for teachers as well as for students. Today's teachers not only must understand their content area, but also must understand child development, differentiation of instruction for individual students and the social/cultural barriers and issues of their communities. Measurable student learning must occur despite the growing numbers of students falling into special needs groups including the economically disadvantaged, second language learners, and those with identifiable disabilities. Teachers may recognize individual student learning needs, but without clearly identified teaching strategies and methods that result in improved in student outcomes, educational decision-making is often left to politicians who advocate for mandated curriculum materials as the method of insuring student achievement.

Conversations surrounding the issue of teacher quality are at the forefront. There is no doubt that nationwide, teachers are being called to meet high standards of quality, and rightfully so. All children deserve a quality education delivered by capable teachers.

Reflective Practice: Abundant research has identified deliberate reflection as a characteristic of effective teachers. The practice implies that such teachers know the needs of their students, implement lessons that are designed to address those needs, assess student progress, and think about what they might do differently to improve their students' learning. Though the average teacher thinks about his or her classroom far beyond the hours spent on campus, reflective practice suggests conscious and deliberate thinking that includes seeking new information and constantly striving to improve one's impact on student learning. It strives to answer the question: *How can I better address the learning needs of each of my students?*

Reflective practice is inherent in the National Board Certification process as prompting questions ask teachers to explain and justify their professional decisions in each of the required entries. Teachers who do not regularly reflect on their teaching will learn to do so during their candidacy. Due to this aspect of the Certification process, it has become recognized as a powerful professional development tool that helps develop, as well as identify, accomplished teaching practices that result in improved student learning.

Professional Learning Communities: It is well documented that rich reflective practice does not occur in isolation.   Professional dialogue among committed teachers is both enriching and energizing as teachers feel empowered to positively impact student learning. Such dialogue is fostered when teachers are able to meet frequently and purposefully.

A group of teachers that meets regularly to talk about effective teaching practices is popularly described in current literature as a professional learning community (PLC), and is cited as a key element for school reform and the improvement of instructional practices. As defined by school reform specialist Mike Schmoker, professional learning communities have the greatest impact on student learning when teachers establish and teach to a common, concise set of essential curricular standards, make use of common assessments, and meet regularly to analyze and share teaching practices. They are often organized for the purpose of analyzing student work samples and discussing strategies to meet specific learning targets.[7]

In the best of circumstances, professional learning communities generate small, but frequent "wins" that initiate and sustain continuous improvement. They create a culture where monitoring is not necessary and real professionals are best left alone to engage in seeking answers to powerful reflective questions. They:

- Engage educators in dialogue
- Encourage teachers in leadership practices for new team structures
- Allow evaluation to be owned by the teacher teams
- Reward, recognize and celebrate teachers to promote further enthusiastic work

While not identical to the classic model, a professional learning community that focuses on the National Board Portfolio requirements is similarly specific, providing forums for reflective dialogue to explore the NBPTS Standards and the meaning of "evidence" as applied to those Standards.

For this reason, many educational leaders are looking to the National Board portfolio as the shared project for a school or district-based professional learning community. Participants may or may not be candidates for National Board Certification, but have the shared desire to improve their teaching practices and measure themselves against the NBPTS Standards for accomplished teaching. The questions imbedded in the Portfolio entries are used to prompt reflections on teaching and learning. As they are open-ended, they invite dialogue on diverse issues related to professional practice.

Whatever the basis for discussion, the professional learning community concept assumes the experts are among us. They are the teachers. Through rich discussion in a community of fellow professionals, they shine the light on their own instructional practices for the purpose of improving their services to students.

> *When teachers recognize that knowledge for improvement is something they can generate rather than something that must be handed to them by so-called experts they are on a new professional trajectory. They are on the way to building a true profession of teaching. In a profession where the members take responsibility for steady and lasting improvement, they are building a new culture of teaching.*
>
> *-Heibert and Stigler* [8]

Teacher Quality and Professionalism: Nationwide, there is a renewed emphasis on teacher quality and conversations surrounding this issue are at the forefront. There is no doubt that all teachers are being called to meet high standards of effectiveness, and rightfully so, as all children deserve a quality education.

We believe the National Board Teaching Standards provide educators with a common language to describe accomplished teaching, and that the

Standards are sorely needed to improve the status and quality of the profession.

> *Teachers stand very little chance of improving their salaries and working conditions if policymakers and the public accept the idea that teaching requires little more than enthusiasm, knowledge of a subject, and a dollop of coaching or night courses.*
>
> *-John O'Neil[9]*

The present climate of reform was fueled in part by the 1983 report, *A Nation at Risk: The Imperative for Educational Reform* produced by the President's National Commission on Excellence in Education.[10] Three years later an equally significant report was issued by the Carnegie Task Force on Teaching as a Profession, *A Nation Prepared: Teachers for the 21st Century.*[11] Just as standards define what students should know and be able to do, the report declared that as is the case in other professions, there must be standards for what accomplished teachers should know and be able to do.

Following the recommendations of this report, a panel of educational professionals met to establish the National Board for Professional Teaching Standards and to develop standards and an assessment to define accomplished teaching. In 1994, the first group of 86 teachers to demonstrate evidence of teaching to these Standards became NBCTs, and the movement for voluntary National Board Certification was born. Since then, the number of teachers seeking NBPTS certification has grown each year. In twelve years, there were over 55,000 National Board Certified Teachers.[12]

The National Board for Professional Teaching Standards

The mission of NBPTS is to establish high and rigorous Standards for what accomplished teachers should know and be able to do; to develop and operate a national, voluntary system to assess and certify teachers who meet these Standards; and to advance related education reforms for the purpose of improving student learning in American schools.[13]

Through the National Board Certification process and related research, NBPTS has raised awareness of the profession and the expertise of teachers. With a common language about what teachers should know and be able to do, The Five Core Propositions and Standards help us define our profession. The NBPTS Standards have been infused into teacher education programs at colleges and universities. National Board has partnered with the National Council for Accreditation of Teacher Education (NCATE) and the Interstate New Teacher Assessment and Support Consortium (INTASC) to help institutions modify existing teacher preparation programs to be clearly aligned with The NBPTS Five

Core Propositions for accomplished teaching.[14] In many states, elements of the National Board Certification process are finding a way into teacher licensing and renewal requirements and master's degree programs.[15]

> *The great promise of the National Board is that it clearly delineates standards for accomplished teaching and creates the prospect for a career continuum from entry to expert practice.*
>
> *-The National Commission on Teaching and America's Future[16]*

At the heart of National Board Certification is deep reflective practice—a vital aspect of the profession, effecting and sustaining improvements in practice for both beginning and veteran teachers. Elements of the NBPTS Certification process, which require teachers to look critically at their work, find evidence of good practice, and use that information to improve teaching in the classroom, are found in education reform nationwide.

> *The accomplishments of these teachers represent the best of the profession, the path we could choose to take in meeting the challenge of finding highly qualified teachers. As a group, they demonstrate how investing in teachers' professional knowledge and development can pay off, not only in the classroom but in the profession as a whole.*
>
> *-Pam Grossman[17]*

The NBPTS invites research to measure the impact of the assessment process. With more than 150 studies, reports, and papers as of August, 2006, National Board Certification is the most thoroughly grounded, in research terms, of any assessment program in the teaching profession. Numerous studies have confirmed that, in comparison to non-NBCTs, National Board Certified Teachers make a positive impact on student achievement gains, sustained school improvement efforts, and closing the achievement gap between students of higher and lower socio-economic status. In one multi-year study of over 600,000 students, independently funded by the U.S. Department of Education, the learning gains of students taught by NBCTs were most pronounced for younger and lower-income students.[18]

In addition, research supports the value of the National Board Certification process as a tool for professional development. In various studies, NBCTs scored higher than their peers on identified dimensions of teaching expertise, demonstrated dispositions and skills that were in alignment with high-quality teaching, and used student assessment tools more effectively and consistently. Studies have shown that teachers who pursued National Board Certification showed significant improvements in their teaching practices, whether they achieved certification or not.

When surveyed, teachers overwhelmingly agreed that the National Board Certification process was better than other professional development experiences, and had positively impacted their teaching practices. The process is increasingly recognized as an effective, cost efficient avenue for professional development.[19]

With few exceptions, our candidates consistently tell us that, regardless of their success in achieving National Board Certification, the experience is the most valuable professional development work they have ever done. Over and over, teachers indicate that they have taken the first steps on a life-long journey toward the improvement of student learning.

> *I am so glad that I challenged myself to pursue the NBPTS certification. The process was rigorous, much like getting a master's degree; however this was much more self-directed and self-reflective. The NBPTS certification process has inspired me to become much more aware of my classroom teaching practices in engaging my students to do their best.... I believe that I have a much more critical eye in creating and presenting relevant and appropriate lessons to my students. The NBPTS process has reshaped me as a teacher and as a learner.*
>
> *-Judy Locke, NBCT Hawaii*

What Every Teacher Should Know

The National Board Certification process is time-consuming, rigorous, and entirely voluntary. Pursuit of National Board Certification is a personal decision, above and beyond licensure, that must be based to a great extent on an individual's circumstances and readiness for the process. No teacher "needs" to become National Board Certified, and many highly capable teachers will not choose to seek National Board Certification.

It is important, however, that educators become familiar with the NBPTS Standards and that they are able to participate in the professional dialogue that is generated among accomplished teachers. It is important that, NBCT or not, they are empowered by the dignity conferred by the Standards, and as professionals constantly strive to improve teaching and learning for their students.

In the 2002–2003 school year, NBPTS made the certification materials available to anyone with an Internet connection. Now, any interested teacher may access the Standards documents and National Board Certification materials by visiting the website of the National Board for Professional Teaching Standards.

Whether they intend to pursue National Board Certification or not, we believe all teachers can and should become familiar with their subject area Standards. Those interested in delving deeper into the National Board Standards are encouraged to participate in study groups that help teachers develop analytic and reflective skills as they practice with the assessment materials. Practicing with the materials in a pre-candidacy period can give teachers a head-start on the process and may increase their chances for success as candidates.

Among NBPTS candidate support providers, there is general recognition of three phases in a teacher's progress toward National Board Certification:

1. *Pre-candidacy* - the teacher learns about National Board Certification requirements and practices the thinking and writing skills demanded by the process;

2. *Candidacy* - the teacher submits the application and completes and submits all sections of the assessment;

3. *Advanced candidacy* - teachers who do not initially achieve National Board Certification are supported through the process of re-submitting selected sections of the assessment.

Some universities have developed programs that anticipate and address the needs of teachers in each of the above phases of the process. Advocates view all teachers as being on a continuum that leads to National Board Certification from the moment they first set foot in a classroom. The NBPTS Teaching Standards provide the context for developing professional excellence in teachers at all phases of their careers.

Fundamentally, National Board Certification is a professional development experience. Most candidates have said it is the most powerful and meaningful professional experience they have ever had. It is a journey through a teacher's practice, involving analysis of one's impact on student learning and documenting practice through reflective writing and related artifacts.

Certification is valid for a ten-year period. The renewal window opens in the eighth year of certification and NBCTs can only renew certification in their original certificate area. Recertification requires classroom teaching in the area of the original certificate and teachers must complete a *profile of professional growth (PPG)*. The recertification process highlights ways the NBCT has continued to demonstrate accomplished teaching as a teacher leader.

Readiness for National Board Certification

Though demanding, the period of candidacy is also very exciting as teachers delve deeply into their practices and recreate themselves as professionals. Although we encourage any teacher to study the National Board materials for professional development purposes, teachers who lack the necessary experience or circumstances for candidacy may soon feel overwhelmed. We encourage teachers to read through the assessment materials to understand the task; then reflect on their ability to commit formally to the certification process.

If, after familiarizing yourself with the assessment task, you are interested in pursuing National Board Certification, it is important for you to determine whether or not you are ready to be candidate at this time. In *The Life Cycle of A Career Teacher*, the authors provide a useful model for self-assessment. Teaching is described as a developmental career with six possible progressive phases: Novice, apprentice, professional, expert, distinguished, and emeritus. At all levels, reflective practice is the catalyst for moving forward as a professional. The authors identify reflective practice as the key to rejuvenating, sustaining, and promoting effectiveness in teachers throughout their careers.[20]

In the first two phases of this model, novice and apprentice, teachers are just learning the basic content and skills for working with students. Usually in their first three years, they are gaining self-confidence, acquiring new strategies, and learning how to respond to the many demands of the profession. These teachers lack the depth of experience needed for candidacy. This explains why NBPTS requires teachers to have at least three years of documented teaching experience in order to be eligible. Even when teachers have more than three years of experience, they should not attempt to pursue National Board Certification unless they can identify themselves as being at or beyond the professional phase.

Teachers move to the professional phase as a result of a conscious effort to improve their practices, and work confidently and effectively with their students. They have acquired a deep understanding of the developmental needs of students and have a wealth of strategies to employ in the classroom. They network with colleagues on a regular basis and take advantage of professional development opportunities.

Expert teachers, according to the authors, "…meet the expectations required for national certification"[21] even if they do not choose to seek it. They continually reflect on their practice and modify instruction to meet individual and group learning needs. They actively seek new ideas through interaction with other expert teachers, apply research findings, and often assume leadership roles in local educational organizations.

The last two phases on the continuum, distinguished and emeritus, describe teachers who may be nearing the close of their careers as they take their vast teaching expertise above and beyond the walls of their school buildings to impact policy, lead by example, and support the careers of those who follow them. Emeritus teachers are those who continue to serve the profession after they have retired from active employment. Few teachers reach the distinguished and emeritus phases.

Using this model, the skills required in the process of National Board Certification are consistent with the phase of the professional teacher. While some candidate support providers believe one should demonstrate expert qualities before seeking National Board Certification, many others regard the process as a tool to reach this level. As the National Board assessment materials are readily available to all interested teachers, they have become tools that help teachers reach and refine their practices at the professional and expert levels.

If you are a teacher who is simply practicing with the portfolio materials before seeking National Board Certification, you have the luxury of stopping any time that other commitments make demands on you. However, if you intend to commit yourself to candidacy, it is critical to make sure you thoroughly understand the task ahead, and are ready in every sense of the word. Here are a few key questions to ask yourself:

1) Are you willing to invest in the process?

The cost for the first year of candidacy is currently $2500 (January 2007). Candidates who need to retake sections in a second or third year of candidacy will pay additional fees.[22] Many states provide fee subsidies and or fee reimbursements for candidates who complete the process of National Board Certification; however in some cases you must be prepared to advance the fees yourself. Check the NBPTS website, www.nbpts.org, for programs and scholarships available in your state.

2) Do you have a computer with Internet access?

You MUST have basic computer literacy skills and Internet service to access and utilize the resources available from NBPTS. The chapters that follow in this book will direct you to download and work with these materials systematically to examine and write about your teaching. You will need a computer to obtain resources and complete parts of the assessment, in addition to making multiple revisions of your written work. As a professional educator, knowledge and use of technology should be part of your practice. If you are not yet comfortable on a computer, you should take a basic skills course before becoming a candidate. Having your own at-home computer is strongly recommended. You will be spending hours at your keyboard, and it will be especially critical to have round-the-clock access as you near your deadline.

3) Can you make the time commitment?

National Board Certification is intensive and time-consuming. Successful certification rests, in part, on the amount of time you are able to devote to the work. It is important to be ready, not only in terms of professional preparedness, but also in terms of other personal and professional commitments you may have.

Consider your schedule and prepare to eliminate unnecessary activities before undertaking National Board Certification. Candidates report that they have spent 200–400 hours on portfolio entries. This translates to time each and every week, producing video recordings, writing papers and reviewing student work.   Teachers are expected to think and write analytically throughout the process, requiring large blocks of uninterrupted time. Teachers often wonder if they will be able to do the assessment work while teaching full time; however, this is a normal and necessary requirement of the process. You may need to find other ways to adjust your level of activity.

Teachers who seek National Board Certification are often highly involved with their students, parents, and colleagues, and are often sought to provide leadership for school improvement efforts. However, this is the year to try to clear your schedule, not to take on additional activities, or become coordinator of a major school project. It is not the year to do major remodeling on your house, add a new family member, or increase your household activity level.

There is never going to be a time when your life is completely empty and you will be looking to fill it with a portfolio for National Board Certification but, realistically, you may need to determine if there is a better year or a better time for you to enter the process.

4) Do you have enough teaching experience in your certificate area?

Teaching involves the acquisition of a variety and range of skills, and National Board Certification is intended for experienced teachers who have developed those skills. National Board Certified Teachers are recognized for accomplished teaching above and beyond licensure, based on deep reflection on their teaching practices. NBPTS requires teachers to have, at minimum, three years of state-licensed teaching experience before applying for candidacy.

No matter how many years you have put in, it is important to strongly consider your strengths and weaknesses in the classroom. Ask yourself:

- How well do I know my students?

- How well do I know my content area?

- Do I thoughtfully select my instructional methods and monitor the learning of individual students?

- Do I adjust my teaching to address student needs?

- Do I collaborate with colleagues?

- Do I work with parents and with the community to enhance my students' learning?

Few of us do it all as well as we would like to, but these are important aspects of your teaching that will be showcased in the work required of a candidate. The National Board Certification process will ask you to describe and explain who you are as a teacher and to demonstrate the depth and breadth of your practice.

5) Is your teaching situation appropriate for completion of your portfolio requirements?

It is important to select the certificate area in which you are most proficient and to read the NBPTS Standards for that area. Candidates who seek National Board Certification out of their primary area of experience are significantly disadvantaged in the process.

Portfolio requirements are specific to content areas and age groups. Candidates must conduct lessons and provide evidence of teaching in the area selected. Although out-of-classroom resource teachers and others may complete the portfolio requirements by making arrangements to work with the appropriate group of students, the task is likely to be more challenging under these circumstances. The teacher who is experienced and currently teaching in the chosen certificate area is best positioned for success.

The Assessment

At this writing, Standards have been developed for certificates that cover numerous subject areas and student developmental levels. More than 95 percent of the nation's teachers will find a certificate for their teaching situation. NBPTS Standards share a common vision of accomplished teaching as conscious and deliberate pedagogical decision-making, based on a deep knowledge of the particulars of content and context. Underlying principles guiding the development of assessments include:

- tasks should be authentic and, therefore, complex;
- tasks should be open-ended, allowing teachers to show their own practice;
- tasks should provide ample opportunity and encouragement for analysis and reflection;
- subject-matter knowledge should underlie all performances;
- tasks should encourage teachers to exemplify good practice;
- each task should assess a cluster of standards, and each standard should be assessed by more than one task.[23]

The National Board assessment materials are designed to produce evidence of accomplished teaching by prompting candidates to describe, analyze, and reflect deeply on the educational choices they make for students within the specific teaching context; and by testing the candidates on their content knowledge for the certificate area.

In addition to the Standards, overarching principles that apply to all certificate areas and Standards are The Five Core Propositions. Candidates must demonstrate an internal structure for their teaching practices based on these Five Core Propositions of accomplished teaching described by NBPTS. The study of practice in relationship to these principles is the subject of this book, and will be addressed in detail as readers progress through each chapter.

The process of National Board Certification is designed for completion during the course of a single year of teaching, although some candidates may take two to three years to achieve success. The task, in its entirety, is referred to as "the assessment," and it is based on area-specific Standards developed by NBPTS. As shown in Figure 1, it consists of two parts, a portfolio with four written entries and a set of six exercises conducted at a testing center. Each piece of the assessment is scored separately to yield a total of ten scores.

After the assessment is completed, the candidate may wait several months before the results are announced. One or more trained assessors, who are practicing classroom teachers from the same field as the candidate, will score each of the ten pieces. The combined total of scores from all ten pieces will determine whether or not National Board Certification is achieved.

The following is a general overview of the ten pieces that comprise the National Board assessment. As changes may be made from one year to the next, candidates should always verify requirements for the current year directly with NBPTS.

The Assessment

I. The Portfolio	II. The Assessment Center
Written description, analysis, and reflection on classroom and professional practices with supporting evidence.	Computer-response assessments of content knowledge.
Entry 1: Classroom-based Entry 2: Classroom-based Entry 3: Classroom-based Entry 4: Professional work with families and community	Exercise 1 Exercise 2 Exercise 3 Exercise 4 Exercise 5 Exercise 6

Figure 1. Components of the Assessment for National Board Certification.
Four portfolio entries and six assessment center exercises make up the ten parts of the assessment.

Part I: The Portfolio

Specific guidelines are provided for the four written entries, which are approximately twelve pages each in double-spaced text. The text will be accompanied by required documentation specific to the particular entry. Most candidates will spend approximately five months working intensively on the portfolio entries.

Entries 1, 2, and 3 are based on the candidate's classroom teaching practices. Each will require a short videotape and/or student work samples and instructional materials in addition to the Written Commentary.

Entry 4: Documented Accomplishments: Contributions to Student Learning, will ask the candidate to describe work during the past one to five years with parents, community, and/or professional colleagues that has helped to support and enhance student learning.

Part II: The Assessment Center

Candidates are required to complete six 30-minute assessment center exercises that are specific to their certificate areas. Exercises are focused on content knowledge for the area. They consist of written responses to test prompts, which may include student work samples and/or teaching scenarios.

The National Board provides the candidate with an overview of the prompts that will be given, and an online tutorial is provided to simulate testing conditions. The candidate must schedule an appointment at a certified assessment center during a specific calendar window. At the testing center, the candidate will read and respond to each exercise on a computer. Nearly all certificate areas require use of the computer for the assessment center exercises; however there may be exceptions for specific certificates (e.g. Music, World Languages) or for candidates requiring special accommodations. All six 30-minute assessment center exercises are completed during a single half-day session.

Becoming a Candidate

We believe that any interested teacher should have an opportunity to learn about National Board Certification and work on portfolio entries as a professional development opportunity before making the commitment to candidacy. NBPTS has made this possible by providing free access to the Portfolio Instructions and other candidate materials on the NBPTS website. Internet access is a must for candidates and pre-candidates alike, as the website is the primary source for information and access to resources.

In the pages that follow, we will tell you how to download the information you need, and will encourage you to utilize all available support and begin practicing with the portfolio materials before sending in the initial non-refundable application and processing fees. We also encourage you to begin working the materials well ahead of the due date for your application fee to ensure that you will have a thorough understanding of the task and are in every sense ready for the commitment to candidacy.

The formal commitment to candidacy is made when you submit your application and initial fee to NBPTS. All information for doing so can be found on the NBPTS website. Be sure to follow the provided links to find out what subsidies and support programs are available in your state, as eligibility for these supports may also affect your application date. Once you pay your initial fees, you will receive a CD customized for your certificate area that includes the same downloadable materials that can be found on the NBPTS website.

What if I Do not Achieve National Board Certification in the First Year of Candidacy?

When a candidate does not achieve National Board Certification in the first year it does not mean he or she is not a good teacher. It means only that, on the basis of the information received through the assessment, there was not enough evidence to make a determination of accomplished teaching. Few teachers are accustomed to writing to the degree of detail needed to produce evidence, and many may need to spend more time to develop this skill.

The candidate will receive a report listing the ten individual scores for the portfolio entries and assessment center exercises. Although one does not need to earn a passing score in each entry, the combined total of the scores must meet or exceed the established threshold for National Board Certification. Candidates whose combined scores are below the threshold have the option to continue the process as advanced candidates, retaking one or more of the pieces which they did not pass and "banking" the remaining scores for a maximum of two additional years. It is not uncommon for candidates to work on their assessments for two to three years before becoming certified.

Professional Development and Support

In your work with the National Board Standards and assessment materials, we strongly encourage you to develop or join a support group. Professional dialogue among group members stimulates reflection and new perspectives on teaching. As previously noted, reflective practice is imbedded in the certification process. When teachers make time for focused dialogue with their colleagues, they benefit immensely from sharing ideas and strategies and are motivated to continue the self-improvement process.

An experienced candidate support provider can clarify expectations, help teachers develop needed skills, and keep candidates focused on the most important aspects of the work. Process-focused professional learning communities provide invaluable support and skill development for candidates, and a rich experience for pre-candidates who benefit from sharing perspectives on teaching and learning with other educators.

Support groups and programs are available throughout the country. However, because candidate support groups may differ in philosophy and experience, it is important that you define how and why you will study the National Board Certification materials and then determine a course of study that suits your purposes.

The *Take One* Option

The NBPTS has developed *Take One* as an alternative way for interested parties to experience the certification process. For a fee, one pre-selected portfolio entry may be purchased, completed, and submitted for scoring. Through this option, a teacher, administrator, or anyone else can explore the process without the commitment of candidacy. *Take One* offers an opportunity for teachers to "test" their readiness and to apply the resulting score to candidacy in the next certification cycle if they so choose.

In some states, *Take One* has been selected as a tool for professional development or as a requirement for license renewal. More information about *Take One* can be found on the NBPTS website.

How to Use This Book

Whether or not you have decided to be a candidate for National Board Certification, we believe this book serves as a useful tool for you to study the National Board Teaching Standards and to improve your professional work. Our goal is to help you develop your abilities to analyze, reflect, and write about your teaching practices, and encourage you to think deeply about how student learning can be improved in your classroom. No matter what your current level of expertise, your commitment to professional development through a study of the National Board Teaching Standards will lead you closer to accomplished teaching.

If you have chosen to embark on the journey of a candidate, you will find this a valuable guide to the meaning and development of evidence for your portfolio entries, as each step is discussed in detail. If you are an advanced candidate, it will lead you to a deeper understanding of your requirements and of the structure of your teaching that must be visible in your entries.

If you are a candidate support provider (CSP), this book is also for you. Although our discussion is directed primarily to candidates, key points for facilitators are included at the end of each chapter as suggestions for those who are leading candidate groups. As the text provides unlimited opportunities for candidates to review information about the process, they can more readily pace themselves through the work. Participants may find the exercises throughout the text useful to prompt reflective thinking and dialogue during or between sessions. By enabling candidates to work with greater independence, more time in support sessions may be used to clarify questions and to engage in rich conversations about accomplished teaching practices. The CD that accompanies this edition includes working copies of all the exercise templates found in the text, as well as other selected material. The exercises are intended to support teachers as they reflect and write about their teaching for the portfolio entries. They may be used by candidates as visual organizers to clarify understanding or as pre-writing worksheets to help focus and organize their responses.

The book will be helpful to others working in teacher professional development programs including facilitators, administrators, and other leaders in higher education. Those who are new to the National Board Certification process will gain a deeper understanding of how to encourage and support the growth of all teachers by studying the National Board Teaching Standards.

While NBPTS recognizes the growth factor inherent in the process by allowing candidates up to three years to successfully achieve National Board Certification, we recommend interested teachers practice with the materials before committing to candidacy in order to "front-end" this growth process. It is our intention to provide interested teachers, pre-candidates, and candidates with a guided experience of the National Board materials through the chapters that follow.

Organization of the Book

The chapters are organized to lead you from the beginning of your work with the portfolio entries to the end, with a number of exercises provided in each chapter to prompt and deepen your thinking. Some chapters should be revisited for each entry, to remind you how to effectively write about your teaching. We have also included a discussion about the importance of support systems for candidates and information about the assessment center and scoring procedures for the assessment. Our last chapter is written for candidate support providers, but may also be of interest to candidates themselves.

Candidates, pre-candidates and other interested educators may use the chapter resources to prompt deep analysis of and reflection on teaching and learning. In order to make meaning from the text and use the suggested exercises, you will need to obtain a few important documents from the NBPTS website. Refer to Chapter 3: Organizing Your Resources for information on locating and downloading the materials you will need. You will be able to access and work with all the featured materials even if you have not yet decided to formally begin the National Board Certification process. However, to simplify our discussion and guide your work with the materials, we will refer to you and all our readers as candidates from this point forward.

Overview of the Chapters

In this first chapter, we have given you a bit of history and an overview of the National Board Certification process. The next two chapters will help you prepare for your work with the assessment materials. In Chapter 2: Support Systems, you will find an in-depth discussion about the importance of support and considerations for seeking support. In Chapter 3: Organizing Your Resources, we will provide you with a list of the materials you will need and directions on how to obtain them. We will also provide suggestions for getting organized, and an overview of the skills you will use to provide evidence of the Standards in your teaching.

Chapter 4: Starting at the Core will introduce you to The Five Core Propositions of accomplished teaching, and prompt you to identify evidence in your teaching practices. This chapter can provide the basis for professional development through on-going discussion in the context of a non-candidate study group. For candidates, it lays a critical foundation for the work that will follow.

Chapters 5 through 12 address the specific requirements of the portfolio entries for teachers engaged in the process as candidates or pre-candidates. Each chapter will help candidates focus on the most important aspects of the entries. Planning lessons, writing about teaching, and developing evidence of teaching to Standards will be discussed in detail.
The remaining chapters provide other important information including preparing for the assessment center, scoring, and advanced candidacy.

A number of exercises are provided throughout the text. These are not meant to be prescriptive, but are intended to prompt your thinking and help you develop your portfolio entries. We have found them useful in our work with candidates and will refer to them to help illustrate key points in each chapter. They may be helpful as concept maps for the process, whether or not you choose to use them as described.

Candidates are encouraged to read the entire text for an overview of the assessment process, and then return to Chapters 3 and 4 to get started. This will give you the "big picture" of the process and show you where to access information as you need it. You may be anxious to begin working directly with the portfolio materials, and this book will help you to recognize the importance of pacing yourself in order to comfortably complete your work before your deadline.

Clear your desk, take a deep breath, and enjoy your journey!

Key Points for Candidate Support Providers

In these "Key Points" located at the end of each chapter, we have included some suggestions, comments and tips just for candidate support providers. As you begin:

- Read both Chapter 2 and Chapter 17 on the topic of candidate support to help you define the nature and limitations of your work with candidates. You will also find information that will help you conference with candidates about their work.

- Help candidates assess their readiness and level of commitment to National Board Certification by walking them through the "Readiness" section in this chapter.

- Use the following chapters to supplement your candidate support sessions. The material will help build candidates' understanding and skills outside of sessions, and enable them to participate in valuable discussions of accomplished teaching during your meetings.

- Visit the NBPTS website often for the most current information about National Board Certification. You will find information for candidates as well as additional resources to assist you in your role as a candidate support provider.

2

Support Systems

Featured Resource:

Guide for Ethical Candidate Support

Whether you are a candidate seeking National Board Certification or a pre-candidate practicing with the materials, it is important to talk about support. You may or may not be an active candidate, but if you are working with the National Board Portfolio materials, this discussion applies to you.

What does candidate support look like and why do you need it? How can candidate support providers (CSPs) help you enhance the quality of your work? Although there are certainly candidates who have completed the assessment on their own, we believe support networks are a tremendous help to candidates and may increase their chances for success in the National Board Certification process. CSPs can prompt candidates to look at their work from new perspectives, and can help them develop needed analytical thinking and writing skills.

In this chapter, we will identify some common models of candidate support. We will discuss the advantages of different kinds of support opportunities, as well as some of the issues and considerations for candidates and for CSPs.

This chapter is written primarily for candidates, but will also be of interest to support providers to help them better define the purpose and nature of their relationships with candidates. More information for support providers can be found in Chapter 17: Providing Candidate Support. Before engaging in a support relationship, both candidates and providers should be sure to read the *Guide for Ethical Candidate Support*, available on the NBPTS website.

Types of Candidate Support

Why should you be concerned with support systems? A candidate's support community can help them understand and focus on the most essential aspects of the certification process, develop new ways of thinking and writing about their teaching, and may help candidates achieve success.

Whether you engage in a one-to-one support relationship or participate in a candidate support group, an experienced CSP can lead you to think more critically about your teaching practices, understand the key elements of the certification process, and help you develop the precision writing skills required for National Board Certification. Your CSP may offer new perspectives and prompt you to think more deeply about your instructional practices as you analyze and reflect on your featured entries. Working on their own, new candidates often focus on aspects of the task that may be less important while missing critical areas. Many advanced candidates have expressed regret they did not take advantage of available support in the first year, and are more likely to do so in their second or third year of the process.

Group Support

Core Proposition 5: *Teachers are members of learning communities*
As you will see in the chapters ahead, participation in learning communities is a valued attribute of National Board Certified Teachers. When you join a candidate support group you participate as a member of a powerful professional learning community to examine and understand the core principles of accomplished teaching practice. Traditionally, teachers have thought about their professional skill development as a private matter, developed over their years of experience in the classroom. However, current perspectives suggest a collaborative approach to the development of accomplished teaching. Reflective practice, an inherent part of instructional improvement and the National Board Certification process, can be effectively developed through facilitated professional dialogue in candidate support groups.

Groups build a sense of collegiality and caring among candidates that is important for sustaining participants through the challenges of the National Board Certification process. New candidates should be encouraged to participate in support groups led by an experienced CSP who helps them understand and build the skills they will need to successfully complete the portfolio requirements. Advanced candidates, in their second or third year of the process, will benefit from groups designed especially for their needs, to reach deeper levels of understanding about their work.

In some groups, teachers will be asked to apply for membership and be fully committed to candidacy before beginning their study. Funding sources for such groups may be dependent on a high rate of successful National Board Certification among participants each year. In this case, prospective candidates are often "screened" and accepted as group members based on the perceived likelihood of their success.

On the other hand, study of the National Board Certification materials is often regarded as a form of professional development in and of itself, with candidacy an option for those who feel ready. In some cases, teachers can earn credits by studying the National Board Standards in pre-candidate courses offered by universities. Opportunities for studying the National Board Standards, including online coursework and degree programs,[24] are on the rise across the country.

When professional development is offered to teachers who are undecided about the process of National Board Certification, it serves as a valuable training ground for acquisition of understanding and skills. When teachers are ready to begin, they can submit the candidate application with confidence, knowing they have learned many of the basic elements that are necessary to successfully complete the portfolio entries.

Facilitator-Led Groups

In most areas of the country, support groups are available to assist declared candidates. Ideally, the facilitator of such a group has been trained by NBPTS as a candidate support provider to help insure quality support and attention to the ethics involved in the support relationship. Whether trained as a CSP by the National Board or not, a support group facilitator should have a deep understanding of the process and a wealth of experience that will be helpful to candidates. Focused on process, the facilitator will help candidates analyze and understand the requirements, including both the Portfolio Instructions and the assessment center exercises. An experienced CSP can clarify procedural issues and may help candidates develop skills for richer responses to prompts.

> *Things really did become more clear and organized after I started attending...classes. I learned how to dissect and fully understand what was being asked of me. This is essential to being able to answer a question correctly.*
>
> *-Dr. Robert O'Boyle, NBCT New Jersey*

Many universities have developed graduate level courses for National Board Certification with faculty members acting as facilitators for candidates. In other situations, CSPs may be educators from state or district offices or others who have learned about the process in order to help candidates. Many are National Board Certified Teachers (NBCTs) who want to help other teachers attain Certification.

Support groups provide valuable insights to candidates by clarifying requirements and helping them practice critical skills. They are often very structured, with a series of presentations designed to help candidates understand and complete their requirements. Candidates are guided through the process of responding to portfolio prompts and learning how to provide evidence of their teaching practices. A facilitator-led group can make the difference for candidates who have a tendency to procrastinate, as they will be expected to begin teaching and writing to the portfolio entries in order to participate in group discussions and activities.

Depending on the size of the group and the style of the CSP, groups may or may not be able to provide needed emotional or professional support. In some groups, participants bond easily and help sustain one another through the certification process. In others, members may be at very different stages and levels of understanding in the process and may differ in their levels of personal and professional maturity. A large group may include several candidates working in the same certificate area, while members of a smaller group may benefit from more personal attention from the CSP.

In the best of circumstances, participants rarely work at the same pace, and it is often difficult for a facilitator to respond to the individual needs and concerns of each group member. This can be mitigated if group time includes opportunities for professional dialogue and debate, helping candidates develop new perspectives on their work. Once candidates understand task requirements, they need to shift the focus from process to content and quality of the writing with regard to providing evidence.

Generous opportunity for professional dialogue can help develop a true professional learning community, encouraging individual responsibility while helping candidates address the deeper aspects of the task, and raising the level of performance for all participants. Many group members find it valuable to view candidate video recordings together, and look for evidence based on the scoring criteria for the entry.

...We were all from different schools and taught different ages and subjects, but found enough in common with the process that we could help each other..... As tough and independent as I am in just about everything I pursue, I don't know if I would have made it through the process without the support of the group and our leaders.

- Colleen Collins, NBCT, Hawaii

Candidate Cohorts

When an experienced CSP is not available, a cohort study group can be a good way for candidates to obtain support. Whether organized by a college instructor or constructed by candidates themselves, teachers who are going through the National Board Certification process at the same time often choose to form their own support groups. The cohort members agree to a schedule of meetings, follow a similar schedule, and bring task-related materials to share at each meeting.

In some cases such groups may be certificate-specific for deeper study of the content area, such as *Early Childhood Generalist* or *Early Adolescent Science*. Or, candidates may attend facilitator-led sessions for general information, and arrange additional certificate-specific cohort meetings for further dialogue about their specific Standards and entry requirements.

Professional dialogue prompting deeper reflection is at the heart of successful cohorts. The candidate has an opportunity to present an entry to colleagues who may prompt deeper thinking or clarification through focused questioning. As videos and writing are shared, participants benefit from seeing and hearing positive examples of evidence from others.

The cohort model works best when candidates know the process and task requirements, and have developed good questioning strategies focused on content and quality of evidence. Advanced candidates in their second or third year of candidacy are often attracted to the cohort model, as they already know the logistics of the task and want to develop their capacity for analysis and reflection.

There are many positive aspects to cohort study groups; however, participants must conscientiously avoid the potential drawbacks. Without experienced leadership, the cohort is susceptible to shortcomings that can negatively impact its members. If a cohort does not hold regularly scheduled meetings or have regular agendas, members may not realize the expected benefits. Implicit in the cohort model is the assumption of an interdependent relationship among the members: Each member will be prepared with something to share and will in turn benefit from the sharing of others. If one or more members continually come to meetings unprepared with material to share, it is no longer mutually beneficial for all and the model quickly breaks down. To be successful, cohort members will need to organize, schedule, and agree to explicit expectations and ground rules.

Ideally, cohort members should participate in sessions led by an experienced CSP in addition to the study group. When members of the cohort are not sufficiently familiar with the process and the task requirements, they may be unwittingly misdirected by one or more strong personalities in the group, and may develop common misunderstandings based on poor examples of evidence.

Both individualized and group support experiences are helpful for candidates at all levels. Group support sessions provide opportunities for collegiality and professional dialogue, while individualized support may be customized to help a candidate think more critically about the quality of the work.

I am an introspective learner. Though I like to share in a group, I do much of my reflection personally and do not really like to share the intimate details of my thought processes. This was a handicap for me as I went through Certification. In one case, I did not want to share my interpretation of an entry with my colleagues. I designed my lesson, wrote my commentary, and received positive feedback from my pedagogy specialist. When I received my scores I found that I had completely misread the question. Had I bounced my ideas off of my fellow candidates, I might have gotten a more accurate perspective on the entry.

- MaryAnn

Considerations for Participating in a Candidate Support Group

Now that you know more about the types of group support that may be available to you, here are some additional considerations, based on your personal needs and preferences:

- How much time have you already spent on understanding National Board Certification? How much time does this group plan to spend on preparatory exercises?
- How much time will you want to spend in dialogue with other candidates? Are there other people in your certificate area in the group?
- Do you want a personal relationship with a reader or support provider? How large is this group? How many CSPs will facilitate?
- Are the facilitators NBCTs? Are they CSPs trained by NBPTS? What is their background and experience?
- What is your work style? Do you need a lot of meetings, few meetings? How often does this group meet? In person? Online? Does this group offer a variety of options for candidate support?
- Are you interested in obtaining credit hours for the process of certification? Does this support group offer college credit? Professional development/continuing education credits? No credit?

Individualized Support

Candidate support providers include those who help with clarification of process and content, as well as those who provide personal and technical assistance. As a candidate, you will often want someone to be a "sounding board" when you have questions about your work. One supporter may be a person who knows you well, providing emotional support and encouragement. Another may be a respected fellow professional who can prompt you to examine your pedagogical practices.

Still others may be experts in your content area who can guide you to current research and practice in your field. Although these areas of support may overlap and one person may fulfill more than a single role, we will discuss four aspects of candidate support: personal, technical, process, and content.

Personal Support

A friend, family member, or close colleague often provides personal support by helping you through the ups and downs of the National Board Certification process. Someone who knows and cares about you personally, who sees you on a regular basis and can "read" your need for rest and recovery should provide this support. He or she can give you a "reality check" when you feel overwhelmed, or remind you that you need to take a break and get away from the process to renew and refresh yourself. Constant intense reflection of the work requires an investment of energy from a candidate that can be exhausting. Someone who respects the task, but will remind you to take time for recreation will help you sustain yourself over the months of work.

As you identify people who can provide you with personal support, it is important to take time to discuss your task with them and to establish a mutual understanding of the time commitment and nature of assistance you would like from them. When another person (such as your spouse) will be significantly affected by your candidacy, it is important to ensure you have their full support and willingness to assist.

> *As my husband sat next to me with the Standards to help analyze the tape, he developed an even stronger appreciation of what I do. At one point he said, "Did you just count [the number of] times that you facilitated a student in two minutes?!" He also served as an editor to help me see what I could eliminate (the fluff).*
>
> *- Christine Rodek, NBCT, New Jersey*

You may identify more than one personal supporter, and might ask for help with any or all of the following: Staying on track with your master calendar and schedule for completing entries; reading entries for voice and clarity; making copies; and double-checking as you pack your entries for submittal. Help with household tasks such as cooking, shopping, laundry, and childcare may be even more important as this can provide you with invaluable writing time. You will want to make sure your personal supporters are especially prepared to assist you during the "home stretch" in the weeks just before your deadline.

Technical Support

You may need someone to record your videos for you, and may need help locating, setting up, and operating appropriate equipment for the video recording process. Many candidates seek help for duplication of their selected segments. Some teachers may be able to recruit a media-experienced student for technical support and/or videography. However, not everyone will have a "techie" to help them and in many cases a willing colleague, friend, or spouse fills this role.

Your video recordings, though not professionally produced, must capture appropriate content with good sound and picture qualities. You will find valuable guidelines and recommendations for video recording in your Portfolio Instructions to share with your technical support person. Your videographer should be available to assist you during your class sessions, and should be prepared to do multiple video recording sessions for you. The months immediately preceding your deadline will be especially important.

Process Support

If you are participating in a support group with an experienced leader, your CSP is providing process support. This supporter understands the process and requirements of the National Board assessment and provides useful guidance to candidates. Although process support is often given in a group setting, others can provide individual assistance to candidates by reading and discussing their entries with them.

We encourage candidates both to attend support groups and to locate CSPs who can give them individualized feedback. The National Board encourages teachers to be members of learning communities. If local support is not available, process support can even be found on the Internet. Some candidates have found and interacted with online chat groups on National Board Certification. While such groups may fulfill a lone candidate's need for support, many CSPs advise against them out of concern that misinformation can be circulated too easily. Check the NBPTS website for candidate resources, including the directory of NBCTs, which may help you locate someone knowledgeable in your area.

Process mentors are extremely important, as they help guide candidates through fundamental understanding of the assessment requirements and, in many cases, have personally experienced it. In seeking a process mentor, the candidate should ask about a person's background and level of experience with National Board Certification. Is he or she an NBCT? Trained as a CSP by the National Board? Experienced at reading candidate entries? Recommended by others? Candidates may consult the NBPTS website for a certified CSP who is well-grounded in the ethics and limitations of acceptable candidate support.

Content Support

You may also seek support from someone who can assist you with an understanding of the most current research in content and pedagogy for your area of teaching. Many candidates find such professionals in local colleges, among their school colleagues, or in their district-level resource teachers. Some states and districts provide "Teaching Mentors" to new teachers in the district, to teachers with emergency certificates, and to National Board Candidates. These professionals serve similar purposes, helping teachers through a new learning process.

Some candidates feel uncomfortable seeking out assistance from the field if they do not already know someone, but we urge you to get beyond such feelings and locate one or more content support providers. If you cannot find someone in your area, check the NBPTS website. You may be able to find an NBCT in your field who will act in this capacity for you.

The content specialist knows your subject area and students' developmental characteristics within that area. Your Standards should be shared and discussed with your content specialists, as they may help you identify aspects of your teaching to provide evidence of the Standards. They may also be able to direct you to helpful resource material such as guidelines from national organizations or cutting edge research in your field.

The assessment center exercises are focused primarily on knowledge of content, and may ask you to discuss issues involving specific theories, events, and/or people that are central to your certificate area. While, to some extent, you must already "know" this material to be effective in your field most teachers should brush up on current issues in their fields. A content specialist in your field may be able to help you identify the most important material to study in your assessment center preparation.

Readers

After you have written drafts of one or more portfolio entries, you may want to have someone read and give you feedback on your written commentaries. It has been our experience that the majority of candidates who successfully certify in their first year have made good use of both process and content supporters as readers. Most candidates want and need feedback on their entries, so it is important to have access to one or more readers, and to understand both how they can help you and what their limitations may be.

Reading candidate entries and giving feedback on them is a time-consuming task that brings up a number of issues. How much time does your reader have? What is the focus of the reading? Does she/he understand what is valued in the entry? How many different people will you ask to read and provide feedback on a given entry?

CSPs who facilitate groups clearly understand the process and requirements of National Board Certification. As they come to know and trust their facilitators, candidates naturally turn to these supporters to read for them. It is important to know groups vary widely and, although some CSPs will read for candidates, others will not. In a university course for candidates where the facilitator is a regular faculty member, the instructor can be expected to read entries as he or she would read any other course assignments.

While some support groups may take place in the context of a university classroom, others may be lead by volunteer NBCTs or others who are paid only a nominal fee for conducting group sessions. In this case, it may not be practical for the facilitator to read all the entries for an entire group.

Some CSPs are adamant about reading and giving feedback on each entry produced by their candidates, while others are equally adamant about limiting their reading and feedback. A facilitator may agree to guide the candidate through several drafts of the first entry only, or may agree to read one draft of each entry. In some groups candidates read for one another, while in other groups facilitators feel that it can be detrimental to have candidates reading one another's work.

Some candidates may have limited access to experienced readers and will need to seek outside perspectives from professionals in other positions and capacities.   There are hazards to be considered when working with well-intentioned but inexperienced readers who may unintentionally misdirect the work. Feedback focused on irrelevancies like writing style, details of a featured teaching activity, or style of dress in a videotape may unnecessarily distract the candidate from what is most important. Candidate support providers will agree poor feedback is worse than no feedback.

Ultimately, the candidate must weigh the value of seeking input from less experienced readers. If you are able to filter out less useful comments from your readers, you can benefit from different perspectives and you will not be left without any feedback in the event your preferred reader is unavailable. You must understand what is valued in the entry and have an overall sense of responsibility for the final piece.

You may find that, from two different readers, you get pieces of advice that are in direct opposition to one another. Remember that YOU, not your reader, are the final authority for the entry you submit. In your Portfolio Instructions: **Get Started**, you will want to reread the section called Reviewing Your Writing for important information about using feedback. As stated in this section:

Once you have received feedback, understand that it is simply the opinions of unique readers of your writing, and that it is up to you to decide how to use this information.

- NBPTS Portfolio Instructions[25]

Reader Feedback

No matter how experienced, your reader cannot provide you with effective feedback unless he or she knows what to look for in your entry. Your job is to tell the reader what aspects of the writing you would like feedback on. For example, you might ask your reader to look for one or more of the following:

1) Clear goals for the learning sequence; cohesiveness through the alignment of goals, instruction, and assessment.
2) A clear, direct response to each prompt for the Written Commentary, including a focused analysis of student learning, and an in-depth reflection.
3) A sense of authenticity provided by rich details and examples to illustrate key points.
4) Evidence that meets the descriptors in the Level 4 Rubric for the entry, illustrated by rich details and examples.

Simply asking someone to "read" for you is not helpful to your reader, and the resulting feedback may not be focused on what is valued in the entry. You have the primary responsibility to know what is valued, and to ask a reader to critique specific aspects of your entry. A graphic organizer can be very helpful for this purpose, as it provides a focus for reading and thus increases the likelihood that the feedback will be useful to you. Samples of graphic organizers can be found in Chapter 17: Providing Candidate Support.

In addition to your written feedback and a focus for the reading, the materials that you provide to your reader might include the prompts from the Portfolio Instructions, the relevant Standards, and/or the Level 4 Rubric descriptors. These will be discussed thoroughly in the chapters that follow.

As a candidate, you must be mindful that the reader is only giving a perspective and is not qualified to judge whether or not the entry meets or does not meet the Standards for accomplished teaching. The best that the candidate has provided is not necessarily adequate according to the Standards. Your reader should never attempt to "score" an entry, or in any way indicate whether it will or will not be scored as accomplished by NBPTS.

In the final analysis, you have the sole responsibility for determining if you have adequately met the criteria for each entry. When this is not clearly understood by candidates, CSPs, and readers, candidates may mistakenly expect these others to ensure that he or she will attain National Board Certification.

Under ideal circumstances, experienced readers meet with candidates to discuss the work. This requires readers to have a thorough understanding of the task requirements and strategies to help candidates develop new perspectives. Skilled readers often use questioning strategies to help a candidate develop the all-important and often under-utilized skill of reflective practice.

Letting Go

One of the unfortunate characteristics of the teaching profession is that so many teachers continue to work in isolation, and are reluctant to discuss their professional concerns with colleagues. One of the greatest challenges for many candidates is to overcome this reluctance to share their work with other candidates or with their support providers.

Professional development rests, in part, on teachers' willingness to be candid about their practices. Teachers who discuss their decisions on planning and assessment or their instructional delivery as shown on video expose both their strengths and their weaknesses. They give up anonymity by allowing their work to be seen and dialoguing about it with colleagues. In doing so, they invite others to break through the isolation of traditional practice. The experience is valuable for the teachers who share and for their colleagues who, while viewing and discussing someone else's work, see their own from new perspectives.

> *...the process [of examining the quality of teaching] starts by learning to analyze the details of ordinary classroom instruction, with all its warts and foibles, and the learning to see more effective ways of teaching. To do this, ...(teachers) must be willing to allow others to use their lessons as data that can be examined and discussed over and over.*
>
> *-The New Heroes of Teaching*[26]

The learning community surrounding National Board Certification can help us overcome the reluctance to share as we recognize and appreciate that:

- Each teacher brings unique, positive qualities to the profession;

- Accomplished teaching is the result of classroom experience and prolonged engagement in reflective practice in reference to the NBPTS Standards;

- National Board Certified or not, every teacher has the ability and professional responsibility to continually improve his or her ability to help students learn. Letting go of self-consciousness is an important part of your professional growth in the National Board Certification process.

Now that we have discussed different types of candidate support, can you "dare to share?" Can you identify your available options and arrange support that is right for you? Your personality and work style may lead you to prefer one type of support to another. Figure 2 (Selecting the Right Support for You) may help you determine what will best suit your circumstances and needs. We recommend you take advantage of both group and individualized support opportunities.

Considerations for Candidates

The development of entries to showcase your evidence of accomplished teaching to the National Board Standards is a satisfying, but rigorous task. As you enter the deeply reflective process of developing a National Board Portfolio, it is important to consider your work style and what will best support you in your course of study. Are you a teacher who often engages in professional dialogue with others? How do you feel about sharing your writing, your thoughts, and your questions? All candidates will write and reflect on paper, but it is the rich dialogue among participants that truly encourages candidates to grow as professionals.

In Figure 2, we have provided a tool that may help you identify your best support options, given your personal situation and preferences. While it may seem easiest to make your journey "solo," without the constraints of scheduled meetings and expectations from others, you are far more likely to develop your reflective capabilities when participating as a member of a professional learning community. If this is a new experience for you, consider the following aspects of your participation.

Learning in a Group

As a member of a learning community, you will need to think, talk and share. Do you resist sharing specific information? Do you like to wait to be sure you are right before you share? These are tendencies that will work against the value to be found in a support group. If you are not entirely comfortable at first, remember—your contributions to the group study will foster your ability to reflect deeply on your work and consider new perspectives. Come prepared to share with others. Each candidate is responsible for his or her own entries, but when joining a professional learning community or support group, members have a responsibility to come prepared and to share their responses to the entry questions.

Selecting the Right Support for You

Options ←	NO	Question	YES	→ Options
Choose a personal CSP who knows your work style, will help you plan your calendar and will give you a nudge when you need it to stay on course. Join a group.		*Are you self-motivating? Can you set your own schedule and stick to it?*		Use your master calendar to determine your schedule for teaching and writing about your entries. Review the entire portfolio to see what you can do ahead of time.
Check your local college or university for a course on reflective writing, or incorporating Standards into your teaching. Join a professional learning community .		*Are you inherently self-reflective?*		Use journaling or other reflection to begin recording your daily thoughts about your teaching.
Locate process and/or content specialists who will work with you. Check into online support resources thru the NBPTS website.		*Do you like to work in a group?*		Check institutions of higher education, your DOE or other resources to find a support group.
A group support situation that includes dialogue about Standards-based teaching may provide you with most of the information you need. You should still seek a reader for feedback on your entries.		*Do you want face-to-face, individualized communication and feedback?*		Seek a CSP who will read for you and can schedule time to meet with you personally.
Let your CSP or reader know that you would like to meet with them in person. Discuss the ground rules of your relationship—your meeting schedule and the nature of the feedback.		*Are you comfortable with feedback by fax and/or e-mail?*		Locate a fax machine you can use for this purpose. Learn how to send your work as an attachment to an e-mail message. Be prepared to wait for feedback, as CSPs who use this method often work with multiple candidates.

Figure 2. Selecting the Right Support for You.
Options for types of support are presented for candidates with different work styles and preferences.

Thinking and Talking about Your Teaching

A professional learning community can be an excellent venue for helping you develop an evidence-based thought process to guide your writing in the portfolio, as you will be expected to share your thoughts and ideas with others. Learning communities encourage teachers to share what they already know. However, there may be many good answers to a single question, and this may feel frustrating. Teachers are usually "good students" who are accustomed to knowing the "right" answer, but in this process, it is not the answer that counts. You will be asked to tell not only what you do, but how and why you do it. You must be prepared to analyze, describe, and rationalize the most fundamental aspects of your teaching practices. Details and examples that illustrate your commitment to student learning are central to your sharing.

You may feel uncomfortable if your opinions differ from the rest of your group. Others may read an entry question differently than you do, and, while it is important to consider the perspectives of others, ultimately you must determine your own interpretation and response to the instructions for each entry.

It is important to have a facilitator who can ensure that the group discussion stays focused on the Standards, and who encourages the discussion of different kinds of teaching styles. No particular style is "right" or "wrong," but teachers are expected to be knowledgeable of current research and able to justify their instructional choices. The discussion is grounded in the Standards and in the Architecture of Accomplished Teaching, to be described further in the chapters ahead.

Staying on Task: Responsibility to Your Group

Members of candidate support groups will realize the greatest benefits when they agree to and follow a similar schedule for completing entries. When you join a group, be mindful of your responsibilities so that your fellow candidates can depend upon you. If you tend to procrastinate, your membership in a group may help you stay on task.

As sharing and dialogue is dependent on the sharing of work by group members, you must be prepared to bring a written entry, or part of one, to share at each session. Sometimes online posting will be a part of the support group design. Bringing your work and your questions to each session will support the entire group in the goal of defining accomplished teaching.

Responsibility to Your Support Provider

Whether your support is individualized or with a group, it is important to clarify the expectations of each role group. Candidates often look to a support provider to make the process work for them without first attending

Guiding Principles

*...to support each candidate's unique and distinct journey
to find their own evidence of accomplished teaching...*

Support Providers

- Make an investment of time, schedule meetings, remain committed to the schedule
- Offer challenging ideas
- Help build self-confidence
- Encourage thoughtful reflection
- Ask probing questions to prompt thinking
- Offer friendship and support
- Read/review at least one entry for each candidate
- Provide resources/materials
- Make time available for support
- Answer questions related to the process
- Maintain confidentiality
- Be familiar with the standards; Be familiar with portfolio instructions
- Celebrate the steps along the journey
- Help clarify goals
- Come to support sessions prepared

Signature_____

Candidates

- Make an investment of time, attend meetings, remain committed to the schedule
- Accept the challenge ahead
- Share fears, concerns, issues
- Listen and ask follow-up questions
- Bring work and questions to sessions
- Accept friendship and support
- Prepare drafts well ahead of deadlines
- Visit the website, access and use resources
- Commit time to the process
- Listen with an open mind
- Maintain confidentiality
- Know your standards; Know your portfolio instructions
- Celebrate the steps along the journey
- Set goals
- Come to support sessions prepared

Signature_____

Figure 3: Sample "Contract" for Candidates and Support Providers.
An agreement such as this will help establish ground rules for the support relationship and clarify the expectations for both candidates and support providers.

to their own responsibilities. When agreements are clearly stated, as shown in Figure 3, disappointments are avoided and leadership skills are fostered in candidates.

Candidate Support and Professional Growth

As a candidate, you expect to be successful in achieving National Board Certification, but statistically we know that success is not guaranteed. After sharing your work with your CSP and peers in support groups, what if you do not become a NBCT?

Our work with candidates has assured us that, whether or not National Board Certification is achieved, the vast majority of candidates feel a great sense of personal accomplishment. If candidates focus on the process of becoming accomplished teachers through professional dialogue with the CSP and other candidates, rather than on the outcome of National Board Certification, they feel comfortable with their results. When teachers discuss their teaching with CSPs and colleagues, they feel renewed as they consider new directions, strategies, and approaches to student learning. The support group becomes a learning community, and seeds are sown that eventually grow and blossom in the teacher's work with students.

Connecting to support is especially important for advanced candidates, who engage in the process for a second or third year. Those who made their first attempt alone often regret they did not seek assistance. Even if you normally prefer to work alone, think about how you can be involved in a support group and take advantage of the tremendous benefits they have to offer you. Many candidates have stated that the most beneficial part of the process was the sense of community and professional collegiality of the support group.

Your understanding must go beyond National Board Certification to the bigger picture of what it means to demonstrate accomplished teaching. Continuous learning through reflective practice, a critical feature of your portfolio entries, is one of the most important attributes of the accomplished teacher.

Key Points for Candidate Support Providers

- As a metaphor for the National Board Certification process, MaryAnn likes to use *Finding the Green Stone,* a children's story by Alice Walker, with her candidate groups. In the story, each member of a group must find his or her own magical green stone. A little boy, Harry, sets out to find his stone and, after attempting many shortcuts to avoid the labor of searching, finds he cannot borrow or steal a stone, but must find his own. Others may help him, but can not do the work for him. This book illustrates both the task of the candidate and the role of the facilitator. National Board Certification is an individual endeavor resulting from a candidate's deep search into his or her teaching practices. Candidate support providers and colleagues help support the candidate and guide the search, but each teacher must find his or her own "green stone" for success.

- You need to be sure that you have carefully defined your role and limitations for yourself and for your candidates. Reading entries for several candidates may seem manageable at first, but may quickly become overwhelming as deadlines approach. You may wish to encourage candidates to find other readers, and offer training for those without prior experience.

- Encourage candidates to call NBPTS directly at 1-800-22-TEACH or use the e-mail connection to NBPTS found at the website when they have specific questions about an entry. No facilitator will know all the answers, and candidates should be encouraged to take responsibility for finding the information they need.

- Many candidates will not use the web site as much as they should, and you will need to alert them to important changes and available resources. Changes to procedures and requirements, errors found in materials, and other important candidate information will be posted as it becomes available.

3

Organizing Your Resources

Featured Resource:

www.nbpts.org

The National Board materials are designed to help you provide evidence of your accomplished teaching practices. In this chapter we will discuss the materials, the task, and the skills you will need for the work ahead. Selecting, obtaining and organizing your materials is the first step in the certification process.

The Materials

In the past, prospective candidates had no access to the materials without paying non-refundable application fees to the NBPTS. The fees were sent in, and then candidates received a specially designed box containing all the printed materials. "The Box" seemed to take on a life of its own as candidates shared their reactions to receiving it. Some felt too intimidated to open it and stuck it away in a closet for several weeks, while others could not wait to tackle the materials and get started.

Today, any interested person can download the materials from the website, and NBPTS has developed and made available a number of resources to assist candidates. If you have already submitted your application to NBPTS you have received, or will receive, candidate information and materials that will include instructions for printing from a provided CD along with a box for returning the materials to be scored. However, if you want to work with the materials before committing to candidacy, you can obtain them from the NBPTS website at no cost other than your own ink and paper. Whether downloading from the website, or working from the provided candidate CD, lengthy printouts are unavoidable.

Even if you know a former candidate in your certificate area, requirements for National Board Certification may vary slightly or significantly from year to year, so it is important that you obtain current information directly from NBPTS. Once you have printed your materials, you will need to create an organizational system that enables you to identify, access, and use them effectively.

Download Your Documents: www.nbpts.org

Your first task is to determine your eligibility for candidacy and to identify the certificate area that best matches your professional expertise and current teaching assignment. On the NBPTS website, www.nbpts.org, locate the following sections: *Become a Candidate* and *For Candidates*. Follow the provided links to read the eligibility requirements and to find a list of available certificate areas. Review descriptions and materials until you find the certificate area that seems right to you.

Whether actual or virtual, your first encounter with the materials may be daunting. There are documents that are essential for the task, including the Standards and Portfolio Instructions,[27] as well as many other resources that can help you to understand and complete your requirements successfully. The NBPTS website has a wealth of information for candidates and other professionals. We will guide you through the use of several of these resources in the chapters ahead.

It is important to determine the range of the knowledge and content required by your certificate. Generalists will need knowledge of all subject areas and how to teach them for several grade levels. Content area specialists must know sub-topics within the content area. For example, a social studies teacher may be accustomed to teaching U.S. history but, for National Board Certification, must also demonstrate knowledge of content for world history, political science, economics, and geography.

A list of required and recommended materials is found below, with instructions on how to locate them. It should be noted that, at any time, NBPTS might add new materials or rearrange the location of the materials on the website. If you cannot find the documents as described here, then use the website search tool on the home page, and look for them by title.

To find your certificate-specific documents:

1. Go online and open the home page for the National Board for Professional Teaching Standards: www.nbpts.org. From the NBPTS home page, locate and select the tab **For Candidates.** From this page, choose **Certificate Areas**, and select the appropriate information on the drop down menus to open to the certificate materials that are right for you.

2. Your page will provide links to the following documents specific to your certificate area:

- Standards
- Portfolio Instructions (Be sure to download instructions for the most current year of candidacy)
- Assessment Exercises
- Scoring Guide

3. You may begin with your Standards and Portfolio Instructions, but will eventually need to print all of the above materials to assist you in your work. Do not let the length of the document prevent you from printing. You will want all documents in hard copy for easy access, highlighting, note taking, etc. It would be far too cumbersome to attempt to work with them as electronic files only.

4. In addition to the documents listed on your certificate menu, you may also wish to view and/or print the *Online Guide to National Board Certification,* listed as a resource on the Assessment Center page in **For Candidates** section. Though intended for candidates, pre-candidates may find it useful for informational purposes.

When you are ready to print your materials, find a reasonably fast computer, purchase a 3" binder, a ream of pre-punched paper and a new ink cartridge for the printer, and "just do it!" There is no reason to handicap yourself by trying to work without the materials you need. If, for some reason, you are not able to download the materials as directed in this chapter, order them by calling NBPTS at 1-800-22-TEACH.

As you open and view each document, check the number of pages before printing. The documents are lengthy. You can expect to print four to five hundred pages of material.

Getting Organized

Candidates will have different styles in their approaches to completing the entry requirements. Some will complete one entry before beginning the next, while others will develop two or more entries simultaneously. No matter what your style, you need to be organized in order to access and work with your materials easily. See the "Tips for Candidates" page at the end of this chapter for suggestions from other candidates.

Create a Master Calendar

Time management is crucial for success. Use a master calendar to notate your important dates including both personal and professional commitments. After reviewing your entry requirements (see Chapter 5: Mapping Your Entries and Standards), you will need to determine your schedule for teaching and writing about your entries. You may need to do some backward mapping and juggle your teaching schedule as needed to ensure all teaching for your entries will be completed at least a month before your portfolio due date. Plan to spend about two months on the Written Commentary for each of your entries, including time for multiple drafts and feedback from readers. See Chapter 2: Support Systems for more information on readers.

Review Your Requirements

After printing, organize your documents for easy reference. Begin by reading the *Portfolio Instructions: Introduction* for an overview of your certificate area and other helpful information. Forms are provided in this section to help you organize your work, including:

1. Entry Tracking Form

2. Summary of the Portfolio Entries

3. Time Requirements for the Assessment

You will also need to think about your assessment center appointment for example, whether you will schedule before or after completion of your portfolio work. NBPTS maintains that there is no disadvantage to candidates to take the assessment center exercises before beginning the written work, but some experienced candidate support providers will argue that, no matter how capable you are in your content area, you will improve your knowledge, skills, and writing ability in the course of completing the portfolio entries. In any case, it is important to schedule your assessment center appointment early as your center may have limited appointment times available. Record all important dates on your master calendar.

Your Portfolio Instructions also include directions for submission of your completed work to the NBPTS. There are specific requirements for formatting, page length, and packaging that must be followed in order for NBPTS to receive and score your work.

Return Forms

All registered candidates are required to complete and return specific forms immediately after obtaining the materials from NBPTS. You will need to locate, complete, and promptly return the necessary forms, found on the candidate CD and in the Portfolio Instructions.

Set Up Your NBPTS Mailbox

Candidates should be sure to set up a profile in the For Candidates section of the NBPTS website. Select "My Profile" from the menu and use your candidate ID number to set up an account. This will allow you to check the status of your candidacy, including fees, materials and, eventually, your score report. You will be able to verify that NBPTS receives your payments and portfolio in a timely manner, and will be able to follow-up promptly if there are delays.

Locate Support

You may work on National Board Certification by yourself or with a support group. Any teacher who has a baccalaureate degree and has been licensed by the state to teach for at least three years can work directly with NBPTS to seek and complete the National Board Certification requirements. However, we highly recommend that you locate and participate in a candidate support group for National Board Certification. (See Chapter 2: Support Systems.)

Set Up a Schedule

Plan to designate a specific time and place for writing. You will need to find time each week, including large blocks of uninterrupted time for your analytical and reflective tasks, in order to develop your understanding and produce the necessary quality in your entries. It is critical to establish a regular schedule for work on your portfolio over a period of time. This is not a task that can be completed as a "rush job" in a few days.

Candidates often underestimate the time they will need to finish the work, and quality suffers accordingly. Build regular blocks of time into your weekly schedule, and plan on completing all the written work at least a month before your deadline in order to allow time for feedback from readers and subsequent revisions.

Understanding the Task

Many teachers are concerned that, in the year of candidacy, the time spent on portfolio work will detract from their normal teaching routines. While it is true that many hours will be spent thinking and writing about your teaching, the focus is on student learning and the process should enhance rather than detract from your teaching.

Although you must select and/or design a lesson that meets the entry requirements, you have many options within the given framework for an entry. In most cases, you will be teaching to familiar topics and using strategies proven effective with your students in the past.

How Will My Teaching Be Different?

What is different about teaching for National Board Certification? Your teaching may or may not be very different, but you will be asked to

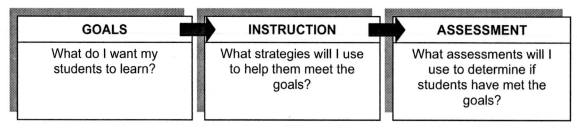

Figure 4. Questions for Traditional Lesson Planning.

write about what you do in such a way that your professional thinking processes are made evident to your reader. You will be asked to think more deeply than ever before about what you do in the classroom and about how you enhance student learning through your relationships with families and fellow professionals.

Teachers at all levels of experience are very familiar with the traditional lesson planning process as shown in Figure 4 (Questions for Traditional Lesson Planning). However, for National Board Certification, you will be asked to demonstrate thinking that is much deeper and more detailed than shown in Figure 4. Accomplished teachers must show they plan for the learning needs of individuals as well as the group; have a broad range of strategies upon which to draw; can adjust as needed during the course of instruction; and use multiple measures to monitor and assess student learning.

Figure 5 (Lesson Planning, Instruction, Assessment, and Reflection for National Board Certification), illustrates the depth of thinking required by the candidate for National Board Certification with an additional series of questions that might be used to prompt thinking and writing. As you can see, candidates must reveal and justify the reasons behind selected goals and strategies. They must manage and monitor student learning through constant analysis and reflection.

National Board Certification requires you to demonstrate *what you know*, and to show *how you use what you know* by making your thinking processes visible to your reader. As for many experienced teachers, this meta-cognitive process in which you "think about your thinking" may be a new skill for you.

You will be asked to analyze and reflect on your teaching more deeply than you may have done in the past. You must be prepared to think and write carefully, explain your specific teaching decisions and behaviors, and discuss the outcomes of your teaching in reference to both individual and group needs.

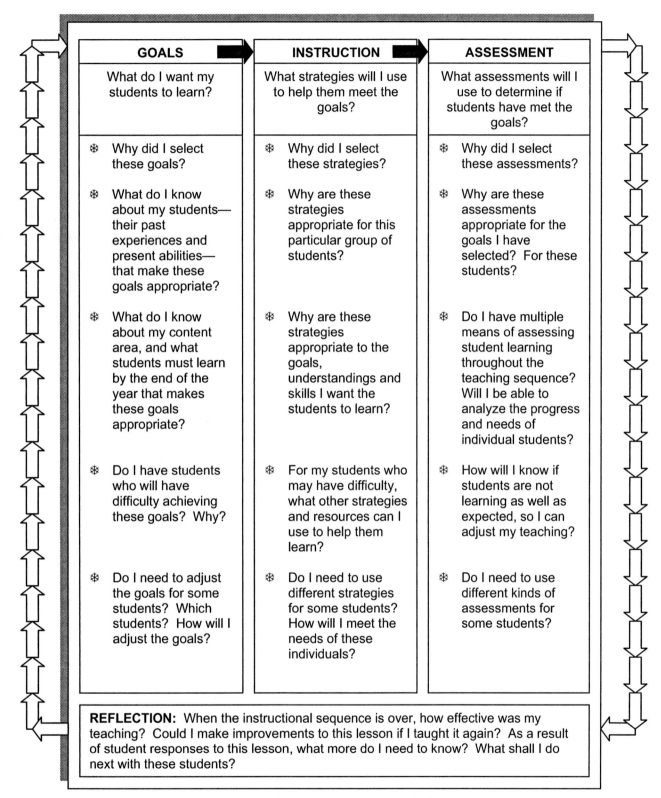

GOALS	INSTRUCTION	ASSESSMENT
What do I want my students to learn?	What strategies will I use to help them meet the goals?	What assessments will I use to determine if students have met the goals?
❊ Why did I select these goals?	❊ Why did I select these strategies?	❊ Why did I select these assessments?
❊ What do I know about my students—their past experiences and present abilities—that make these goals appropriate?	❊ Why are these strategies appropriate for this particular group of students?	❊ Why are these assessments appropriate for the goals I have selected? For these students?
❊ What do I know about my content area, and what students must learn by the end of the year that makes these goals appropriate?	❊ Why are these strategies appropriate to the goals, understandings and skills I want the students to learn?	❊ Do I have multiple means of assessing student learning throughout the teaching sequence? Will I be able to analyze the progress and needs of individual students?
❊ Do I have students who will have difficulty achieving these goals? Why?	❊ For my students who may have difficulty, what other strategies and resources can I use to help them learn?	❊ How will I know if students are not learning as well as expected, so I can adjust my teaching?
❊ Do I need to adjust the goals for some students? Which students? How will I adjust the goals?	❊ Do I need to use different strategies for some students? How will I meet the needs of these individuals?	❊ Do I need to use different kinds of assessments for some students?

REFLECTION: When the instructional sequence is over, how effective was my teaching? Could I make improvements to this lesson if I taught it again? As a result of student responses to this lesson, what more do I need to know? What shall I do next with these students?

Figure 5. Lesson Planning, Instruction, Assessment, and Reflection for National Board Certification.

The first time I read my Standards, I remember reading this thick document and wondering how much more could be asked of teachers. But then I remembered how I work every day to help students meet state standards and persuade teachers to provide clear expectations, focused lessons, and high expectations for their students. So then, how could I not support the same for teachers? Wouldn't it be easier for them, for me to have clear targets? How could I not hold myself to the same standards and still call myself a professional?

-Nina Garcia, Pre-candidate, Hawaii 2006

What Skills Will I Need?

In each entry you will need to demonstrate your ability to align your goals, strategies, and assessments with what you know about your students and your subject area. You will also need to describe your teaching practices in enough detail to provide "evidence" that you meet the Standards described for a teacher in your certificate area. In addition, you must demonstrate that you engage in conscious reflection about your teaching practices.

It is the purpose of this book to assist you with these skills as you learn more about the certification process in the chapters that follow. Here, we will describe each very briefly:

Alignment of Instruction

In each entry, the teacher's knowledge of content and instructional strategies must be integrated with knowledge of *these students, at this time, in this setting.*[28] Goals are focused, strategies scaffold students to higher levels of learning, and assessments inform the teacher's instructional decisions. All are aligned to produce specific learning outcomes for all students.

Evidence-Based Writing

One of the greatest difficulties for teachers beginning the National Board Certification process is learning to how to provide evidence of their Standards-based teaching practices. New candidates rarely understand the degree of specificity that is needed to produce such evidence, and often struggle to move beyond general statements when describing their teaching. Candidates must first read and internalize their Standards, align their teaching with those Standards, and then learn how to share details and examples of their teaching to illustrate standards-based practices in their entries.

Reflective Practice

Enough cannot be said about reflective practice—the habit of regularly thinking about and analyzing the things you have done for the purpose of improving your teaching practices. From professional literature to a variety of self-help books, the benefits of journal writing and other reflective practices are touted as the means to effect significant changes for personal or professional improvement. Reflective practice is an intrinsic characteristic of the accomplished teacher and an integral part of the National Board Certification process.

If you do not currently engage in regular conscious reflection, it will be important for you to train yourself to do so as you work on your portfolio entries. Although some people prefer keeping daily journals, if that is not your style, there are a variety of other ways to reflect on your teaching. You may use sticky notes on your calendar or plan book, jot notes about individual students on a clipboard, or record your thoughts on a battery-operated cassette player. What is important is to find a method that works for you and do it regularly. By doing so, you will create a "bank" of rich details that may be used as evidence of accomplished teaching as you write about the lessons in your portfolio entries.

> *Teachers who think that they know all there is to know about children and curriculum—who don't get excited by new insights into learning, by new approaches to subject matter, or by new ways of working with materials—will not serve children well. Advisors constantly challenge their advisees to become more thoughtful and reflective individuals who will remain learners for the rest of their lives. Teachers need to be learners not only to experience the excitement and the satisfaction of gaining new insights and knowledge, but also because being engaged in their own learning will help them to understand and respect the many varied ways in which children learn—and that is critical for successful teaching.*
>
> *- Maja Apleman[29]*

Accomplished teachers demonstrate the habit of lifelong learning as they *think systematically and learn from their experiences.* Reflection implies a willing attitude and an open mind to new possibilities. It means you will continually make changes as a result of thinking about your teaching. It assumes you have a responsibility and commitment to improving your practice for the benefit of your students.

Occasionally, we meet teacher candidates who self-confidently indicate they know everything they need to know, their ideas are always the best, and there is little they can learn from others. Those who think they "know it all" will have difficulty with the National Board Certification process, for those who have nothing to learn have nothing for which to strive, and this is not the mark of an accomplished teacher. Life-long learners understand their horizons have no limits and that, in fact, it is a challenge to keep up with the latest research and developments in the profession.

Reflection and Experience

While reflection is an important tool for new teachers as well as for veterans, the quality and focus of the reflection will differ, depending on one's experience and career phase as described in *The Life Cycle of a Career Teacher*. NBPTS requires a teacher have at least three years of experience before applying for certification *because the quality of the reflection must be that of an accomplished professional.* What is the difference? MaryAnn shares this example from her early years in teaching:

In my last year of student teaching, I worked as a partner teacher with an eighth grade teacher. My assignment was to re-teach concepts with a few students who had difficulty. I reviewed the lesson objectives, assessed the students' needs, planned instruction in a game-like format, and delivered the lesson. Afterwards, my reflection went something like this: "Did the game I designed hold students' attention? Did it help them learn the science objectives? What else could I do to instruct and assess these students and their learning?" My reflection was valid, but only at a beginning teacher level.

I was fortunate I had a mentor teacher who guided me to consider broader perspectives. Now, as an experienced teacher, I ask and seek answers to other questions including: "What prevented these students from learning in the regular classroom setting? What skills and understandings do these students have and need in terms of the bigger picture of the eighth grade science curriculum? Did the missed objectives imply a need to remediate basic misunderstandings, or are there other issues to consider?"

- MaryAnn

Like most novice teachers, MaryAnn followed procedures and designed instruction to meet certain goals. Because she did not have much classroom experience, her understanding of the particular students' abilities and interests was limited, she did not have a solid grasp of the "big picture" of the content area, and she did not have a wealth of instructional strategies to draw upon or the ability to make on-the-spot adjustments to meet student needs. She focused more on her teaching than on the students' learning.

Her mentor was able to help her consider new perspectives and assess herself more effectively than she might have been able to do on her own, but only time and experience would help her build the skills that exemplify accomplished teaching.

Three years' teaching experience is considered the minimum for a candidate, but it is important for a teacher to assess personal readiness for the process in terms of collective knowledge and skills as well as his or her ability to reflect on teaching and learning. A mentorship experience during the early years of teaching, or on-going membership in a nurturing professional learning community can help a teacher develop these important skills.

Read for Information

Ethics Policy: Anyone working with the National Board materials, including candidates, pre-candidates, and support providers, must read and adhere to the Guidelines for Ethical Candidate Support published by NBPTS. Infringements to the policy can result in permanent denial or revocation of National Board Certification. This policy can be found on the website: www.nbpts.org.

Standards: Read the Standards for your certificate area, and begin to think about your practice in reference to these Standards. You may wish to use highlighter pens in different colors, or other notations, to distinguish key words and phrases describing practices that you can easily demonstrate versus those in which you need to improve. The chapters that follow will guide in continued analysis of your teaching in reference to the Standards and The Five Core Propositions of accomplished teaching.

Portfolio Instructions: Before beginning the guided work in the text, we recommend that you review the entire Portfolio Instructions document in order to get a "big picture" of the task ahead. The first part of the document contains a section called **Get Started**. Read this thoroughly, as it will be an important reference for you during the course of your work.

The Five Core Propositions: This document, also known as *What Teachers Should Know and Be Able to Do* is the foundation of the Standards for accomplished teaching developed by the National Board for Professional Teaching Standards. They are at the heart of successful National Board Certification. You should be able to recall, articulate, and explain the meaning of each proposition in reference to your teaching practice. The text for this document can be found in your Portfolio Instructions: Introduction and on the National Board website.

This Book: In the chapters that follow, we will systematically guide you through your resources as you complete the portfolio work and prepare for the assessment center. A number of optional exercises are provided that may help you analyze and provide evidence of teaching according to your Standards. Exercise worksheets are provided at the end of each chapter and on the CD that accompanies the book. Should you choose to use them, we recommend that you use the electronic versions on the CD, as this will allow you to cut and paste text that is used in more than one exercise.

We suggest you begin with a quick read of the entire book in order to familiarize yourself with the style and content of the text, then open to Chapter 4: Starting at the Core to begin your deliberate work with the materials. Each chapter is directly related to your work, and designed to lead you from the beginning of the National Board Certification task to the end, introducing increased complexity as the work progresses.

Having said this, we know that the depth and direction of your study will be influenced by your time frame and working style. In the best of circumstances, candidates will take a full calendar year to complete and submit all the assessment materials. Teachers can even begin the process while on a vacation break when they have time to study, reflect, and deepen the analysis of their teaching, and may be able to draft much of Entry 4: Documented Accomplishments before resuming classes. If your time frame is shorter or it is simply your style, you may be working on several entries and chapters simultaneously.

Other Resources

The NBPTS Website: www.nbpts.org. We have given you some specific instructions for locating documents and other resources on the National Board website, but would like you to know what else is available. We encourage you to explore, become familiar with all the information available, and know how to find it. You will find information on application procedures and timelines, scholarships, descriptions, and instructions for available certificates, specific directions for completing the assessment process and more.

You should visit the website often to check for news and updates, and learn how to navigate through various sections. Candidates often fail to make use of available resources from NBPTS simply because they have not spent time exploring the website information.

NBPTS invites ongoing research related to National Board Certification and the Teaching Standards. There are state affiliate organizations and many institutions of Higher Education that have incorporated the National Board Teaching Standards into pre-service, graduate, and professional development programs for practicing teachers. More information about research, affiliates, and higher education programs can be found on the website.

University Sites: Some universities have created their own candidate support websites with a wealth of resources and information. An Internet search using "University National Board Certification" will lift out a number of sites for you to explore. We are aware of one university that offers an online master's degree program built around completion of the National Board Portfolio, and others may soon follow.[30]

National Standards: To strengthen content knowledge, teachers may wish to obtain and study standards and policy statements from nationally recognized professional organizations. These may assist teachers in selecting high, worthwhile goals for selected lessons, and may suggest useful instructional and assessment strategies. However, it is important that candidates understand the National Board Certification process will assess them *only* on their evidence of teaching to the National Board Teaching Standards.

Professional Organizations and Journals: Regular review of one or more professional journals may help you stay current with trends and issues in your content area or in education generally. Some organizations, such as the Association for Supervision and Curriculum Development (see below), may offer online resources that enable you to search for research on various topics. This is by no means a complete list, but may give you a starting place if you are searching for resources or policy statements related to a particular content area:

- Association for Supervision and Curriculum Development (ASCD) www.ascd.org
- Council for Exceptional Children (CEC) www.cec.sped.org
- International Reading Association (IRA) www.reading.org
- Kennedy Center Arts Edge www.artsedge.kennedy-center.org
- National Association for the Education of Young Children (NAEYC) www.naeyc.org
- National Council for the Social Studies (NCSS) www.ncss.org
- National Council of Teachers of English (NCTE) www.ncte.org
- National Council of Teachers of Mathematics (NCTM) www.nctm.org
- National Middle School Association (NMSA) www.nmsa.org
- National Science Teachers Association (NSTA) www.nsta.org

Tips for Candidates

◎ Read everything thoroughly. Use highlighters and sticky notes to tag and label sections you will want to revisit for specific information. Read your Standards (again and again and again…).

◎ Organize your materials. Set up an organizational system as soon as you begin your work. Some candidates like to keep all portfolio materials in a single binder, while others prefer a binder for each entry. Others choose to use file folders. Some candidates also use color codes for different entries. In any case, you will want to keep your planning notes, drafts, work samples, reflections, and professional articles organized and easily accessible. Binders are recommended for the downloaded materials, as you will be referring to them often, and may be using some of the documents side by side. Choose a system that works for you. The following ideas have been suggested by other candidates:

- Separate file folders for each entry OR
- A separate file box for each entry OR
- A binder with separate sections for each entry OR
- Separate binders for each entry
- Folders or binders for articles and resources relating to your assessment center exercises

◎ Designate the NBPTS website as your homepage (www.nbpts.org). Use the settings on your computer's web browser to do this. Every time you connect to the Internet, this page will open first. This will help you stay abreast of the latest news from NBPTS, and will help you become accustomed to the site as a source of information. It will also serve to remind you to stay on task and avoid unnecessary procrastination.

◎ Locate online sites that may be helpful for your area. Bookmark these on your computer for rapid access.

◎ As you work on the computer, save everything to both removable storage and hard drive, setting your computer to save automatically every five minutes or less. Keep the removable versions in a separate location. (One candidate we know had all his work on a school computer. The classroom was vandalized and the computer stolen—all the work was lost.)

◎ If you do not mind reading from "draft quality" print, use this setting on your computer to print your Portfolio Instructions and your working entry drafts. This will conserve ink and print your documents more quickly. Be sure to print your final copies in "normal" mode for submission.

Key Points for Candidate Support Providers

As a CSP, you are entering into professional relationships of at least one to three years with each person in your group. You will share their ups and downs and will have the joy of watching each grow through the National Board Certification process. It is important to have both patience and clarity in your work with candidates. Your role is not to lead, but to guide teachers through the deep, reflective experience ahead, and to help them develop the skills they need to demonstrate accomplished teaching practice. Begin with these points in mind:

- Set the tone with warmth, acceptance, and a shared sense of purpose among group members. Trust is critical for meaningful dialogue and growth. Some CSPs open their sessions with an icebreaker so that candidates have an opportunity to connect and begin relationship building.

- Recognize that, like their students, teachers have different skills, learning styles, and levels of understanding. They will be at different points on the career continuum and may need different degrees of support.

- Establish your ground rules clearly from the beginning to define your expectations and limits for support to candidates. (Chapter 2: Support Systems)

- Guide, but do not spoon-feed. This is a learning community of professionals, each of whom bears the ultimate responsibility for his or her experience and degree of success at National Board Certification.

- Expect members to obtain materials, read, and complete portfolio-related assignments for your group in a timely manner. When members arrive unprepared for sessions, it is a disservice to the whole group.

- Use the exercises in these chapters to prompt candidates' analysis and reflection and prepare them for meaningful dialogue during sessions.

- Hit the ground running—start teachers writing, analyzing, reflecting and dialoguing at your first session. (Chapter 4: Starting at the Core)

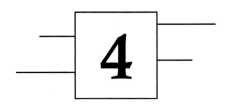

4

Starting at the Core

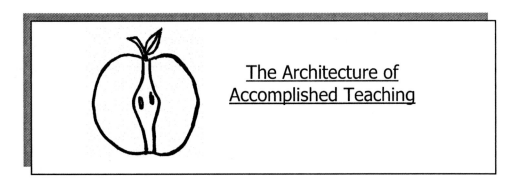

The Architecture of
Accomplished Teaching

Your responses to the National Board assessment materials must answer a single, fundamental question: "What are the things that <u>you</u> do to help your students learn meaningful and appropriate concepts and skills?"

Student learning is at the core of accomplished teaching. The Five Core Propositions developed by NBPTS describe key professional practices that support student learning for all certificate areas. This chapter is designed to introduce you to The Five Core Propositions and to help you begin to develop your evidence of accomplished teaching as defined by them. In order to respond appropriately to the portfolio entry requirements, you will need to have a deep understanding of these principles, know how to personalize them, and know how to provide evidence of teaching to them. We will revisit The Five Core Propositions several times in the chapters that follow to help you deepen your understanding as you review them from a variety of perspectives.

The Five Core Propositions

The National Board assessment requires teachers to provide evidence of teaching to The Five Core Propositions and the National Board Teaching Standards for their chosen certificate area. The evidence provided is the only basis used to determine whether or not the teacher has met the criteria for accomplished teaching. Learning *how* to provide a strong, clear and authentic picture of their teaching is often the biggest challenge for teachers in the assessment process.

Each portfolio entry includes a substantial written commentary that is the most important source for evidence. It must be supported with artifacts such as video recordings, instructional materials, and/or student work samples. Teachers are asked to describe, analyze, and reflect on authentic instructional sequences in their classroom. Teachers often fall short in this area by making general comments about a teaching activity rather than providing the specific details and examples from the activity that illustrate their Standards-based practices. To provide evidence of accomplished teaching, you must be able to provide a clear picture of *your* students in *your* classroom, learning as a result of *your* knowledge and skills.

The Five Core Propositions

1. Teachers are committed to students and their learning.

2. Teachers know the subjects they teach and how to teach those subjects to students.

3. Teachers are responsible for managing and monitoring student learning.

4. Teachers think systematically about their practice and learn from experience.

5. Teachers are members of learning communities.

Figure 6. The Five Core Propositions of the National Board for Professional Teaching Standards

While the Standards are specific for each certificate area, all Standards are derived from The Five Core Propositions. Shown in Figure 6, they are thoroughly discussed in the NBPTS document called *What Teachers Should Know and Be Able to Do* found in your Portfolio Instructions: Introduction.

Typically, beginning candidates will read the core statements, nod their heads in agreement, and then move on to look for what they think is the "real" content they will need. **Stop right there!** The Five Core Propositions *are* the "real" content of National Board Certification. They form the basis for the Standards documents developed for each certificate area, for the Portfolio Instructions, assessment center exercises, and rubrics used to score each piece of the assessment. Your job as a candidate is to provide evidence that these Five Core Propositions form the basis of *your* teaching and that you implement them to a degree that is "accomplished" in your field as described in your Standards.

The ability to provide evidence is increasingly important for all teachers, whether or not they are candidates for National Board Certification. In the current politicized climate for educational reform, "accountability" applies to teaching practice as well as to student learning. When test scores do not accurately portray a student's progress and skills, we must look to other sources for evidence of the student's accomplishments. Likewise, when called upon to do so, teachers should be able to provide evidence of their teaching abilities in a variety of ways that go beyond the performance of their students on standardized tests. Most teachers are familiar with conversations about Standards for students, which describe what *students should know and be able to do*. However the NBPTS has developed The Five Core Propositions and Teaching Standards to describe *what teachers should know and be able to do*.

The National Board Portfolio assessment is an excellent tool that all teachers may use to analyze and improve their practices. In developing the portfolio, teachers engage in a deep study of their work with students and seek to provide evidence of demonstrating The Five Core Propositions and the Standards for accomplished teaching.

The *Architecture of Accomplished Teaching*

Location, climate, purpose, and fashion may influence the design and selection of materials for a building, but basic principles insure that a well-constructed log cabin is as architecturally sound as a high-rise condominium. In the same way, accomplished teaching may occur within many different contexts, teaching styles, and philosophical stances; but, underlying these differences, a structure based on The Five Core Propositions ensures effective learning experiences for students.

National Board refers to this underlying structure as the *architecture of accomplished teaching*.[31] The structure is evident no matter what topics, goals, and strategies are selected for instruction. The assessment process is designed to help you reveal the architecture of *your* teaching.

In Figure 7 (The Architecture of Accomplished Teaching: Structural Components), this structure is represented as a brick building. In this analogy, bricks represent the collected knowledge and skills of the experienced teacher. Levels of learning rise like the floors of the building through effective instructional sequences. The Five Core Propositions are the blueprint that guides the teacher's thinking processes through planning, instruction, and assessment of student learning.

The Five Core Propositions: Lesson Planning and Student Learning

The architecture of the teaching process begins with a solid foundation based on teachers' knowledge of the subject area and knowledge of the students. These correspond with the principles of accomplished teaching as follows:

> ***Core Proposition 1****: Teachers are committed to students and their learning.*

Accomplished teachers know the developmental characteristics and learning needs of their students, based on social and cultural contexts, students' past experiences, and current levels of ability. Teachers answer questions such as these to effectively design appropriate instruction: *What are the backgrounds, interests, and learning characteristics of my students? Where are they now? How do they learn best?*

Core Proposition 2: *Teachers know the subjects they teach and how to teach those subjects to students.*

Based on knowledge of the students, the teacher must determine how best to advance their learning in the content area. He or she must know the essential concepts and skills in the subject area, have end year (or end course) targets for students, and know how to effectively move students toward specific goals. The teacher considers questions such as *What should students know and be able to do in this subject area at the end of the course? What do they need and in what order do they need it? What are the goals of my current instructional unit? How can I design a lesson to scaffold students' concepts and skills toward those goals?*

With an understanding of student needs, knowledge of the content area, and a range of instructional strategies from which to choose, the teacher sets high and worthwhile goals for *these* students, at *this time,* and in *this setting*. This notion is critical, as the teaching process is always based on a specific context involving the needs of real students, not on theoretical work with a group of ideal learners.

Core Proposition 3: *Teachers are responsible for managing and monitoring student learning.*

Teachers are attentive to student progress as they plan for and utilize embedded formative assessments. They observe, dialogue, and review student work to give them information about how well students are performing in relation to the selected goals. They are responsive to individual needs and often seek resources, adjust instruction, and provide specific feedback to support the learning of all students throughout the instructional sequence.

The teacher considers: *What instructional strategies will best help students meet the goals? How can I vary the learning experiences to meet the needs of different kinds of learners? How will I know how* well *my students are learning during the course of my instruction?*

Clear outcomes for the instructional sequence are established and communicated to students, assignments are aligned, and the teacher plans a series of scaffolded learning experiences to help students meet the selected goals. Learning is monitored throughout the lesson sequence by consciously assessing student progress and adjusting instruction as needed. The teacher considers both group and individual student responses to the instruction to determine progress toward the selected goals, and makes an effort to support learning for all students.

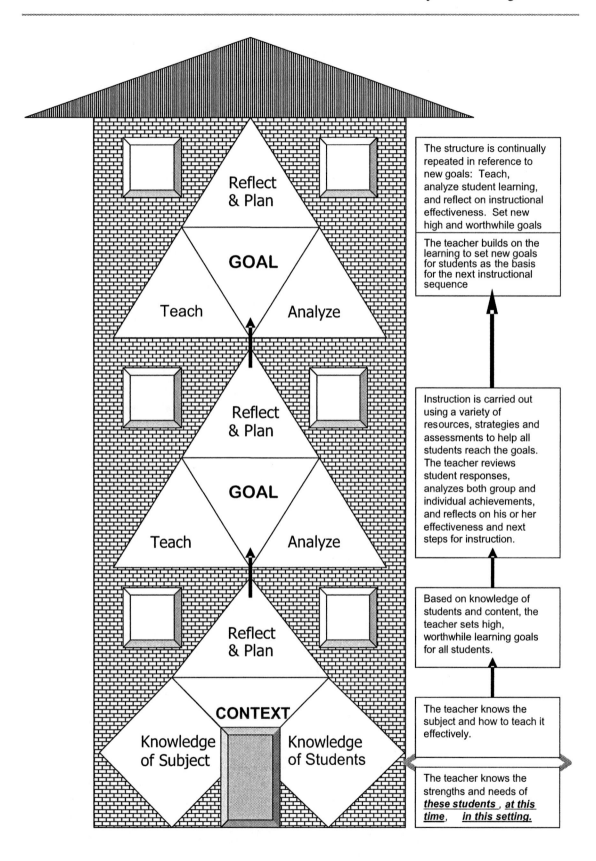

Figure 7. The Architecture of Accomplished Teaching: Structural Components.

Core Proposition 4: Teachers think systematically about their practice and learn from experience.

Following the lesson, the teacher analyzes student learning and reflects on his or her teaching: *Was the instruction effective?   Are there issues or concerns that should be addressed in the next session?   Are there other resources that I could use to enhance student learning?   What shall I do next?*   Another set of high and worthwhile goals is determined for students, instruction is implemented, student responses analyzed and assessed, and the teacher once again reflects on the effectiveness of his or her teaching as the basis for new goals.

Core Proposition 5: Teachers are members of learning communities.

At each step, the accomplished teacher might ask, *What materials, people, or places in the school or community could I utilize to enhance students' learning experiences?* All available resources are accessed to support and enhance student achievement, including work with parents, colleagues, community members, and technology.   Regular communication with parents to share information and involve them in the learning experiences of their children is especially important.

Research tells us that learning communities should also be part of a teacher's professional growth.   Conscious reflection to improve teaching is often deeper and richer when prompted by colleagues.   In the certification process, support sessions provide candidates with opportunities to discuss the meaning of high and worthwhile goals for students and the strength of evidence provided by written analysis of student work samples, videotapes, and other documentation.   Through interaction with others, candidates often gain new perspectives on their own work.

Examining Practice

The exercises that follow are intended to stimulate reflection, dialogue, and sharing of "best practices" among teachers.   Exercises are sequenced to lead you from general to more specific understandings, and to help you translate The Five Core Propositions into actual practices in the classroom and learning community.

You may or may not have the time and inclination to give a written response to each of the suggested exercises below.   However, it is essential to recognize the importance of The Five Core Propositions, their relationship to the Standards for a given certificate area, and the degree of detail that is necessary to provide written evidence of the propositions in your teaching practice.   A thorough study of The Five Core Propositions and Standards can also help you take stock of your strengths as a teacher, and identify areas in which you may wish to improve.

If you choose to complete each of these exercises, you will be building a collection of evidence of teaching to Standards in your practice. You will also find that you will be able to draw upon these examples as you begin your work on the portfolio entries in the chapters that follow. We will continue to help you develop both the quantity and quality of your evidence throughout the book.

Exercise 4-1: Describing the Qualities of an Accomplished Teacher

As experienced professionals, we each have our beliefs about what it means to be an exemplary teacher. This exercise provides a link between personal, individual perspectives and The Five Core Propositions that form the basis for accomplished teaching as defined by the NBPTS Standards.

To use the worksheet for Exercise 4-1, ask yourself, "What are the qualities of an accomplished teacher?" and brainstorm a list of all the important qualities that come to mind. Think about memorable teachers you have had, peers that you admire, and your own strengths in the classroom. After completing the list, refer to The Five Core Propositions, and see how the qualities you listed align with one or more of them.

In a study group, you may wish to do this activity first as partners, then share and chart ideas as a large group. In Figure 8, a sample chart

Qualities of an Accomplished Teacher	Five Core Propositions
• Knows content area (2) • Uses effective teaching strategies (2) • Organized (3) • Understands how to motivate students (1) • Has good classroom management (1) (3) • Flexible (1) • Has high expectations of students (1) (2) • Has lots of patience (1) • Provides for individual differences (1) (2) • Pursues on-going professional development (4) (5) • Innovative, creative (2) (4) • Continually improves lessons (4) • Uses assessment to inform instruction (3) • Involves parents (5)	1. Committed to Students 2. Knows Subject and How to Teach It 3. Manages and Monitors Student Learning 4. Thinks About Practice & Learns from Experience 5. Member of Learning Communities

Figure 8. Sample: Exercise 4-1: Describing the Qualities of an Accomplished Teacher.
Teachers' current beliefs about accomplished teaching practices are connected to The Five Core Propositions of NBPTS.

generated from a discussion group is compared to a list of The Five Core Propositions. The "most fitting" propositions are noted in parentheses after each phrase on the chart.

In the sample we have provided a very short list of qualities, but you can see that these are a starting point for discussing the attributes that lie behind each one of The Five Core Propositions. It also allows teachers to see that no one proposition is a stand-alone statement.

Accomplished teaching occurs in many different types of classrooms, with many different kinds of teachers. Although every teacher will have his or her own philosophy of teaching and style in the classroom, the underlying structure for planning and managing the learning experience must be apparent in fundamental attributes of the teacher's practice.

Exercise 4-2: Reflecting on The Five Core Propositions: *What Teachers Should Know and Be Able to Do*

In the NBPTS document describing The Five Core Propositions, *What Teachers Should Know and Be Able to Do*, each of the propositions is described in detail. The worksheet for Exercise 4-2 (Reflecting on The Five Core Propositions) is designed to prompt your thinking as you read and reflect on each proposition, and help you build a richer, more personal

	Core Proposition	My Reflection
1	I show that I am committed to students and their learning when I.....	*...learn as much as I can about each student. I find time to talk with each student personally at least once a week. I learn about their families, their interests, and their out of school activities. This helps me maintain a personal relationship with each student and gives me insights into possible motivational learning activities.*
2	I demonstrate that I know my subject and how to teach it by...	*...introducing my students to the lives, perspectives and styles of famous authors. Throughout the year, I've worked with my students to read, reflect, and write together as an authentic community of writers, producing work for various purposes.*
3	I display my ability to manage and monitor student learning when I....	*...plan my goals, assessments, and instructional strategies to challenge and encourage student learning. I monitor my students' progress by reviewing their drafts with them on a regular basis and prompting them to make their own choices about revisions, rather than telling them what I think they should do.*

Figure 9. Sample: Exercise 4-2: Reflecting on The Five Core Propositions.
Specific examples from a teacher's practice are described in response to each of the core proposition prompts. The first three of The Five Core Propositions are shown in this sample.

Key Words and Phrases	General Statement	Specific Statement
Monitor what students see and hear. Understand developmental characteristics. Extend efforts beyond cognitive learning to address the whole child.	*I hold a group circle every day. This allows me to listen to my students and learn more about them so that I can address their needs and interests.*	*My class begins with a daily group "circle" to discuss news, events, and concerns that students may want to share. This gives me insight into things that influence my students outside of class. In one case, students wanted to talk about the recent death of a tutor from the school. Although she hadn't worked with our class, she had tutored many of the children in past years, and from the discussion, I found that several students were profoundly affected, and in need of extra TLC and emotional support. I arranged for our school counselor to lead a discussion with them, and to give me advice on how to respond to their questions…*
Understand cultural and social characteristics of students' families and communities.	*I make an effort to learn about the diverse cultural backgrounds of my students so that I can make my teaching relevant for them.*	*Though my school is known for its cultural diversity, for the first time last year we began to enroll increasing numbers of students from M__. As this was a new cultural group for me, I asked for assistance from my ESL resource teacher, who arranged for me to meet with Mrs. A, a parent who became a valuable source of information for me throughout the year as follows… The insights I gained from Mrs. A were invaluable in helping me address student needs, for example…*

Figure 10. Example of General vs. Specific Statements.
Key words and phrases from Core Proposition 1: *Teachers are committed to students and their learning* are provided with contrasting descriptions of practice.

view of each. Think about how you demonstrate these qualities in your classroom. A written reflection on each of The Five Core Propositions as shown in Figure 9 (Sample Exercise 4-2) will provide a starting place for your collection of evidence for your Standards. In this sample, we show only brief responses to each proposition, but we encourage you to write at length about each one.

Exercise 4-3: Analyzing Practice

In Exercise 4-2 you are asked write a holistic reflection in response to each of The Five Core Propositions. Exercise 4-3 will ask you to be more specific—to highlight and list the key words and phrases from the text for each chapter and describe authentic examples of each from your practice. This exercise is designed to help you think and write about your teaching in such a way that you demonstrate evidence of the specific behaviors described in The Five Core Propositions.

When you write about your teaching practices, you must provide enough detail to clearly and convincingly illustrate situations in your classroom. Candidates often provide very general statements about what they do that contain little or no evidence.

The responses to "Key Words and Phrases" from Core Proposition 1 in Figure 10 (Example of General vs. Specific Statements) illustrate the difference in the quality of evidence provided by detailed descriptions from classroom practice versus general, unembellished statements that are common to beginning candidates. In Exercise 4-3, try writing concise, but detailed descriptions of your classroom practices that correspond directly to the key words and phrases of each proposition. Use authentic examples of teaching to the core proposition whenever possible. An example of this exercise is shown in Figure 11.

To use the worksheet for Exercise 4-3, write key words and phrases from the selected proposition in the left column. Personalize each by rephrasing it as an "I" statement as shown in Figure 11. In the right column, describe a specific example from your classroom as evidence that you exemplify this practice in your teaching.

If used in a study group, participants might work individually or as partners to do an in-depth study of one proposition, using the complete text. For each proposition, key words and phrases from the chapter can be charted and shared with other participants. Group sharing can be followed by a few minutes of quiet time for personal reflective writing. Using this strategy will provide everyone with an overview of the key words and phrases in addition to practice at how to study them.

For pre-candidate study groups this exercise can provide the foundation for a series of sessions in which teachers examine, analyze, and reflect on their personal teaching practices. For most teachers, the notion of providing evidence through writing is new and practice is needed to develop this important skill. When teachers practice writing with specific details and examples and share these pieces with others, they develop an understanding about the meaning and quality of evidence.

Many candidates will feel they lack the time to do a complete written analysis of each of The Five Core Propositions, and may choose to practice these exercises mentally rather than literally. However, if you generate numerous specific examples for each of The Five Core Propositions, you will make great strides in understanding and accumulating evidence of accomplished teaching that may later be embedded in your portfolio entries. At the very least, practice the writing with one or two examples, then share your results with a friend. Refer to the samples provided, and ask if your description is detailed and specific enough to serve as evidence of your practice.

Proposition #1:
I Am Committed to Students and Their Learning

Key Words and Phrases

I believe that all students can learn.	*I started the year with several new ESL students who knew little or no English. I knew that I would need more information about their culture and families in order to help them learn, so I enlisted the help of my ESL teacher. I asked everyone who saw them during the day including my principal and cafeteria workers to make a special point of talking to these students using short words and phrases in order to support their language acquisition. The students were shy at first, but with the help and interest from everyone, they showed rapid improvement in language and learning...*
I appreciate individual traits and talents.	*Sammy is an active and talkative child. Although he can be disruptive, he really has a talent for making people laugh. He is often the first child to make a new student feel welcome.*
I monitor what students see and hear.	*Every day we open with a group "circle" to discuss news, events, and concerns that students may want to share. This has given me insight into things that influence my students outside of my class. It also allows me to help the students process experiences that cause concern. For example....*
I understand my students' developmental characteristics.	*Sammy's "disruptive" behavior is very normal for his age. At six years old, he is exploring his social relationships with peers, and his ability to control his natural impulses is limited. Small group discussions are the key to many learning experiences in my class, as they provide Sammy and others with the social opportunities they crave.*

Figure 11. Sample: Exercise 4-3: Analyzing Practice.
Actual teaching practices of an *Early Childhood Generalist* are described with reference to key words and phrases from Core Proposition 1.

Sharing and discussing examples of evidence with others is a valuable way to build your understanding of how to provide evidence in the Written Commentary. You will need multiple examples of teaching to each of The Five Core Propositions that, in turn, provide evidence of teaching to your Standards. Descriptive details that illustrate what, why, and how learning activities took place in the classroom provide the authenticity sought by an assessor.

Exercise 4-4: The Whole Picture

Exercise 4-4 (The Whole Picture) returns us to the *architecture of accomplished teaching*. Accomplished teaching rests on a purposeful structure exemplified by The Five Core Propositions. In Figure 12, questions for each of The Five Core Propositions are shown to guide your thinking about the architecture of your teaching.

Use Exercise 4-4 to describe teaching practices that *work together* to support student learning. Like the puzzle pieces in the figure, your practices must fit smoothly together to create a cohesive, effective learning environment focused on student learning. Taken together, your evidence of The Five Core Propositions will create a structure that illustrates alignment of your accomplished teaching decisions and practices.

Core Teaching Practices

The exercises in this chapter have illustrated ways for you to think in detail about what you do in the classroom. Very experienced teachers often have difficulty analyzing their practice simply because their teaching behaviors have become very automatic and intuitive over the years. In order to provide evidence, you must be able to break down your specific teaching actions and explain how they help students learn.

Some teachers will feel that they do not have much evidence, because what they do in the classroom just is not that special. Although many of our teaching practices seem very routine, there are important reasons for everything we do. The National Board Certification process will ask you to analyze in detail *what* you do and *why* you do it. Remember—this process is about analyzing your everyday teaching practices. What are the things you do in your classes that help your students learn? What are some of the routines you have developed over the years that help you know your students and their families better? How do you organize activities to meet the developmental needs of your students? How do such routines help improve student learning? How do your routines and practices support your personal *architecture of accomplished teaching*? As you write about your classroom practices in the portfolio entries, you will be asked not only to describe what you do, but also to analyze and reflect about your activities.

At each step in the process of National Board Certification, you will be asked to justify the decisions you make about planning and conducting your lessons, and to discuss your thoughts about your work with students. Exercises such as those provided in this chapter may help you begin the reflective practice that is key to a successful portfolio entry.

Prompts for Exercise 4-4: Fitting the Pieces Together

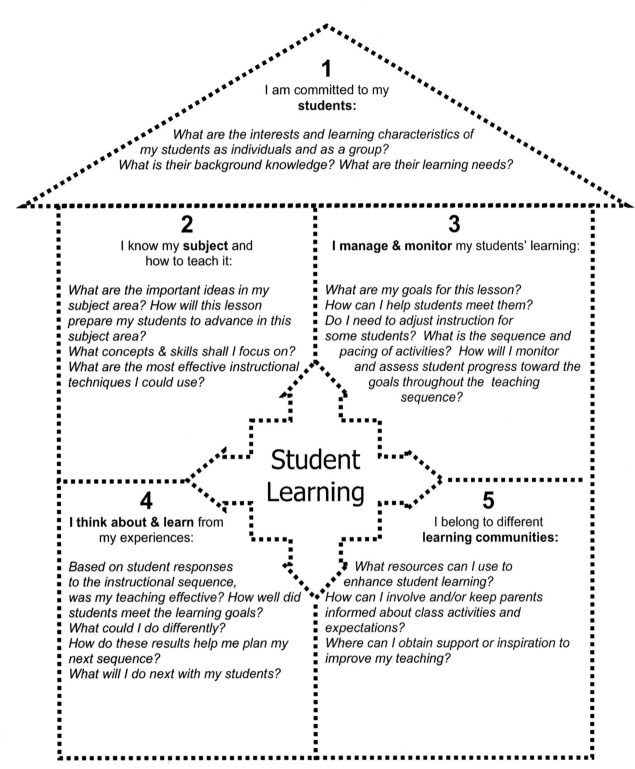

1
I am committed to my
students:

What are the interests and learning characteristics of
my students as individuals and as a group?
What is their background knowledge? What are their learning needs?

2
I know my **subject** and
how to teach it:

What are the important ideas in my
subject area? How will this lesson
prepare my students to advance in this
subject area?
What concepts & skills shall I focus on?
What are the most effective instructional
techniques I could use?

3
I manage & monitor my students' learning:

What are my goals for this lesson?
How can I help students meet them?
Do I need to adjust instruction for
some students? What is the sequence and
pacing of activities? How will I monitor
and assess student progress toward the
goals throughout the teaching
sequence?

Student Learning

4
I think about & learn from
my experiences:

Based on student responses
to the instructional sequence,
was my teaching effective? How well did
students meet the learning goals?
What could I do differently?
How do these results help me plan my
next sequence?
What will I do next with my students?

5
I belong to different
learning communities:

What resources can I use to
enhance student learning?
How can I involve and/or keep parents
informed about class activities and
expectations?
Where can I obtain support or inspiration to
improve my teaching?

Figure 12. Prompts for Exercise 4-4: Fitting the Pieces Together.
Use these prompts to help you complete your exercise.

Accomplished Teaching Permit Quiz

Without looking back through the text, list The Five Core Propositions in order:

1.

2.

3.

4.

5.

Reflection:
What implications do The Five Core Propositions have for your teaching?

If this is difficult, you need to go back and review.
You should know The Five Core Propositions by heart in order to continue.

Key Points for Candidate Support Providers

Exercise 4-1: Qualities of an Accomplished Teacher is an excellent way to introduce The Five Core Propositions to a new National Board study group. Candidates will make the connection from real, familiar classroom practices to the teaching behaviors described in the text.

Have your candidates work in a small group or as partners first, listing exemplary practices that come to mind. Then ask groups to share as many ideas as possible, "round robin style," while you chart the responses on a large chart or overhead transparency. Introduce The Five Core Propositions, and ask candidates to connect the charted behaviors to one or more of the propositions.

You may want to follow with Exercise 4-2 (Reflecting on The Five Core Propositions: *What Teachers Should Know and Be Able to Do*) in the same session, having candidates reflect, write, and discuss what they do in practice as examples of each proposition. It is critical to make the propositions "come alive" by connecting them to real classroom practices. At the same time, you will be introducing candidates to the notion of providing evidence by describing their specific teaching behaviors. You may suggest Exercise 4-3 with one or more of the propositions as a more in-depth reflective writing exercise for homework, which will provide the basis for a comprehensive discussion of evidence at your next session.

Though all the core propositions are important, initially candidates may find it easiest to reflect and write about Core Proposition 3: *Teachers Are Responsible for Managing and Monitoring Student Learning.* This proposition refers to lesson planning, instruction, and assessment, which involve concrete behaviors performed routinely in every classroom. Through continued reading, writing, and reflection, candidates will soon discover how the other propositions contribute to the effectiveness of the familiar instructional sequence.

Exercises 4-2 and 4-3 help candidates understand what is meant by evidence. As shown, one descriptive paragraph may address several aspects of accomplished teaching. Candidates must learn to provide rich, concise descriptions of practice, with specific examples that demonstrate teaching to the core propositions and Standards. Ask group members to bring their examples of evidence to every support session to share and discuss as a strategy for developing descriptive writing skills.

The chapter begins and ends with the *architecture of accomplished teaching.* Exercise 4-4 leads the candidates to consider how his or her examples of evidence must be unified by the demonstration of a systematic approach to student learning that addresses the needs of *these students, at this time, in this setting.*

The exercises in Chapter 4 can be used as the foundation for discussion in study groups for candidates and non-candidates alike. Groups composed of teachers without the time constraints of candidates can use these exercises as the basis for discussion over many sessions.

Exercise 4-1: Qualities of an Accomplished Teacher

Brainstorm List	Five Core Propositions
	1. Teachers are committed to students and their learning.
	2. Teachers know the subjects they teach and how to teach those subjects to students.
	3. Teachers are responsible for managing and monitoring student learning.
	4. Teachers think systematically about their practice and learn from experience.
	5. Teachers are members of learning communities.

Directions: In the first column, brainstorm actions and behaviors that you think are demonstrated by exemplary teachers. Then see if you can connect each of these qualities to one or more of The Five Core Propositions.

Exercise 4-2: Reflecting on The Five Core Propositions
What Teachers Should Know and Be Able to Do

	The Five Core Propositions	My Reflection
1	*I show that I am committed to students and their learning when I…..*	
2	*I demonstrate that I know my subject and how to teach it by….*	
3	*I display my ability to manage and monitor student learning when I….*	
4	*I demonstrate that I think systematically about my practice and learn from experience when I….*	
5	*I work with different learning communities in the following ways:*	

Directions: Before you read more about The Five Core Propositions, *What Teachers Should Know and Be Able to Do,* respond to each of the prompts above as you reflect on your teaching practices. Give as many examples as possible.

Exercise 4-3: Analyzing Practice

Core Proposition:	
Key Words and Phrases	My Evidence

Directions: This exercise calls for multiple and specific examples of your teaching that provide evidence of the proposition as described in the key words and phrases from *What Teachers Should Know and Be Able to Do*. Give the proposition title in the form of an "I" statement at the top of the page. List key words and phrases in the left column. In the right column, describe specific examples from your practice. You may need to use several pages for each proposition.

Exercise 4-4: Fitting the Pieces Together

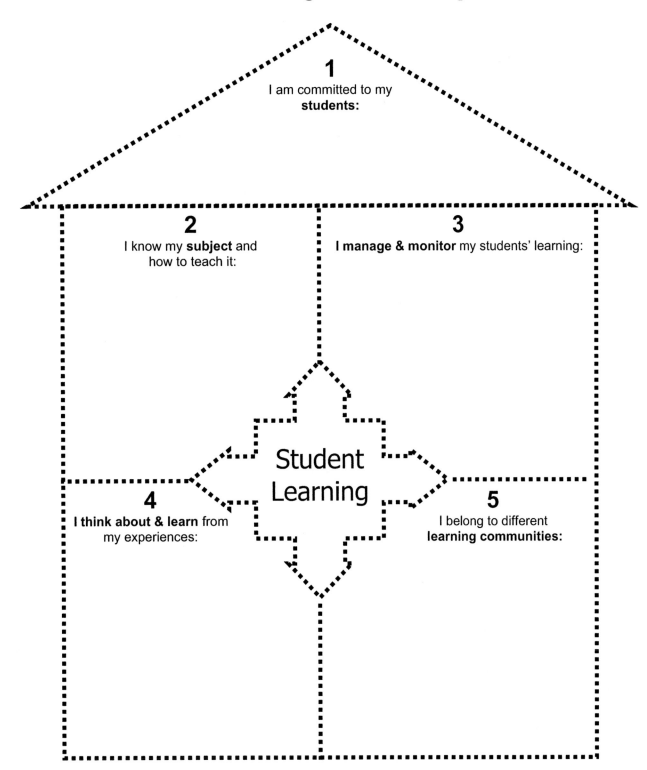

1

I am committed to my **students:**

2

I know my **subject** and how to teach it:

3

I **manage & monitor** my students' learning:

Student Learning

4

I think about & learn from my experiences:

5

I belong to different **learning communities:**

Directions: Each piece of the puzzle represents one of The Five Core Propositions. On each piece, use the prompts in the chapter to write about evidence of your practice. Your pieces of evidence should work together to demonstrate a cohesive approach to student learning in your classroom. Think of this as the blueprint for your personal *architecture of accomplished teaching.*

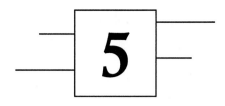

Mapping Your Entries
and Standards

Featured Resources:

- Standards
- Portfolio Instructions

Every traveler needs a map when entering unfamiliar territory, and the same is true for your journey toward National Board Certification. In this chapter, we will describe "the big picture" of your Portfolio, which consists of four separate entries. We will show you how to locate key information and encourage you to create a summary "map" as a visual aid and reference for the requirements of each entry.

These requirements are found in the certificate-specific Portfolio Instructions provided by NBPTS. Each entry consists of a double-spaced Written Commentary approximately eleven pages long accompanied by supporting artifacts in the form of videotapes, student work, instructional materials, and/or other items.

The Portfolio Instructions are very explicit, with prompts designed to help you provide the information needed for assessors to determine that your entry meets the criteria for accomplished teaching according to the Standards for your certificate area. Each entry is intended to help you produce different kinds of evidence so that you may demonstrate a broad range of capabilities.

There are three types of entries:

1.   An entry that requires you to analyze and submit student work samples with a discussion of a lesson that is carried out in the classroom during the course of your candidacy. For most candidates, this is Entry 1.

2. Entries that require you to submit short, unedited videotapes with a discussion of lessons that you will carry out in the classroom during the course of your candidacy. For most candidates, these are Entries 2 and 3.

3. An entry in which you will be asked to describe work during the past one to five years with parents, community, and/or professional colleagues that has helped to support and enhance student learning. This is Entry 4, Documented Accomplishments: Contributions to Student Learning. This entry includes a specific requirement for evidence of on-going communication with students' families during your current teaching year.

All entries require supporting documentation in the form of work samples, video recordings, instructional materials, or other artifacts. The mapping process will help you determine the specific materials required for each of your entries.

Unpacking the Entry

Faced with 300 or so pages of text in the Portfolio Instructions, candidates often feel overwhelmed with the enormity of the task ahead. We encourage candidates to look at each entry and, one at a time, locate the critical features and create a summary of the entry for convenient reference. In doing so, anxiety is reduced through clear understanding of the assessment task.

Instructions for each of the four entries are formatted similarly. The entry opens with a brief overview that describes the "big picture" or essence of what the entry is designed to capture. The instructions for each entry also list the required Standards, for which evidence must be provided, and the following sections to guide your work:

What Do I Need To Do?
This section describes the specific items that must be submitted for scoring of the entry, as well as any other relevant requirements.

How Will My Response Be Scored?
The criteria for assessing the entry are listed here. These include the Standards for the entry, a statement about how the candidate's response will be judged, which we refer to as a "Summary Statement," and the Level 4 Rubric based on the Standards for the entry.

Composing My Written Commentary
In this section, specific prompts for developing the Written Commentary are provided to guide the candidate's response. These prompts are

designed to help the writer describe teaching practices with the necessary degree of detail to produce evidence of the Core Propositions and Standards. Headers within the Written Commentary usually designate three to four subsections for context, planning and instruction, analysis of student learning, and reflection on teaching. Suggested page lengths to guide the writer are given for each subsection.

The remaining sections in the entry instructions provide additional information to support the candidate. These are self-explanatory as follows:

- Making Good Choices
- Format Specifications
- Cover Sheets and Forms

In the exercise that follows, we will help you locate the key features for an entry, and show you one way to summarize them using the Entry Map template provided here. You might choose to use a different format to summarize your own entry requirements, but we encourage you to create similar overviews, as we have found them to be very helpful for candidates.

We will use the *Early Childhood Through Young Adult Library Media 2006–07* Portfolio Instructions for Entry 4, Documented Accomplishments, to guide you through a sample entry analysis and mapping in the exercise below. Entry 4 is the one entry in which candidates describe their professional work outside of the classroom, and instructions for Entry 4 are similar for all certificate areas. After walking through this exercise with Entry 4, try making your own summary of this entry, as well as for Entries 1, 2, and 3.

Exercise 5-1: Entry Mapping

To use Exercise 5-1, refer to Figure 13 and locate the template for the exercise at the end of the chapter. Open your Portfolio Instructions to Entry 4: Documented Accomplishments to identify the referenced information.

Although Entry 4 is similar for all certificate areas, there are differences, and you must locate the key information in your own portfolio instructions to insure accuracy. On our template, the sample map contains four boxes. Each box will be filled with key information about the entry task, found in the sections **What Do I Need To Do?** and **How Will My Response Be Scored?** [32]

Sample: Exercise 5-1 Entry Mapping

Entry#: 4	Title: Documented Accomplishments (Early Childhood Through Young Adult Library Media 2006–07)

Box1: What Do I Need To Do?	Box 2: Standards For This Entry
1. Written Commentary: 10-page maximum Description & Analysis of Accomplishments 2. Reflective Summary: 2 pages maximum 3. Documentation: 16-page maximum	VII. Reflective Practice VIII. Professional Growth X. Leadership, Advocacy, and Community Partnerships *(Note: These Standards are specific to the Library Media certificate area)*

Box 3: Summary Statement:

I must provide clear, convincing and consistent evidence…of my ability to further student learning through my work with families and the community, with colleagues and other professionals, and as a learner.

Box 4: How Will My Response Be Scored?(Level 4 rubric - Scoring Criteria)

- Treat parents and other interested adults as valued partners in students' development and education;

- Use thoughtfully chosen, appropriate strategies that may or may not be original, but are effective in engaging parents and other adults in two-way communication focused primarily on substantive teaching and learning issues and individual student progress;

- Facilitate ongoing, mutually beneficial interactions between the students and the wider community in a way that enhances teaching and learning;

- Engage in conscious and deliberate ongoing professional development to strengthen my knowledge, skills, and abilities relevant to my teaching context;

- Work collaboratively with colleagues to improve teaching and learning within my school or in the wider professional community;

- Share my expertise in a leadership role with other educators through facilitating professional development of other teachers, improving instructional practices, or advocacy for positive change in educational policy;

- Accurately analyze and thoughtfully reflect on the significance of all my accomplishments taken together, and appropriately plan for future opportunities to impact student learning;

Figure 13. Sample: Exercise 5-1: Entry Mapping.
In this sample, key elements for the NBPTS *Early Childhood Through Young Adult Library Media certificate, 2006–07*, Entry 4, 2007 are shown.

Box 1: What Do I Need To Do?

Referring to the first five pages of your Portfolio Instructions for Entry 4, find the heading **What Do I Need To Do?** A bulleted list describes each item that must be submitted for scoring. In our sample map of Entry 4, the following task requirements are listed in Box 1:

1. Written Commentary; Description & Analysis of Accomplishments – 10 pages maximum;
2. Reflective Summary – 2 pages maximum; and
3. Documentation – 16 pages maximum.

Box 2: Standards For This Entry

For each entry, specific Standards must be addressed. These will be found under the next bold heading in the Entry Instructions: **How Will My Response Be Scored?** The Standards referenced for Entry 4 will differ in number and title, depending on the certificate area. In our sample entry, we have referenced the Standards listed for the *Early Childhood Through Young Adult Library Media 2006–07* certificate. There are three Standards listed for this certificate area:

VII. Reflective Practice
VIII. Professional Growth
X. Leadership, Advocacy, and Community Partnerships

Now find *your* required Standards for this entry. Look at your instructions for Entry 4 under the bold heading **How Will My Response Be Scored?** Your instructions may list one or more Standards, with titles that are different from those shown in our sample. To create a summary sheet for *your* entry 4, be sure to list the Standards required by your own Portfolio Instructions.

Box 3: Summary Statement

The summary statement will be found in bold type, following the Standards noted in the section **How Will My Response Be Scored?** It begins with the phrase:

> *Your response will be judged on the extent to which it provides* ***clear, convincing, and consistent evidence...***

In the sample shown here, we have phrased the statement in first person:

> *I must provide clear, convincing, and consistent evidence of my ability to further student learning through my work with families*

and the community, with colleagues and other professionals, and as a learner.

Be sure to check the wording of your Entry 4 summary statement before including it on your outline.

Box 4: Scoring Criteria

It is very important to locate the scoring criteria for each entry, as these will guide your selection of evidence. We will refer to these same criteria in several subsequent exercises. Immediately following the summary statement in the **How Will My Response Be Scored?** section, you will find this phrase:

> *The Level 4 Rubric, the highest level of the rubric, specifically requires **clear, convincing, and consistent evidence** in your response that you...*

The phrase will be followed by a bulleted list. This is a list of criteria from the highest level of the rubric that will be used to score the entry. The rubrics are drawn directly from the Standards for each certificate area. In our sample, we have paraphrased and placed the scoring criteria found in the bulleted list from **How Will My Response Be Scored?** in Box 4 of our summary sheet. Be sure to check the criteria listed in your Portfolio Instructions for Entry 4 and check them against those we have paraphrased in our sample. As you create an Entry 4 summary, you may need to revise the rubric shown here to make it more accurate for your specific instructions.

If you create your own Entry 4 map, be sure to locate and correctly list the Standards required for the entry *in your certificate area*, and check the accuracy of our sample map against your Portfolio Instructions. When you have done so, you will have a complete map for Entry 4, Documented Accomplishments: Contributions to Student Learning.

Mapping Entries 1, 2, and 3

We have walked you through the sample to show you how to summarize your instructions for an entry. We recommend that you follow a similar process to summarize, or "map," each of your remaining portfolio tasks.

You will find such maps will provide you with one to two page reference sheets for each of the individual entries and, taken together, an overview of the most relevant aspects of each entry and of the entire portfolio. They will also be useful to provide to supporters who may read and give feedback on your work

A blank, reproducible template for Exercise 5-1 (Entry Mapping) is provided for your use at the end of this chapter and in electronic form on the CD. Whether you use these templates or create your own entry outlines, we recommend that you save them in electronic form, as you will be able to copy and transfer information as needed to subsequent exercise sheets, if desired.

To summarize, using the provided templates:

In Box 1: Each entry will require a Written Commentary in addition to other evidence, which may include videotape, student work, instructional materials, and/or other artifacts. List the specific requirements for the entry.

In Box 2: List the specific Standards required for each entry.

In Box 3: Include the bold-type summary statement found in the section **How Will My Response Be Scored?** If you prefer, rewrite it in first-person format.

In Box 4: List the specific scoring criteria for the entry from the Level 4 Rubric, found immediately after the summary statement.

It is possible that the NBPTS Portfolio Instructions document format may change in future years, but it will always be important to locate and focus on the key elements of your task. Be sure to follow the directions provided in *your* Portfolio Instructions.

Once you understand the requirements for your classroom-based entries, you will begin to consider specific lessons to fulfill the entry requirements. Scheduling your teaching for these entries on a master calendar will insure completion well ahead of your portfolio due date. (See Chapter 3: Organizing Your Resources.) For entries requiring video recordings, you will want to plan for the possibility that several taping sessions may be necessary before you have a recording that satisfies you.

As you begin to draft your entry pieces, you will find that summaries such as those described in this chapter are useful tools when you ask someone to read and give feedback on your work (See Chapter 2: Support Systems). After you have finished your Written Commentary for an entry, you can provide this overview to your reader with your draft. This tells the reader what is important in the entry, and gives the criteria by which it will be scored.

Exercise 5-2: Standards Mapping

In this next exercise, a one-page overview can be created to show which Standards are most important in each portfolio entry. We encourage you to use the exercise sheet provided or your own version, refer to Figure 14 (Sample Exercise 5-2: Standards Mapping), and list each of *your* Standards by number and title in the first and second columns. Then, using your Portfolio Instructions or summaries such as those created in the previous exercise, mark the Standards that are featured in each entry. Creating this one-page overview will help you to see the distribution of your Standards across different entries, and may help you highlight different aspects of the Standards in your work. The number of Standards will vary, depending on certificate area.

Sample: Exercise 5-2 Standards Mapping
Certificate Area: Early Childhood Through Young Adult Library Media 2006–07

Standard	Title	Entry 1	Entry 2	Entry 3	Entry 4
I	Knowledge of Learners	X	X	X	
II	Knowledge of Teaching and Learning	X	X	X	
III	Knowledge of Library and Information Studies	X	X	X	
IV	Integrating Instruction	X		X	
V	Leading Innovation through the Library Media Program			X	
VI	Administering the Library Media Program	X	X		
VII	Reflective Practice	X	X	X	X
VIII	Professional Growth				X
IX	Ethics, Equity, and Diversity		X	X	
X	Leadership, Advocacy, and Community Partnerships				X

Figure 14. Sample: Exercise 5-2: Standards Mapping.
Shown with the Standards for the *NBPTS Early Childhood Through Young Adult Library Media certificate, 2006–07*

Teaching and Writing - Which Entry First?

Now that you are familiar with some of the key requirements of each entry, where should you begin? Your completed portfolio will consist of three entries that are based on lessons you will plan, teach, and write about (Entries 1, 2, and 3), and one entry in which you describe your work with parents, community, and/or professional colleagues beyond the fundamental requirements of your teaching position (Entry 4).

Should you start with Entry 1 and do each entry in order? Is there another approach? If you are in a structured support program or college credit class, your instructor or facilitator may ask you to begin your work with a particular entry. If your support is more loosely structured, it may be entirely up to you.

Your decision may be influenced by the time of year in which you begin your portfolio work and/or your schedule for teaching particular lessons that you have selected for each entry. Many candidates who start their portfolio work during the summer months begin with Entry 4. This is the only entry which can be substantially developed (though not entirely finished) during a non-teaching period. You can draw upon accomplishments dating back several years, write and collect documentation about them, then finalize the remaining requirements of the entry once the school year resumes.

Many experienced support providers feel strongly that candidates should *not* begin with Entry 4. They believe that it is important for candidates to begin with one of the three teaching entries in order to connect immediately to the most valued aspect of the assessment: Describing, analyzing, and reflecting on classroom practices.

Both approaches have merit. Your professional growth in the certification process will occur through early and continual engagement with the classroom-based entries. Revisions of your entry drafts in which you write about your teaching, analyze student progress, and reflect on the effectiveness of your classroom practices are critical to your success. Your participation in a candidate support group and consideration of feedback from one or more readers will help you consider new perspectives and develop your skills as you write about your work with students. The process of writing, reflecting on your work, and re-writing is your primary tool for learning how to provide clear, convincing, and consistent evidence of your accomplished teaching practices.

That being said, it is also very important that you review the requirements of Entry 4 very early in your portfolio work. Many candidates find they are weak in one or more of the required areas for Entry 4, and must take action during the year of candidacy to strengthen these areas. At a minimum, we recommend that you make a list of accomplishments you might include for Entry 4 and note sources of documentation to accompany them during the beginning stages of your portfolio work. You will want to make sure that you can thoroughly address all requirements and complete Entry 4 well ahead of your deadline for submitting the portfolio.

The next few chapters will support you in your work with Entries 1, 2, and 3. For more information on working with Entry 4, see Chapter 10: Contributions to Student Learning.

Key Points for Candidate Support Providers

- Encourage candidates to complete summaries for each entry so they will be able to see the big picture of the entire portfolio. It is helpful to see the commonalities in the entries in terms of the format used for the Portfolio Instructions, as well as to see how different Standards, or aspects of Standards are featured in the different entries.

- The exercises in this chapter will clarify the task ahead and encourage candidates to work independently between support sessions. Working with Exercises 5-1 and 5-2 will help teachers begin to identify and discuss sources of evidence in their regular classroom routines even if they are not ready to teach the featured lesson.

- The relationship of the Standards to The Five Core Propositions, and the importance of both to the final entry cannot be overstated. The Five Core Propositions provide a structure, or architecture, for the alignment of Standards-based teaching practices. This concept is discussed in more detail in Chapter 9.

- Candidate support providers should remember that when candidates start to write they are simultaneously learning a new process of writing for reflection. This multi-layered task is a difficult one, so the CSP can facilitate the learning by constructing time for candidates to talk with each other, or with a CSP to find evidence of The Five Core Propositions in their writing. Later, when they are beginning to embody the standards in their writing, they can read for evidence of the standards in their writing. Ways to read are presented in a later chapter.

- The importance of mapping the entry cannot be overstated. Mapping helps the candidate see the essential components of the entry and the relationship of the scoring rubric to the prompting questions. Once candidates see that each entry follows a similar format, they are better able to focus on the details that differentiate the rubric for each entry and to understand the evidence that must be provided. Mapping encourages candidates to take the initiative to plan instruction and to work ahead on entries at their own pace.

Exercise 5-1: Entry Mapping

Entry#:	Title:

Box 1: What Do I Need To Do?	Box 2: Standards For This Entry

Box 3: Summary Statement: (finish statement)

I must provide clear, convincing and consistent evidence…

Box 4: How Will My Response Be Scored?(Level 4 Rubric - Scoring Criteria)

-

Directions: This sheet may be copied for each entry: 1, 2, and 3. Locate and fill in the key information from your Portfolio Instructions as described in the chapter.

Exercise 5-2: Standards Mapping

Certificate Area: _____.

Standard	Title	Entry 1	Entry 2	Entry 3	Entry 4
I					
II					
III					
IV					
V					
VI					
VII					
VIII					
IX					
X					
XI					
XII					
XIII					
XIV					
XV					
XVI					

Directions: List each of your Standards in numerical order, then refer to your Portfolio Instructions to mark the Standards required for each of your entries. This will give you an overview of the required Standards for all your portfolio entries.

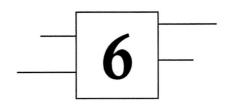

Student-Centered Teaching

<u>Core Proposition 1:</u>

Teachers Are Committed
to Students
and Their Learning

The teacher's commitment to student learning is at the heart of the National Board Certification process. An accomplished teacher must believe he or she can make a difference in the lives of all students, no matter what challenges are presented. Poverty, cultural differences, language barriers, and other social circumstances may drive a teacher to seek solutions, but they do not affect a teacher's belief in the learning ability of all children.

> *Responsive teachers have a vision that places the best interests of students, as those interests are related to their development as complete human beings, and, most essentially as unique human beings, at the center of their practice.*

> *- Shelley Sherman*[33]

Within both large and small group settings, teachers must be sensitive to the individual needs of students and respond appropriately to them. When teachers have high and worthwhile goals for every student and effectively monitor learning, student achievement improves.

Knowing and caring about your students is the foundation for accomplished teaching practices. *Core Proposition 1: Teachers Are Committed to Students and Their Learning* must be *clearly, convincingly and consistently* demonstrated in each portfolio entry. In Entries 1, 2 and 3, it must be apparent in each step of your instructional planning and implementation.

Knowing Your Students

Moving from an instructional paradigm to a learning paradigm is a distinctive mark of a maturing, caring, and competent teacher.

- David Tripp[34]

It should be no surprise that the importance of relationship and knowing your students appears in literature related to school reform, effective teaching, differentiation, and other topics for educational improvement. Accomplished teachers know both general characteristics of their students, such as development and learning theories, as well as specific characteristics of students' families and communities. They also know students' academic and social skills, motivations, learning styles, and interests. They use this knowledge when planning and conducting lessons to help every student be successful.

Conversations

To address the needs of individual learners, teachers must first know their students. This is easier for elementary level teachers who spend all day every day for a year with the same students, but may be far more challenging for secondary teachers with one hundred students or more who rotate through their classroom during several periods per day. In both cases, consider conversations as a first step for building your knowledge of students.

When researchers ask youths who have dropped out of high school why they left school, the young people frequently say it was because no one cared. Those who stayed in school cite meaningful relationships with adults who show an interest in them as individuals.

-Deborah Stipek[35]

Most teachers will have opportunities for conversations with students in non-classroom settings before or after school, or between classes. However, it is also possible to create in-classroom conversation opportunities through your lesson design. When your teaching strategies include dialogue and problem-solving in pairs or small groups, you are able to hold brief conversations with individual students as you circulate from group to group. When the focus is on the learning activity at hand, such conversations provide insights into individual thinking, communication, and problem-solving capabilities. However, students often reveal more personal information that may help you better understand their needs.

Frequent, informal conversations accomplish several important goals: 1) Learning about students' home and family circumstances, interests, talents, and concerns; 2) Conveying an interest in students' thoughts and feelings; 3) Fostering an emotionally safe learning environment where students feel the teacher cares about them, will support their learning needs, and believes in their ability to reach high and worthwhile goals. In most classrooms, student behavior issues are minimized when teachers make a conscious effort to know their students and convey their commitment to students' learning.

When students have a secure relationship with their teachers, they are more comfortable taking risks that enhance learning—tackling challenging tasks, persisting when they run into difficulty, or asking questions when they are confused.

-Deborah Stipek[36]

Social Context: Family and Community

Although we spend enormous amounts of time with students during the course of a school year, we often know little about their lives outside of the school day. It is easy to forget that the realities of their homes and family circumstances may be very different from the middle-class standards and values that are the expected norm at most public schools.

Behavior viewed as "unacceptable" in the school setting, may be normal in a student's home. In some cases, students' most challenging behaviors are symptomatic of survival skills they have developed to cope with difficult living situations. Knowing more about students' families, communities, and other contexts outside of the school setting is critical for engaging them in the learning process and helping them envision a positive and productive future.

Family Culture

Families and their activities outside the classroom are an important part of what each student brings into the classroom. It is important for a teacher to know the family characteristics and cultures represented by his students, and to describe how this influences his teaching. Information about students' home lives will give the teacher guidance in planning for individual students and building a safe, respectful classroom environment for students from different backgrounds.

Accomplished teachers make an effort to involve and partner with family members, particularly when there is a learning concern about a student. Entry 4: Documented Accomplishments, asks a candidate to provide evidence of partnerships with parents and other concerned adults to support students' learning needs. Partnerships mean that communication goes both ways: It is just as important for teachers to learn from families as it is for families to learn from teachers.

Communication systems between students' homes and classrooms are extremely important. Informational flyers serve a good purpose, but are limited in terms of engaging parents in the school lives of their children. More than ever, teachers use e-mail, class websites, or other technology to keep parents informed. E-mail has increased the opportunity for parents to contact teachers directly, but may not be available to every parent, so teachers must continue their efforts to involve families in students' learning.

Knowing the Larger Community

Entry 4 asks candidates to provide evidence of their accomplishments with families and community members. Teachers often tap into community resources to enrich classroom learning experiences and sometimes develop significant projects in partnership with community organizations.

When teachers know the resources and opportunities available in students' home communities, they are better able to integrate these into classroom learning experiences. Local issues and political elections provide authentic topics for dialogue and debate among older students, who can be empowered to influence community planning. Younger students can share about their hobbies and weekend activities. In both cases, the everyday conversation and activities of students will open a window to their social culture and living.

When teachers are able to actively participate in the students' community by attending athletic events, neighborhood fairs, and other gatherings, they have increased opportunities to interact with parents and to see new dimensions of their students. Students are often surprised and flattered to see their teachers take an interest in these non-school events.

As I returned to my apartment after a long Saturday bicycle ride, I happened to see my 4th grade student, Naisha. She saw me, and I made a point to call out to her and wave "Hi," and then I smiled, knowing that this would be her biggest story to tell the class on Monday morning.

-Ben Joseph, Student Teacher

The Importance of Context

Entries 1, 2, and 3 will require two types of contextual information from you. Together your responses to these sections help provide evidence for your Standard on Knowledge of Students and provide the foundation for demonstrating your architecture of accomplished teaching through The Five Core Propositions. The instructional goals you select for your classroom-based entries are determined by the combination of your knowledge of your students and your knowledge of your subject matter. **Your reader will seek a direct connection from your contextual information to your selected goals and strategies.**

This information "sets the stage" by helping a reader understand the circumstances that influence the instructional decisions described in the remainder of the entry. Candidates will be asked to demonstrate that they know their students' strengths, interests, and challenges; and that they use this knowledge to more effectively plan, teach, and assess student learning.

Type 1: Contextual Information Sheet

For each of your four entries, you will be asked to provide the one-page **Contextual Information Sheet** as a cover sheet for the sections that follow. This sheet is separate from the page count of the Written Commentary section and is not scored. However, it is important as it gives you an opportunity to provide the "big picture" of your teaching situation, such as the nature of your community, school configuration, required curriculum, or other external circumstances that may impact your teaching decisions and strategies.

Your response is limited to the space on the provided form, and the prompt instructs you to be "brief and specific" as you provide information that "...you believe would be important for assessors to know *to understand your portfolio entries.*" Candidates frequently provide "laundry lists" of student achievement results, socio-economic statistics, and other information to highlight the less positive aspects of their teaching contexts, and then make no further reference to them. The information is only relevant if you explain how it impacts your instructional decisions in your entry. Do not include this information unless you are prepared to explain it further, as otherwise it does not serve the intended purpose of helping the assessor "...to understand your portfolio entries."

In many cases, teachers will need to complete only one **Contextual Information Sheet**, which can be photocopied and included with each entry, but the **Instructional Context** or **Student Profile** described in the next section must be written specifically for the given entry.

Type 2: Instructional Context or Student Profile

The second type of contextual information is required for Entries 1, 2 and 3, which feature your classroom instruction. Here, you will provide the foundation on which to build evidence throughout the entry that you *....are committed to students and their learning* as you demonstrate that you *know* your students and their learning needs.

You will be prompted to provide this contextual information in the first section of your scored Written Commentary. For most certificate areas, this section is called the **Instructional Context** or **Student Profile.** Questions in your Portfolio Instructions for this section will prompt you to provide more detailed information about the specific class and individual students featured in the entry. Thoughtful responses will help you provide evidence throughout your entry that you know and respond to the needs and learning styles of your students.

You may be directly or indirectly asked to identify students in your class with particular issues or needs, and it is important to so. You may or may not have students who present extreme needs, but you will want to demonstrate your knowledge of your students through examples of your responsiveness to the needs of a few featured individuals or groups of students. In every classroom there are teaching issues presented by groups, such as second language learners or gifted learners; or by individual students, who may exhibit learning or behavioral difficulties, or may have special interests that they wish to pursue.

As you describe your lessons in the remaining sections of the Written Commentary, it will be important to show how the information you have provided in your instructional context guides your teaching decisions for your class and for any individual students you may choose to feature. Accomplished teachers know that learning is optimized when instructional goals and practices are aligned with student needs and interests. Your description of context will help you provide evidence that your instructional sequence was designed and implemented with *these students, at this time, in this place,* in mind.

Relevance is the Key

For both the Contextual Information Sheet and the Instructional Context/Student Profile, you are asked to provide information that is directly relevant to the accompanying Written Commentary. The contextual information sections give teachers an opportunity to describe their unique teaching circumstances and to provide the reader with a better understanding of the reasons for their selection of goals, strategies, and materials in the featured entry. There is no reason to include extraneous information that has no connection to the teaching decisions featured and discussed in the entry.

Will the story about your students that you introduce in the contextual information sections connect to the teaching decisions that you make in the rest of the entry? Readers will seek "connectivity" in your entry as you tell the story of your teaching. In the National Board Assessment, the connectivity of context, goals, strategies, analysis, and reflection are the essence of *clear, consistent, and convincing evidence*, the language of the Level 4 scoring rubric.

These Students, At This Time, In this Place...

Many candidates fail to realize the importance of their contextual information. Accomplished teaching takes place in many different physical, social, and cultural situations, and every student is unique. It is not a one-size-fits-all activity, but involves context-specific actions stemming from knowledge, experience, and a commitment to help all students learn. While planning is critical, some decisions are made in unplanned "teachable moments" that arise spontaneously in the classroom; or when students do not respond to a lesson as anticipated.

No matter what your specific context is like, it has an impact on how you teach. Everything about the National Board Certification process is designed to reveal how you use your given situation, resources, and knowledge to provide the best possible learning experiences for *these students, at this time, in this place*.

As an example, let us suppose you are a sixth grade science teacher and contrast two very different teaching contexts:

> *Context 1*: Last year you taught classes at a large new school located in an upper middle class neighborhood. Most of your students' parents were college graduates and many are successful professionals in the community. The school had several computers in every classroom, as well as a well-equipped science laboratory.

> *Context 2*: This year you are teaching in an old, rather poorly equipped school in a very small rural community. Half of your students are second language learners, and only a few students' parents graduated from high school. You have one sink, very rudimentary equipment and your only access to computers is by appointment at a room across campus. You teach science, math, and reading to the same group of students.

Will you plan differently in these two contexts? How will you determine appropriate goals for your students? Will they be the same in each context? Will students have similar prior knowledge? Will they have the same learning preferences? Will you use different strategies, methodologies, and resources? Clearly, a teacher must adapt instructional strategies to the given context.

Most candidates readily identify challenging circumstances such as high poverty and low literacy rates in their communities. However, if they neglect to make the connection to these conditions as the basis for instructional decision-making, these details are irrelevant to the contextual information for the portfolio entry. The assessor will not award a higher score simply because the candidate works with an especially needy group of students.

Now think about *your* teaching context and the characteristics that may make it different from others across the country. Think about how the community, the school setting, and resources impact your teaching decisions. Be prepared to discuss how the factors you include in your contextual information affect your planning and teaching. These factors should be referenced in your Written Commentary as you plan, carry out, and analyze your instructional sequence.

Exercise 6-1: Your Contextual Information Sheet

The sheet provided for Exercise 6-1 may help you develop your response to the questions you will be asked on the Type 1: Contextual Information Sheet. In the first column on the exercise sheet, the prompts have been broken down and paraphrased to help you respond to each part. These are the responses you will write on the actual Contextual Information Sheet, which is limited to the space provided on a single page.

The second and third columns of the exercise will help you think about the relevance of these features, and how you will explain this relevance throughout your entry. In the second column, you are asked to think about how the features of your particular context influence your planning and instructional decision-making.

The third column asks you to note *where* in your entry you will demonstrate that these aspects of your context influence your decision-making. Remember, you will only provide information that "…you believe would be important for assessors to know *to understand your portfolio entries.*"

Exercise 6-2: Your Instructional Context

Instructions and prompts for the Type 2: Instructional Context will vary from one certificate to another, so before using this exercise, you must first determine if it is a match for your Portfolio Instructions. If so, Exercise 6-2 may be useful to help you think and write about this section of your entry.

In contrast to the Contextual Information, which asks you to describe the broad context of your teaching situation, the Instructional Context is focused on the specific class and students that are featured in the entry. Again, you should only include only information that is relevant to the instructional sequence described in the entry, by showing how

Sample: Exercise 6-2: Your Instructional Context		
Aspects of My Instructional Context	**Implications for My Teaching**	**How and Where This is Shown in My Entry:**
What are the number, ages and grades of the students in the class featured in this entry and subject matter of the class?	How do the class size, ages of students and subject matter impact the nature of the instructional decisions I make and/or my access to resources?	*In the video, I have half the class present for the lesson, while the others are at the computer lab with my part-time assistant.*
Fifth grade self-contained class with 28 students, aged 9–10. A Social Studies lesson will be featured in this entry.	*Planning: The lesson will require students to do a web search for information, and I need to split my class to do this, as our lab does not have that many computers.*	*Because I will only have 14 students at a time, students will have more space at the tables. I can have them complete charts of key ideas as part of the featured small group discussions.*

Figure 15: Sample: Exercise 6-2: Your Instructional Context.
In the first column, direct responses to the Instructional Context prompts are given. The remaining columns remind the teacher to relate her instructional decisions back to this context when writing about the lesson in other parts of the entry.

characteristics of this class and individual students in the class impact your planning and teaching.

In the first column on the exercise sheet, the prompts have been paraphrased to help you respond to each part. These are the responses you will write in the Instructional Context portion of your portfolio entry. Follow your Portfolio Instructions for the page length of this section, as well as for any additional or different prompts required by your entry.

The second and third columns of the exercise will help you think about the relevance of the characteristics you have described, and how you will explain this relevance throughout your entry. In the second column, you are asked to think about how the characteristics of your class and students influence your planning and instructional decision-making.

The third column asks you to note *how* and *where* in your entry you will demonstrate that these class and student characteristics influence your decision-making. Remember, you will only provide information that "…you believe would be important for assessors to know *to understand your portfolio entries.*"

As you complete this exercise, consider the unique characteristics of this class and of some of the individual students. Who are these students? How do you use what you know about them to effectively plan and provide instruction? Do they have preferred learning styles? Do some students need additional supports to access learning? How do you personalize the learning experience to help each student be successful?

Remember, the information you provide in Columns 2 and 3 is not included in the Instructional Context section. These are notes to help you think and write about the influence of your context on your instructional decisions in the remaining sections of the entry.

Applying Your Knowledge: Best Practices

Through relationship-building, accomplished teachers come to know and appreciate students as individuals. Based on that foundation, teachers make an effort to imbed basic elements of good teaching practice into routine practices and interactions with students. As we briefly describe several elements of "best practice" below, you will see they share the common themes of knowing your students and responding to individual student needs.

Most teachers have some familiarity with the following topics and know that there are abundant resources available for deeper study. Our purpose is to highlight areas that are especially relevant to the NBPTS portfolio entries and discuss how these elements may impact your planning and discussion of your teaching practices.

Developmentally Appropriate Practices

In any classroom, students display a wide range of interests, experiences, and abilities. At the same time, among students of a given age or grade level, there are commonalities that have been identified by researchers and theorists in child development and learning. These include cognitive, social-emotional, and physical characteristics associated with different ages and stages. Accomplished teachers know the developmental learning characteristics of their students and use this knowledge to design instructional activities that are relevant and engaging.

The term "Developmentally Appropriate Practice" is often associated with early childhood education, where it serves to remind educators that paper and pencil tasks are not the best avenue to learning for young children. While early childhood specialists are usually well-versed in learning theories and the developmental characteristics of their students, we have found teachers of older students are seldom so knowledgeable. Teachers of all ages and grade levels should know and use the methods that best meet the developmental characteristics of their students. When they do not, students may be penalized for behaviors which are normal and to be expected for their developmental level.

Many accepted school practices that have their roots in the far distant past are driven by the needs of the institutional school setting, and are not necessarily developmentally appropriate according to what is now known about brain functions and learning. Portfolio entries ask candidates to justify their selections of goals, strategies, and assessments; and may specifically ask writers to explain why they are developmentally appropriate for *these students, at this time, in this place.*

I worked with a five year old who came to my attention because he was spending more time with the principal and the counselor than he did in his kindergarten class due to "off task" behavior. I chose him as the subject of my video entry, and was pleased when he readily engaged with a picture book showing close-up photos of insects and other animals. However, I reached to my side to retrieve a tissue and when I looked up, he was GONE! Conscious of the camera running, I was momentarily horrified, but then I saw him on all fours in a plush corner of our library setting. He was role-playing a spider using his preferred learning modality of interacting spontaneously with the text. Although his engagement was genuine and very focused, I realized others might consider him "off task" for similar behaviors in the classroom.

-Ruth Ann Santos, NBCT Hawaii

Multiple Intelligences

Research also tells us that individuals may have strengths or "intelligences" in different realms. We all know people with outstanding athletic or social skills and others who are gifted in mathematics or music. These strengths may be evident even though a person has had no special instruction in the given area. Accomplished teachers seek to identify students' areas of strength and leverage them to build skills in less proficient areas.

An understanding of multiple intelligences theory can help teachers appreciate the diversity of student interests and abilities, and cultivate an environment of acceptance and support for all learners in the classroom. According to Mel Levine, author of *A Mind at a Time*, learners who struggle in the classroom may have highly specialized minds that need to access learning experiences through specific modes and affinities. While they should be exposed to and encouraged to strengthen learning in new ways, they should not be punished for being initially less able in their weaker modes.[37]

The multiple intelligences approach does not require a teacher to design a lesson in nine different ways so that all children can access the material. Rather, it involves creating rich experiences in which students with different intelligence profiles can interact with the materials and ideas using their particular combinations of strengths and weaknesses.

-Seana Moran, Mindy Kornhaber, Howard Gardner
Orchestrating Multiple Intelligences[38]

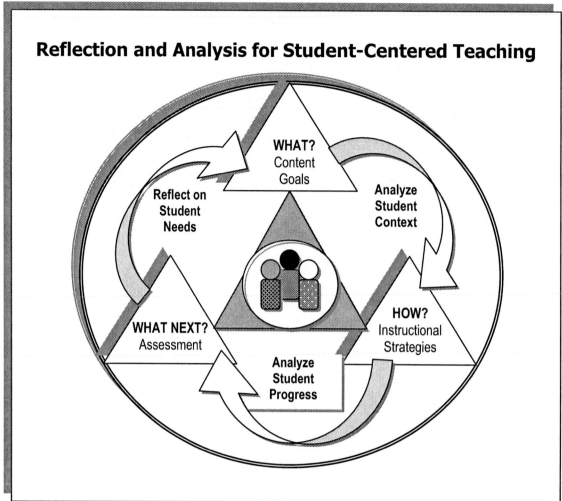

Figure 16: Reflection and Analysis for Student-Centered Teaching.
When teaching is focused on student learning, the characteristics and abilities of both a group and individuals within the group are important. The teacher's mission is to help every student progress toward appropriate learning goals through continuous analysis and reflection based on knowledge of the students and knowledge of the content area.

Diverse Needs of Learners: Fairness, Equity, and Access

When teaching is student-focused, attending to the needs of individuals is imbedded in the teacher's practice. Understandably, many teachers balk when they perceive an implied expectation that they must create individual learning plans for each student in the class. "Differentiation" is often interpreted to mean "too much work!" Fundamentally, differentiation means knowing students, recognizing individual needs, and making reasonable adjustments to insure that every student is presented with appropriate learning tasks. The underlying assumption is that every student deserves to be challenged at his or her optimal learning level, whether that level is lower or higher than the average student in a class. Most teachers will readily acknowledge that, in a given classroom, student learning levels and motivation vary. Teachers commonly differentiate by using grouping strategies, different materials, technology supports, or peers to engage and provide support to less proficient students in their classrooms.

Unfortunately, many teachers still claim to address the issue of fairness by treating every student exactly the same way. This stance is in direct opposition to what is intended by the Standard on equity and diversity found in every certificate area. Equity refers to providing students with equal access to learning opportunities. In order to do so, teachers must often make accommodations, access resources, or provide particular supports to individual students. Insisting that a child perform at a level significantly below or above his or her capabilities because it is "fair" to expect the same performance from all children actually *prevents* many children from learning and may have devastating consequences for some.

In each of the three classroom-based entries, candidates will be asked to identify and discuss strategies to meet the needs of individual learners. It is important that you "see" your students as individuals, demonstrate that you think about how to enhance learning experiences for them, and support their progress toward specific goals. The foundation for this discussion is laid in the first few pages of the entry, as you are asked first to describe the context of the school community, and then the context of your classroom environment, including students who present exceptional challenges. When specific students are featured throughout the entry, candidates are able to demonstrate their concern for and responsiveness to the needs of these individuals.

As you think and write about your teaching, you must consider how you address both the needs of the group as a whole, and the particular needs of some individual students. Exercise 6-3 may help you consider how to address these needs in each part of your entry.

Exercise 6-3: Thinking and Writing about Student Learning

Exercise 6-3 may be used to help you plan, teach, and describe your instruction as you respond to each section of the Written Commentary for a classroom-based entry. Find the template for the exercise at the end of the chapter, and refer to the copy of the exercise shown in Figure 17 (Prompting Questions for Exercise 6-3: Thinking and Writing about Student Learning).

The exercise is designed to help you think of your teaching in terms of a double-strand process. One strand is what you do for your class as a whole, and the other strand is what you may do to provide extra support for individual students. As you think about each section of your Written Commentary for your entry, use the questions shown in Figure 17 to develop an appropriate instructional response that demonstrates how you do your best to meet the needs of all students in your class.

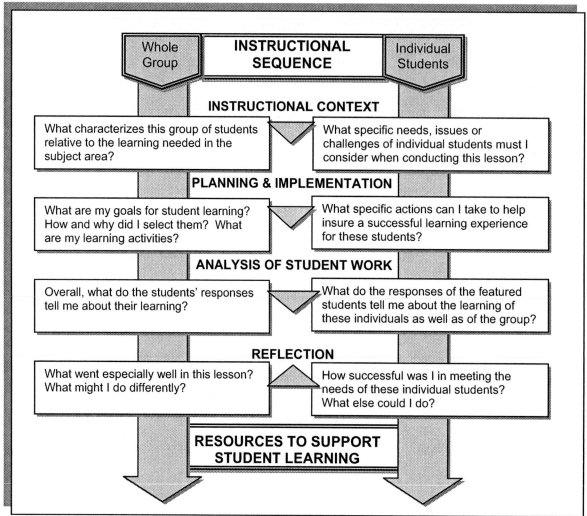

Figure 17: Prompting Questions for Exercise 6-3: Thinking and Writing about Student Learning
Use the questions here to plan, teach, and describe your instruction as you respond to each section of the written commentary for an entry. In most classroom-based entries, teachers will be asked to describe how they meet the needs of the class as a whole, as well as for individual students.

The Responsive Classroom

Accomplished teachers develop supportive learning environments where students feel accepted and respected. The tone of the classroom, including students' tolerance and interest in diverse opinions from their classmates, is important evidence in the video entries. Teachers of younger students may be asked to discuss specifically how they develop the classroom community, including direct teaching of positive social skills.

The nature of the teacher's relationship with students is also an important characteristic of the classroom environment. As shown in the video, is the teacher a "sage on the stage" or a "guide on the side"? Candidates will be asked to explain how and why their selected teaching strategies support student learning in the featured lesson.

In the responsive classroom, physical and instructional design plays a large part in the learning outcomes for students. Consider the role of your instructional materials, supports, and adaptations. Think about how your lesson design addresses different learning modalities and how grouping strategies may help support learning for the whole class and for individual students. Describe classroom behavioral expectations and the role they play in student achievement. The following exercise will help you think about these aspects of your classroom and how they impact student learning.

Exercise 6-4: Reflecting on the Responsive Classroom

Use Exercise 6-4 to help you think about the supports provided to students through aspects of your classroom and lesson design. Several aspects of responsive classrooms and suggestions for addressing them are listed in first and second columns of the template. In the next two columns, think about how and why these aspects support the learning needs of the class as a whole, and of certain students in particular. In the last column, comment on the learning outcomes that result from these responsive elements.

Toward Accomplished Teaching

Students learn best when teachers set high, worthwhile goals, and then help students move incrementally closer to attaining those goals through a sequence of carefully planned activities. However, experienced teachers know that what they teach is not always the same as what students learn. Effective teaching, with demonstrable student outcomes, results when instructional activities are appropriate and engaging. Such activities meet the developmental abilities and interests of the students, provide opportunities for exploration and dialogue about ideas, and support the needs of diverse learners.

Figure 18: Moving toward Accomplished Teaching, illustrates the difference in teaching effectiveness when educators address the specific context presented by *these students at this time in this place*. Student learning increases when instruction is relevant. When teachers match what they do - subject matter and strategies - to what students do – based on their interests, abilities and developmental levels, students are engaged and motivated. [39]

Teachers are able to make this match when they understand and respond to their specific instructional context. They deepen their knowledge of students and their ability to be effective in the classroom through relationship building, information gathering, and continuous analysis of student performances.

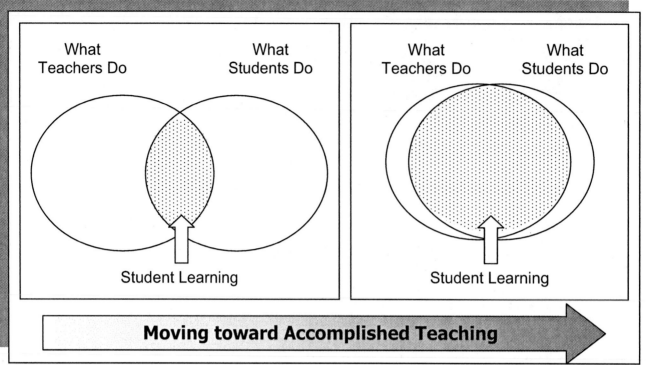

Figure 18: Moving toward Accomplished Teaching
When teachers match goals, strategies, and assessments to the specific needs and characteristics of their students, they are more effective in helping students learn.

Scaffolded Learning Experiences

Good teaching is inevitably the fine art of connecting content and kids—of doing what it takes to adapt how we teach so that what we teach takes hold in the lives and minds of students.

—Carol Ann Tomlinson and Jane Jarvis[40]

Standards-based teaching has swept the nation and classrooms everywhere post exemplary student work samples accompanied by standards and benchmark objectives. Such objectives identify worthy learning outcomes for students and provide a good starting place for teacher planning. However, a benchmark is rarely specific enough to serve as the goal for a single instructional sequence.

Effective learning experiences require the professional judgment of teachers who know their students and subject matter well, and can design lessons that meet the needs of *these students, at this time, in this place.* They know where students are now, and what concepts and skills are needed in order for them to capably meet and internalize the standards and benchmark indicators of the subject area.

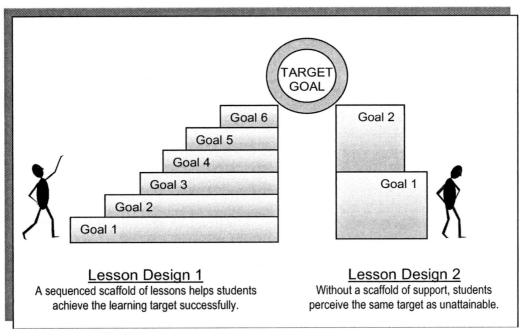

Figure 19: Scaffolding the Learning Experience:
Lesson Design 1 is a scaffolded sequence of instruction, which moves students in small increments toward the target goal, while the learning expectations in Lesson Design 2 require big leaps that are beyond the capabilities of many students

Benchmarks are usually reached through a series of lessons that build students' skills and provide them with multiple opportunities to demonstrate proficiency. Accomplished teachers think in terms of a series of lessons that will scaffold students' understanding toward these loftier goals.

Lev Vygotsky, a prominent Russian psychologist, coined the term "zone of proximal development," a term that describes how children acquire understanding through scaffolded learning experiences.[41] Learning experiences must be "in the zone," within reach for students—neither too easy nor too difficult—to pique their interest and be achievable with adult assistance. When the learning goal is too distant from a student's present level of ability, he or she cannot bridge the gap and is unlikely to engage. Repeated experiences of too-distant goals are disempowering, and cause student motivation to plummet.

As shown in Figure 19, when a goal is high and worthwhile, a sequenced series of learning experiences help students reach target goals. When too much is expected in a single lesson, and the goal is too far away from students' current level of understanding, few students will be able to achieve.

In any given classroom, some students will learn more quickly than their peers while others may need additional steps on the scaffold. The role of the accomplished professional is *know the students* and *know the subject area,* to insure that the provided learning experiences are in the students' zone of proximal development, and move students forward toward the essential understandings expressed by state standards and benchmark indicators.

Depending on the Portfolio Instructions, your featured lesson for an entry may be just one of the steps on your scaffold, or may be an instructional sequence of several steps. In either case, it is important to observe the following:

1) Identify the specific learning outcomes (goals) that will be assessed in each featured lesson.
2) If prompted to do so, describe the overarching or long term goal related to the lesson.
3) Explain how the selected goals help meet the specific learning needs of your students, as described in the instructional context.
4) If applicable, describe how your goals will be modified for specific students.
5) Determine how you will monitor learning and provide feedback to students on their progress toward the goal over the course of an instructional sequence.

The teacher's ability to *manage and monitor* student learning through the use of formative assessments helps determine when students need supplementary scaffolds for support, or are ready to move to the next level. At each step of the learning process, the teacher's knowledge and purposeful selection of strategies produce positive learning outcomes for students. Scaffolded learning experiences increase students' success by providing supports and multiple opportunities for practice of new concepts and skills.

> *Teachers' classroom practice must be seen as an integrated, focused response to student learning rather than as a checklist of teaching behaviors.*
> -Carol R. Rodgers[42]

Analyzing Student Learning

A critical part of the scaffolded learning experience is the analysis of student learning through a variety of formative assessment strategies including observations and student work samples. When students have difficulty, professional judgment is needed to determine where and how the students' difficulties occur. It makes no sense to continue teaching the same material in the same way without determining the cause of students' misunderstandings. Accomplished teachers must be able to make the distinction between what they have *taught* and what students have *learned.*

Ideally, students themselves are encouraged to participate in the assessment process, making judgments about the quality of their work by comparing it to available exemplars, and tracking their progress toward visible targets. They can do so only if targets are clear, if assessment criteria are a match to the target, and if they know how to improve their work. Teachers can foster student self assessment by asking questions such as: *Where are you trying to go? Where are you now? How can you get where you want to be?*

When questions such as these are coupled with specific, descriptive feedback, students are encouraged to take charge of their own learning and set goals for self improvement. Teachers can help build students' confidence by highlighting strengths and focusing feedback for improvement on just one aspect of the work at a time. Scaffolded learning experiences increase students' success by providing supports, feedback on progress toward goal, and many opportunities for practice of new concepts and skills. When teachers routinely assess student learning, they are able to adjust and respond with appropriate teaching strategies.

Teachers at any school seriously engaged in systemic improvement are familiar with data analysis to determine areas in need of improvement. While numerical data is helpful in many respects, as educators, we understand that it does not tell us everything we need to know in order to help individual students make progress.

Student-centered teaching focuses on learning outcomes rather than "covering" curriculum. Whether formal or informal, accomplished teachers continuously analyze student needs to answer the real questions: *Who are these students? How can I best help them learn?*

The Best Thing about My Teacher

"The best thing about my teacher is she is never snappy and mean." (Age 16)

"The best thing about my teacher is when she says, 'Oh, Johnny is absent, I will miss him.'" (Age 5)

"The best thing about my teacher is her ability to teach and care about her students as if they were her own, and not having any favorite." (Age 17)

"The best thing about my teacher is she listens to me." (Age 7)

"The best thing about my teacher is her way of understanding and explaining things." (Age 15)

"The best thing about my teacher is he has a sense of humor." (Age 11)

"The best thing about my teacher is she tells us what to do and doesn't drone on for days." (Age 14)

"The best thing about my teacher is her likes every kid in the class." (Age 11)

-Judy Gordon Morrow[43]

Key Points for Candidate Support Providers

The exercises in this chapter refer to important pieces of the entry that are often under-valued by candidates. Use one or more of these exercises to help candidates distinguish between the two types of contextual information and to practice responding appropriately to the prompts:

- Give the group 15 minutes of writing time to respond to the questions in the first two columns, and then have them share their responses in small groups. They will benefit from hearing how others describe and analyze their teaching contexts, and will better understand how differences in context influence instructional decisions.

- Be sure to emphasize *relevancy* in the information that teachers include in their contextual information. For a given characteristic, such as a large population of ELL students, or a lack of community resources, ask teachers to share "round-robin" or "popcorn" style about how this specific characteristic impacts their classroom practices.

- Build descriptive writing skills by having teachers do a five to ten minute "quick write" about their class or individual students, and then share in small groups. Circulate and listen for "red flag" statements such as "To be fair, I have the same expectations for my students," or "I have no students in my class with any special needs." These misconceptions should be addressed with your group since accomplished teachers know and respond to specific needs and interests of their students.

- Candidate support providers can model and develop teachers' abilities to analyze and respond to student needs by taking time for the group to discuss "case studies" presented by candidates. Teachers can be invited to describe a child for whom they have questions regarding behavior, lesson design, or learning progress and invite perspectives and suggestions from the group. Assure confidentiality by using only first names or initials of the children under discussion.

Exercise 6-1: Your Contextual Information Sheet

What Is My Context?	What Does This Mean For My Teaching?	How/Where Is This Demonstrated In My Entry?
1A. My teaching occurs in the following school or program, grade, or subject configuration:	How does this configuration impact the nature of the instructional decisions I make and/or my access to resources?	
1B. In an average day, I teach the following grades/age levels and courses: The number of students in each class is___. I teach ___ students each day:	How do the grades/age levels, the number of courses I teach, and/or the size of my classes impact my decision-making?	
2A. What state, district, and/or school mandates am I required to meet in terms of curricula, texts, assessments, and/or pacing of instruction?	How do these requirements impact my instructional decisions?	
2B. What is the nature of the school community? (Environmental, cultural, economic, etc.) What resources/technologies are or are not available to support my instruction and students' learning?	How does the nature of my community and availability of resources/technologies impact my instructional decisions?	

Directions: Use this sheet to help you think about how the context influences your teaching, and where this might be shown in your entry.

Accomplished Teaching: The Key to National Board Certification

Exercise 6-2: Your Instructional Context

Aspects of My Instructional Context	Implications for My Teaching	How and Where This is Shown in My Entry:
What are the number, ages, and grades of the students in the class featured in this entry and the subject matter of the class?	How do the class size, ages of students, and subject matter impact the nature of the instructional decisions I make and/or my access to resources?	
What are the relevant characteristics of this class that impact my decision-making?	How have these class characteristics influenced my instructional strategies for this sequence of instruction?	
What are the relevant characteristics and needs of students with exceptional needs and abilities?	How have the needs of these students influenced my instructional strategies for this sequence of instruction?	
What are the relevant features of my teaching context that impact my decision-making?	How have the features of my context influenced my instructional strategies for this sequence of instruction?	

Directions: Please note this exercise will NOT match the requirements for all entries. If it matches your entry, the exercise may help you think about the significant aspects of your Instructional Context, and how you will write about them throughout your entry.

Exercise 6-3: Thinking and Writing about Student Learning

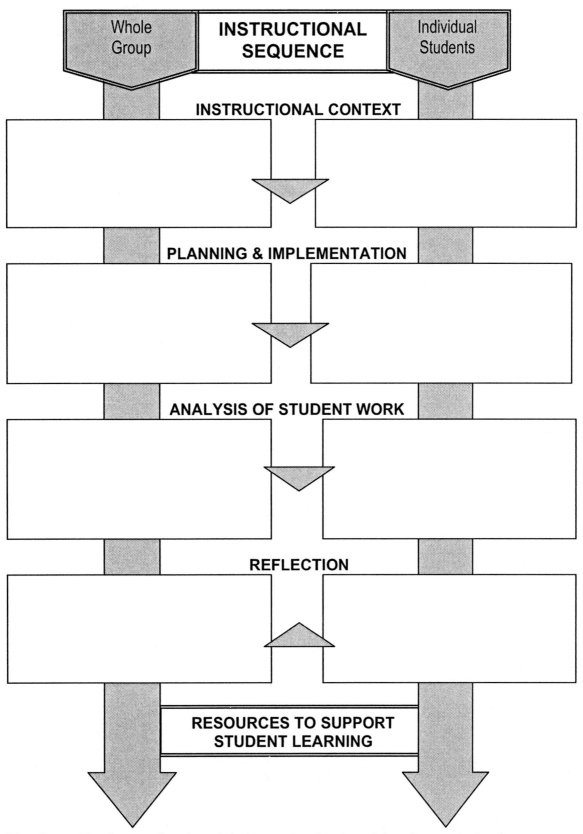

Directions: Use the questions here to help you plan, teach, and describe your instruction as you respond to each section of the Written Commentary for an entry.

Exercise 6-4: Reflecting on the Responsive Classroom

Aspects of a Responsive Classroom	How have I designed my classroom and instruction?	For all students? Why?	For particular students? Why?	How does my design impact student learning?
Environmental print	Examples of classroom print that reflect different learning styles of your students, Supports for schedules, procedures, routines.			
Instructional materials	Stimulating, thought-provoking materials			
Technology supports	Specific supports to address individual student needs			
Lesson adaptations	Specific student needs. At risk students, high achieving students?			
Student learning modalities	Alternative ways to demonstrate learning			
Grouping strategies	Proactive strategies to promote belonging, acceptance, encouragement.			
Distribution of attention	Daily opportunities for each student to receive support.			
Classroom behavioral expectations	Classroom rules or procedures that benefit students. Specific interventions that have helped a student learn.			

Directions: Consider the different aspects of your classroom and instructional design that help support student learning. Comment on how these effectively address needs of the class and of individual students

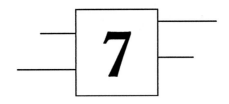

7

Planning Your Featured Lessons

Core Proposition 2:

Teachers Know Their Subject and How to Teach it to Students

Which of the following best describes the assessment task of the National Board for Professional Teaching Standards?

a. National Board requires candidates to showcase some of their best lessons, explaining how they provide evidence of meeting the National Board Standards.

b. National Board requires candidates to demonstrate how they meet the Standards by designing, implementing, and reflecting on lessons according to the specific criteria provided.

c. National Board requires candidates to demonstrate exceptional creativity in designing comprehensive, exciting lessons that relate to the Standards provided.

d. Both a and b

e. a, b, and c

Although "a" and "c" may tempt you, "b" is the correct answer. Your teaching may include many creative and exciting activities, but the only thing that matters for the National Board assessment is that you provide evidence of meeting the Standards for your area as defined by the scoring criteria for the entry. The Portfolio Instructions for Entries 1, 2, and 3 are designed to help you produce the evidence you need if you respond to each prompt with appropriate depth and breadth. It is not necessary to design an elaborate or unusual lesson, and it may be counter-productive to do so.

When a lesson is too elaborate, it may be difficult for you to clearly articulate your goals for student learning. A multi-experience thematic unit usually consists of several instructional sequences that relate to one another. Unless directed otherwise, your portfolio entry should focus on just one sequence with clearly defined goals and methods of assessment. If you try to cover too much, lack of focus will result in poor evidence.

For each entry, your task is to provide your evidence of teaching practices described in your Standards. It is important that you respond directly and completely to each of the prompting questions in your Portfolio Instructions. In doing so, you will tell about the professional decisions you make in the course of an instructional sequence to help students learn. Each entry is structured differently, to ensure that you will have the opportunity to demonstrate a full range of decision-making relating to planning, instruction, assessment, and reflection about your practice.

All ten sections of the assessment—four portfolio entries and six assessment center exercises—have been carefully developed so that different aspects of your professional understanding and proficiency may be demonstrated. However, the classroom-based portfolio sections, Entries 1, 2, and 3, are the most valued in terms of potential points toward your National Board Certification. (See Chapter 14: Scoring) Each of the classroom-based entries will focus on different aspects of your content knowledge and pedagogy for the purpose of revealing the underlying structure or "architecture" of your teaching.

As an experienced teacher, you have undoubtedly developed many lesson plans. How will this lesson plan be different? In this chapter we will look at the lesson planning process through the lens of The Five Core Propositions for accomplished teaching.

Selecting the Featured Lesson

> *"I have a great lesson that I teach every year... the kids respond really well...I'll use that lesson for Entry 1..."*

Most experienced teachers have favorite lessons that they have developed during the course of their teaching, and many candidates are anxious to share such lessons with their assessors. However, it is not uncommon for candidates to find that their expected "best" entry did not score as well as the entry they did in a rush to meet the deadline. In a debriefing session with candidates who had received their scores, here are some explanations that emerged for entries that scored unexpectedly well:

> *"I designed a lesson specifically to meet the requirements of the entry, because it wasn't something I would normally include in my teaching."*

"I did the (high-scoring) entry last. I didn't have time to do anything fancy. In fact, I didn't think the lesson was especially interesting. I just made sure I answered the questions."

The Portfolio Instructions will prompt you to design and carry out lessons that provide evidence of teaching to the Standards for your area. Some unsuccessful candidates fail to follow instructions fully, while others neglect to address the necessary Standards called for in the entry. Some insist that they are going to do the work "their way," or they detour to focus on sharing their "good ideas" through a favorite lesson.

"Good ideas" are just that—ideas that may hold potential for effective teaching. Without analytical planning, instruction, and assessment of student learning, ideas alone provide no evidence of accomplished teaching. Let us take a look at how we might ensure that instructional activities provide such evidence.

Knowing What is Valued

The featured lesson for the entry is selected on the basis of how well it aligns to the guidelines and requirements for the entry. Pay particular attention to the scoring criteria, **How Will My Response Be Scored?** from the Portfolio Instructions for the entry. These are drawn directly from the rubric used by the assessor to score your piece.

Prompts, Propositions, and Practice

To meet the Standards for accomplished teaching established by NBPTS, each of the classroom entries must demonstrate your personal *architecture of accomplished teaching*, with The Five Core Propositions as the underlying structure for your decision-making. We introduced you to The Five Core Propositions in Chapter 4: Starting at the Core, and now we will review them in terms of planning for a specific lesson. We will continue to revisit them in each chapter as you develop your entries and build your understanding of accomplished teaching.

The instructions for each entry will prompt you to provide the evidence you need. You must give a complete, concise response to each question to provide evidence that is *clear, convincing, and consistent* throughout the entry.

Select and plan the lesson to meet the Standards for the entry, which are summarized in your scoring criteria, **How Will My Response Be Scored?** Reading the entry requirements, **What Do I Need To Do?** and questions, **Composing My Written Commentary**, will help you design an appropriate lesson.

In Figure 21 (Planning Your Featured Lesson), The Five Core Propositions are used as an outline for different parts of the lesson planning process and instructional sequence. Let us discuss each of the propositions in terms of the nature of the questions commonly asked of candidates in Entries 1, 2, and 3.

1. Teachers Are Committed to Students and Their Learning.

In each classroom-based entry, you will demonstrate your understanding of your students, their learning needs, and your decision-making in response to those needs. The Written Commentary instructions begin by asking contextual questions. In this first section, often called Student Profile or Instructional Context, candidates are prompted to describe the general characteristics of the class, how features of the class may have influenced the teacher's selection of instructional strategies, and specific challenges represented by the class. In each entry, you should also expect to discuss the unique needs of individual students who present learning challenges. Throughout the entry, the discussion of your planning and instruction to meet the needs of these individuals will help you provide evidence of meeting your Standard for Equity, Fairness, and Diversity.[44]

For some certificate areas, entries are focused specifically on the learning of an individual student rather than of a whole class. Even when you are asked to describe a group lesson, however, it is important that you are able to identify and address individual learning needs. In each entry, you will discuss the learning progress of students through an analysis of student work samples or assessments, or in reference to a video recording of your lesson.

2. Teachers Know the Subjects They Teach and How to Teach Those Subjects to Students.

The entry will ask you to describe your learning goals for students as well as your instructional and assessment strategies. Your goals are expected to be *high and worthwhile* for this particular group of students. You will be asked to explain your selection of goals and strategies in terms of your knowledge of the content area, your long-term goals, and your understanding of your students' readiness and learning characteristics.

Inherent in this proposition is that accomplished teachers have a range of different strategies to draw upon. In teaching, lessons often do not go as planned due to student misconceptions or other unanticipated reasons. When teaching for the entry, you may need to adjust your goals and instruction for certain students or for the whole class if student responses to the lesson indicate they are not learning as expected. It is important to acknowledge and discuss such adjustments, as they help you demonstrate your responsiveness and knowledge of your subject matter.

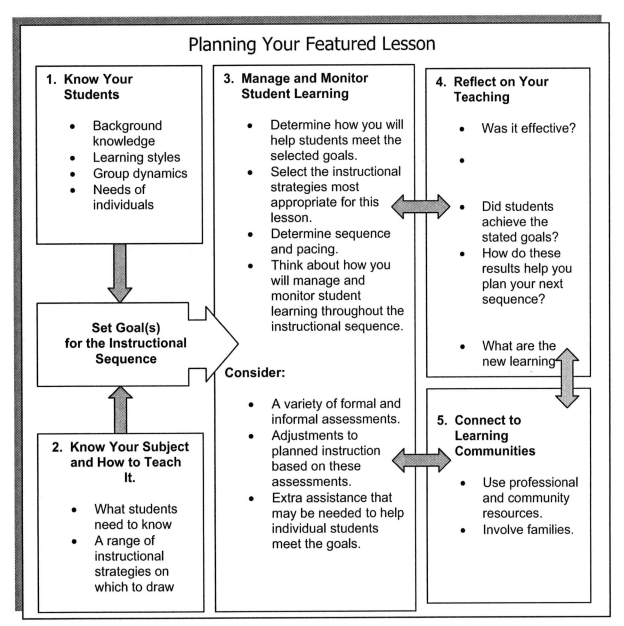

Figure 20. Planning Your Featured Lesson.
The Five Core Propositions provide a framework for accomplished teaching as the teacher plans an instructional sequence.

3. Teachers Are Responsible for Managing and Monitoring Student Learning.

Your selected instructional strategies, organization of the lesson, and assessment methods are part of this proposition. You will be asked to justify the instructional approach you have selected and describe your assessment strategies. Assessment should include a variety of methods to determine student learning, including assessments that inform your instruction during the course of the lesson.

Some entries may also ask you to discuss the organization of the class environment and the routines that are part of your practice. You may also be asked to address the classroom community in terms of building students' social skills and a positive climate for learning.

4. Teachers Think Systematically about Their Practice and Learn from Experience.

Reflective practice is imbedded throughout the entry as you demonstrate your knowledge of your students, thoughtful selection of strategies, and analysis of learning. However, each entry ends with a section for reflection in which you are asked to think about the effectiveness of your teaching. You will be asked to reflect on the results of your instruction for the purpose of improving learning for your current students, as well as for those you might teach in the future. Your reflection should be balanced in terms of what went well in the lesson and what you might improve upon. It might speak to your need to seek more information about the subject, changes you would make to the lesson, or next steps you will take based on the students' responses to the instructional sequence described in the entry.

5. Teachers are Members of Learning Communities.

When prompted to do so, you should be prepared to describe resource materials or personnel employed to assist the class and/or assist individual students during the lesson. This might include your work with other teachers, counselors, paraprofessionals, parents, and/or community organizations. The most important members of your learning community are the families of your students, and some entries may call for specific evidence of parent involvement in the lesson sequence.

Multiple and Varied Assessments

In the past, to many teachers the word "assessment" meant "test." While teacher-created or standardized tests are forms of assessment, we now know there are many other tools teachers use to determine student learning. Less structured, "formative" assessments that inform instruction on an on-going basis are usually most useful to the classroom teacher, while "summative" assessments such as final exams and standardized tests are useful for reporting student progress to other audiences. In Figure 21 we have shown you some common types of assessments, their purposes, and their characteristics.

Assessment: Types, Purposes, and Characteristics

Informal/Formative	Common Types of Assessments	Formal/Summative
Purpose: Inform instruction—Assessment FOR learning	• Observation: Unrecorded quick perceptions	Purpose: Report to external audience–Assessment OF learning
Intuitive and/or based on teacher's knowledge and experience	• Observation: Anecdotal notes or checklist	Objective data measuring uniform standards or criteria for all students
Teacher-determined procedures	• Questionnaire or survey	May include required administration procedures
Flexible; time based on individual needs	• Conference, Interview	May include timed sections
May be impromptu—applied with individuals or groups of students	• Use of rubric for self-assessment.	Pre-determined schedule for testing all students
Focused on customized classroom curriculum	• Portfolio, work samples, student products	Often based on the specific content and skills of a widely applied curriculum.
Provides immediate feedback to guide on-going instruction of individuals or groups	• Culminating product or performance • Criterion-referenced test or performance • Norm-referenced test	Results are tabulated and compiled to compare individual and group student performance to a pre-established norm. Results may not be readily available.
Data are based on teacher-developed criteria; may or may not be recorded.		Data are based on set criteria; formal records are kept, results are reported to outside audiences

Figure 21. Assessment for Different Purposes.
Accomplished teachers plan multiple assessments that will inform instruction prior to, during and at the conclusion of the teaching sequence.

In the center column, some common types of assessments are generally described and listed from least to most structured. In the columns on the left and right, the characteristics of formative (during the course of the instruction) and summative (at the end of the instructional sequence) assessment are described. There is a tendency to think that assessment should be administered to measure learning after instruction has taken place, as shown in the column on the right. However, in order to manage and monitor student learning, assessments such as those described on the left will give the teacher information about how well students are learning throughout the instructional sequence. Formative assessments let the teacher know when modifications to the lesson may be needed, and when individual students need extra support. In the classrooms of accomplished teachers, a variety of assessments including observations and assignments are used throughout an instructional sequence to help the teacher at various stages:

1. Pre-planning: In order to teach effectively, you must know students' levels of understanding and abilities before you can begin your lesson planning. Only when you know where students should begin their learning in the content area can you set appropriate goals.

2. Planning: Once you have selected the goals for the instructional sequence, you must determine how you will measure student learning at the end of the sequence. How will you know if, or how well, students have achieved? What should they know and be able to do? What methods of instruction will help them achieve the goals?

3. Instruction: During instruction, you need to know if your strategies and methodologies are effective. How will you know how well students are learning during the course of instruction? Will you be able to determine if you need to adjust your instruction to meet the needs of individuals or the group?

4. Post Instruction: At the end of the instructional sequence, you will measure achievement using the tools or methodologies selected during the planning phase.

Assessment is an important part of each phase in the lesson sequence—before, during, and after instruction. Assessment reveals your students' abilities and needs for purposes of planning, it informs your instruction as the lesson is being carried out, and it will help you determine how well students have learned at the end of the lesson. Finally, assessment of student responses to the entire instructional sequence will help you plan what you will do next with your students.

As you plan your lesson, consider a variety of sources for determining student progress. For the purposes of your entry, formative assessments are likely to be utilized, as these will give you information about how well students are learning throughout the instructional sequence. Accomplished teachers manage and monitor student learning, and modify their instructional plans when necessary to address unanticipated student learning needs. It is critical to know how well students are learning while instruction is on-going, so that such adjustments may be made. This is assessment *for* learning, as opposed to the assessment *of* learning that is generally reported to an outside audience.

You may find that you do a lot of assessment at an intuitive level, as you interpret and respond to students while you are actively teaching. However, it is also important that students know how well they are learning during the course of the lesson, and that they are provided with useful feedback that encourages and helps them improve.

After context (e.g., knowing your students), assessment is the starting place for lesson planning, as it will determine what you expect students to know and be able to do at the end of the instructional sequence. As you begin the lesson planning process, consider how you will address the following:

- Clear targets for students to achieve
- Explicit criteria for determining levels of proficiency
- Strategies that scaffold student learning toward achievement of the goals
- Student products or performances that will be measured by the stated criteria

Effective teaching practices include the use of rubrics with exemplars of student work, descriptive feedback, and opportunities for students to self-assess against stated criteria. However, the most critical aspect of the instructional sequence is the alignment of the key components of the lesson: goals are based on student needs; strategies help students achieve the stated goals; and assessments show student progress toward the stated goals.

Exercises for Lesson Planning and Review

The three exercises that follow may be used to assist you in planning your featured lesson for an entry. Based on the parts of the plan shown in Figure 20 (Planning Your Featured Lesson), the exercises are designed to help you delve more deeply into each step of planning (Exercise 7-1), instruction (Exercise 7-2), and analysis and reflection (Exercise 7-3).

Exercise 7-1: Setting Goals

Alignment to the selected goals is a critical feature of an accomplished entry. As you outline, think, and write about your teaching, you should be focused on your selected goals at each step. Choose your goals thoughtfully, and then plan your instruction to help each and every student meet the goals. Be sure your assessments help you determine how well students will meet the goals you have chosen.

Think about a lesson or unit you have recently taught or one that you are getting ready to teach. Use the exercise sheet as follows to help you prepare and/or analyze your lesson.

1. **List one to two specific, assessable learning goals for this lesson/unit.**

    Consider: What is the present learning level of the students with regard to the goals? How do you know? What knowledge or skills should students be able to demonstrate after the lesson? Are your goals specific enough for you to assess? Are they high and worthwhile goals?

2. **Explain *why* you selected these particular learning goals.**

    Consider: How do the selected goals relate to school, district, or state expectations/standards for student learning? How do they relate to overarching goals specified in your Standards for the content area? How do the goals relate to your scope and sequence for the year? How are they related to students' background experiences, learning styles, and prior levels of understanding?

3. **Describe your (actual or anticipated) sources of evidence for student learning during the course of this instructional activity. How will you assess whether, and how well, students have met the goal(s)?**

    Consider: Will you observe students applying skills that they have learned in content-focused dialogue or activities? Will there be a project, portfolio, or other samples of student work that may show you what students have come to know and be able to do as a result of this learning experience? Will there be a test, a survey, an essay, or some other summative assessment used at the end of the lesson? Do you have more than one way to determine whether students have met the learning goals selected for this lesson/unit?

The selection of goals and assessments go hand in hand, as you must know how you will determine what students have learned. Clearly defined goals are the basis for the instructional choices, assessments, analysis, and reflection on the entry. Without them, an entry cannot meet the criteria for accomplished teaching. Candidates often have difficulty with goals for three reasons:

1. Lack of visibility: Goals are not explicitly stated. Candidates assume they are "obvious" based on the selected instructional strategies.

2. Lack of focus: This may be due to unclear, "fuzzy" goals such as "Students will have a greater appreciation for…." or "Students will increase knowledge of…." that are very difficult to assess. It may also result from the selection of too many goals, so that alignment to instruction and assessment decisions is not clear. In both cases, the reader is unable to determine what specific student learning is expected as a result of the instruction.

3. Inappropriate: In many cases, candidates will list "goals" that are actually instructional strategies or assessments. For example, a math candidate might state a goal is to have students draw a given geometric figure, "Students will draw and label different types of triangles," rather than stating the goal in terms of broader content knowledge or skills, "Students can describe the attributes of isosceles, scalene, and equilateral triangles." The discussion in the Written Commentary revolves around the selected goals—why they were chosen, what strategies were selected to help students meet them, how they were assessed, and reflection based on the results of the assessments. High and worthwhile goals are based on the acquisition of important concepts and skills, not on performance of discrete tasks or rote learning.

State standards and benchmarks for student learning may provide a starting place for you to think about your lesson design. However, they are generally achieved through multiple learning experiences that engage students over time. For a single lesson or instructional sequence, you will need to define clear targets for your students, and support their learning through thoughtfully selected strategies and assessments.

Exercise 7-2: Instruction and Assessment

Based on the goals you have selected and the sources of evidence you will need to determine student learning, the following exercise sheet may help you describe the process of planning and carrying out instruction. Refer to your Standards to help you select your strategies.

1. **What strategies and activities will be applied in order to help students achieve the selected goals?**

   Consider: Have you chosen strategies and activities that are especially appropriate for your students' learning needs and interests? Will you use more than one strategy to appeal to different kinds of learners? Have you scaffolded learning experiences to lead students to higher levels of understanding?

2. **Explain why you selected these particular strategies and learning experiences.**

   Consider: How/why are the selected strategies effective in helping students learn? How have the characteristics of your students and /or the nature of the task influenced your selection of strategies?

3. **Which students in your class may need "customized" assistance, either because they may have difficulty learning, or because they need more challenging work?**

   Consider: Will you need to provide additional or different strategies in order to meet the learning needs of certain students? Are there resources or technologies that can help these students? Describe how you will meet the needs of specific individuals.

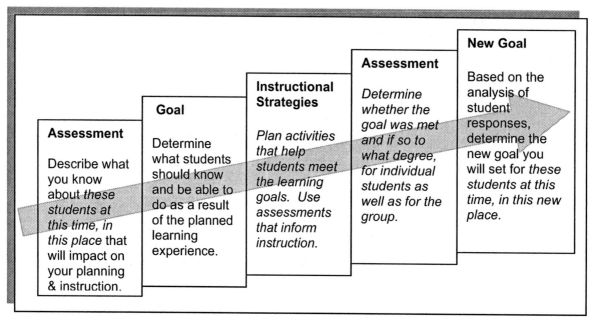

Figure 22. Alignment of the Instructional Sequence.
Alignment is an important feature in the *architecture of accomplished teaching*.

4. **How will you assess student learning during the course of instruction?**

   Consider: Will your formative assessments during the course of the instructional sequence provide feedback to students in terms of their progress toward the stated goals? Will there be opportunities for students to assess themselves? How will you know if your teaching in this lesson helped students attain the goals?

Instruction and assessment must be clearly aligned to the selected goals, as shown in Figure 22. The teacher begins by assessing the knowledge, skills, and predispositions of students in reference to the subject matter. Based on this information, appropriate goals and methods of assessment are selected. The teacher demonstrates knowledge of students, subject, and strategies by selecting methodologies that motivate students and support them in reaching the goals. The needs of individual learners are met by using a range of strategies that appeal to different learning styles, including the use of technology where appropriate. The teacher assesses student progress during the course of instruction and adjusts instruction as needed for individuals or for the group. Assessment and analysis of student learning of the goals is made at the end of the sequence, and new goals are selected based on this information.

Exercise 7-3: Analysis and Reflection
(after instruction has taken place)

Think about what took place during your instruction and assessment of students. Describe your thinking and how it will influence your future planning.

1. What happened during the course of instruction? How did students respond? Was the instruction paced and organized appropriately for optimum learning by students? Did anything unexpected occur? If so, describe the situation and your response to it.

2. Were students effectively engaged in the learning process? How did student responses inform your instruction as the lesson was taking place? Did you make any "adjustments" to your plans as a result of student responses? What is your evidence that students met the goals?

3. Comment on the engagement and learning of individual students with exceptional needs or abilities. Was the learning activity successful for them? How do you know?

4.   What did you like about this lesson and your students' response to it? What would you do differently if you were to teach it again? What else can you do to improve student learning? Could you utilize additional resources or involve parents more?

5.   What insights or new ideas do you have? What will be your next steps with your students as a result of your reflection on this lesson?

Exercise 7-4: Planning the Multi-Lesson Sequence

In some entries you will focus on a single lesson, while in others you must describe an instructional sequence that occurs over time. This is often the case with entries that require student work samples. When the entry requires that you select and discuss a series of work samples taken from different points in the instructional sequence, you will need to plan a multi-lesson sequence that scaffolds student learning toward the selected goal.

Exercise 7-4 is designed to help you plan the main components of such a sequence. When a series of lessons is planned with the intention that students will make progress over time, there is an implication that students will submit work and receive feedback to help them improve on subsequent assignments. Your instructions may require you to collect student work samples and describe your feedback to students whose work is featured in your entry. Developing your evidence based on student work samples is described in more detail in Chapter 11.

Each work sample is produced after new instruction in the form of descriptive feedback, a lesson, or an activity. While Exercise 7-4 may help you plan the big picture of such a sequence, Exercises 7-1 and 7-2 will assist you in planning each individual lesson. The prompts for Exercise 7-3 will help you reflect on the effectiveness of your instruction at the conclusion of the entire sequence.

In each of your portfolio entries you must not only describe *what* you do, but also *why* and *how* you do it. You must think about the particular learning needs of individual students as well as those of the class as a whole. Most importantly, at the conclusion of the teaching sequence you must reflect on the results of your instructional decisions and indicate how your reflection will influence your future planning and instruction.

While you may have a lesson or instructional sequence that is a perfect fit for the entry requirements, it is far more likely your favorite lesson is not an exact match. *It is critical that you design a lesson to fit the entry requirements rather than try to fit the requirements to your lesson.*

In summary, pay close attention to the requirements, scoring criteria, and Standards for the entry. Select your goals carefully and use a range of instruction and assessment methodologies to help students meet the goals.

Key Points for Candidate Support Providers

The exercises in this chapter will help teachers analyze and reflect on their decisions at each point in the instructional sequence. The most important piece of this sequence is goal-setting. We have found many teachers have difficulty setting the clear, appropriate, and assessable goals that are the foundation for a well-written entry. Every part of the instructional sequence must be aligned to the selected goals. Otherwise:

A poorly written goal = a poorly written entry

Use Exercise 7-1 (Setting Goals) to determine the level of understanding among your candidates. You may find responses like these, stated by individual teachers as their lesson goals:

1. **<u>Kindergarten</u>: Develop phonemic awareness though association of letters and sounds. Practice fine motor coordination, write name legibly.** Here, the teacher has listed too many goals. "Develop" and "practice" do not suggest specific outcomes. What will the teacher assess at the end of the sequence? Although writing one's name is important, is it a *high and worthwhile goal* in terms of conceptual development?

2. **<u>Grade 3</u>: Plan, count, organize, and display 1000 items, present and explain method of organization.** Are these instructional activities or goals? What will be assessed—organization, math concepts, or presentation skills?

3. **<u>Intermediate Social Studies</u>: Students will understand that history can be interpreted from different perspectives.** How will the "understanding" be demonstrated? What should students know and be able to do at the end of the instructional sequence?

As they are stated, it would be difficult to develop and write about an instructional sequence based on any one of these "goals." A discussion of responses from your own group can be quite valuable for helping candidates understand how to define and state a goal for the lesson that is:

- high and worthwhile
- clearly assessable
- appropriate for *these students, at this time, in this setting*

All three exercises in this chapter are useful homework assignments for study group members and can be used to prompt small group discussions in subsequent sessions. Such dialogue can help candidates begin the featured lesson on a firm foundation, rather than floundering through an entry that is poorly planned from the beginning.

Exercise 7-1: Setting Goals

Lesson Title: _____

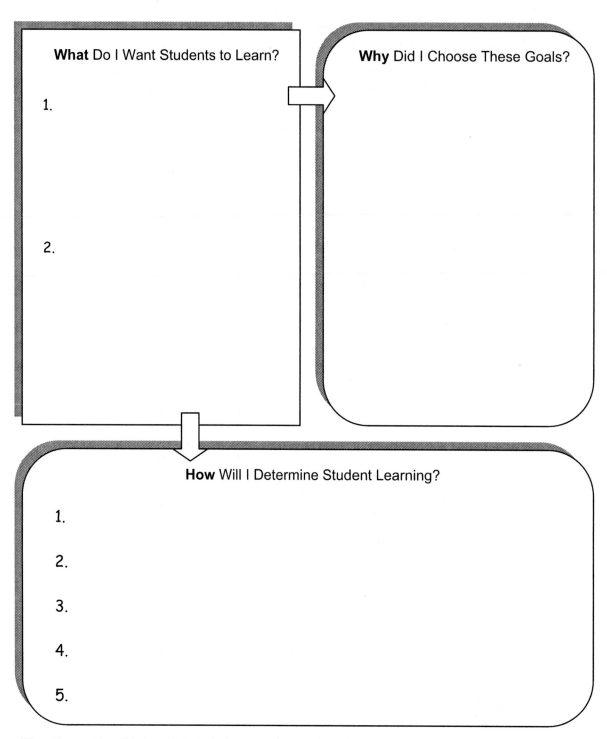

What Do I Want Students to Learn?

1.

2.

Why Did I Choose These Goals?

How Will I Determine Student Learning?

1.

2.

3.

4.

5.

Directions: Use this template to help you select and explain your goals for the lesson. Tell why the goals are important, and how you will assess them.

Exercise 7-2: Instruction and Assessment

Lesson Title: _____

What instructional activities will I use to help students meet the learning goals?

Why did I select these activities?

Which of my students may need "customized" assistance in order to meet the learning goals?

1.

2.

3.

4.

How will I adjust the activities or the environment to enhance success for each of these students?

1.

2.

3.

4.

Directions: Describe the activities you will use to help students meet the goals. Explain why you chose these activities. Explain how you will adjust activities or instruction to meet the needs of certain students.

Exercise 7-3: Analysis and Reflection

Lesson Title_____

How did it go? How well did students progress toward the goals? How do I know? Did I provide a successful experience for my students with exceptional needs and abilities? How do I know? What did I learn from my students?

What I Liked: (If I taught this lesson to a new group of students, I would be sure to do these things again...)

Things To Improve: (If I taught this lesson to a new group of students, I might make these changes/additions...)

Based on the results of this lesson, the next thing I will do is:

Directions: Based on student responses to the instructional sequence, analyze how well they met the goals. Think about how you could improve your instruction, and what you might do next with your students.

Exercise 7-4: Multi-Lesson Sequence Plan

Title_____

Goals for Student Learning

Pre-assessment of current skills and content knowledge: *What information do you currently have about your students?*	Learning goals for this instructional sequence: *How are these goals related to what you know about your students and the subject area?*

Lessons & Strategies Describe the strategies and activities to scaffold student learning toward achievement of the goals.	**Formative Assessments** Indicators of progress toward the goals: *How will you monitor student progress?* Describe your assessments for each lesson.
1.	
2.	
3.	
4.	

Summative Assessment
What will students know and be able to do at the end of this instructional sequence?

Product or performance	Criteria for Assessment/Evaluation

Directions: Use this template to help you think about instruction that occurs over time. When, for example, a series of student work samples will be used to demonstrate student progress toward selected learning targets.

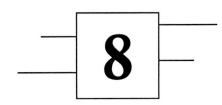

8

Thinking and Writing about Your Teaching

Core Proposition 3:

Teachers Manage and Monitor Student Learning

In the portfolio entries, you will tell the story of your professional decision-making processes in the classroom and in your activities with parents, other professionals, and community members. You will "prove" that you are an accomplished teacher by providing evidence of your Standards-based practices through descriptions of specific interactions with students, parents, colleagues, and others.

In the previous chapters, you were asked to map out the requirements for each of your entries, think about how your teaching context and knowledge of your students impact your instruction, and begin to plan the lessons for your portfolio entries. Now, we will take a closer look at the two types of classroom-based entries and how they are structured. Each entry is organized to help you reveal the "architecture" of your teaching as you demonstrate Standards-based teaching practices.

Entries 1, 2, and 3: Classroom Instruction

In most certificate areas the classroom-based entries are organized in three to four sections similar to the following:

1. Instructional Context (or Student Profile)
2. Planning
3. Instruction and Analysis
4. Reflection

The titles of these sections may differ from those shown here, but each entry will ask you to: 1) identify and describe students for whom you will: 2) plan and deliver instruction and/or assessments, 3) analyze student learning, and 4) reflect on the effectiveness of your selected strategies. Your Portfolio Instructions will provide you with suggested page lengths for each section of your commentary, and each will contain a series of questions or "prompts" to which you must respond.

Candidates are encouraged to respond to the prompts as they are presented in the Portfolio Instructions. Although assessors are trained to credit your evidence no matter where it appears in the entry, your prompts have been purposefully arranged to help you provide the necessary evidence and to reveal your personal architecture of accomplished teaching. Candidates sometimes feel the sequence of the prompts is awkward, and want to rearrange them. Although you may do so, you risk submitting an entry with insufficient evidence.

Writing in the Entry

Before you begin to write, it will be helpful to create a computer file for each of the classroom entries. You can copy and paste from your electronic files, or type in all the prompts listed for the entry as your guide to ensure that you respond directly and completely to each one as you write. The prompts can and should be removed later to maximize your space, but they will guide you during the writing process. When you list your entry prompts on a computer file, you will easily be able to create tools to help your readers, as described in Chapter 2: Support Systems.

Types of Writing

To help you develop evidence of your accomplished teaching practices, you will be prompted to use three types of writing in each of your entries: description, analysis, and reflection. Your Portfolio Instructions discuss these in the section called **Get Started**. We know you must have read this section at least three times by now, but we will go ahead and remind you it contains a very thorough explanation of the three types of writing, with exercises and examples to assist you. We have summarized some of the key points in Figure 23 (Types of Writing).

As you review the examples given in your **Get Started** section, look at (analyze!) the distribution of the descriptive, analytic, and reflective writing in one or more of the samples. Do they appear in equal proportions? Are there patterns in how the types of writing are used? Although there is no one "right" way to complete a portfolio entry, the task is intrinsically analytical, and you will see analytic writing occupies a large part of the overall writing in the sample provided. Likewise, when you look at the instructions for each of your entries, you will find the analysis section required in the Written Commentary is the longest in terms of suggested page length.

Description and Analysis

One cannot begin analyzing without describing the subject to be discussed. You must make the subject of your discussion visible to your reader so your analysis will be meaningful. Each entry will begin with prompts that ask you to describe the teaching situation, the nature of the class, and the challenges presented by individual students. It is critical you provide enough detail that your reader can clearly understand the context upon which your analysis will be based. As you work through your entry, description and analysis will go hand in hand, as your practice and artifacts must be described in full before they can be analyzed.

Candidates often have difficulty distinguishing analytic and reflective writing, perhaps because they are so closely related. Reflective writing is analytical in nature, but what makes it different is its purpose. In your entries, analysis will be used to think about, diagnose, and explain *student* responses to the instruction, while reflection will be used to think about, improve, and build upon *your teaching*. Reflection always implies a direction for future action.

Reflection

The reflective process always includes the aspect of teacher as learner in reference to outcomes for students: "What can I do differently so my students' learning is improved?" It implies the teacher is able to describe the instruction, analyze the effectiveness of the instruction in light of students' responses, and determine the next steps to take in order to continue to advance student learning. In the case of a classroom lesson, the analysis will likely include a discussion of individual student responses to the lesson as well as an assessment of the learning that has occurred for the group as a whole.

After analyzing what occurred during instruction, the teacher will examine the selected strategies in terms of student learning, and consider possible modifications to the lesson in the future and/or how to build upon the learning that has occurred. The reflection might also address the teacher's need to seek more information or assistance in order to increase his or her effectiveness in the classroom.

Although reflective thinking occurs in the process of analysis, typically you will be directed to respond to specific prompts on reflection at the end of each entry. Do not skimp on this section! Your personal thoughts are not visible to others unless you make them so. Your "visible" reflections about your teaching—why you do what you do in your classroom and how you continue to move forward—are what the National Board Certification process is all about. You should use the maximum suggested page limit

	Describe	Analyze	Reflect
Key Questions	What? Which?	How? Why? In what way? What does it mean?	What Now?
Key Verbs	Describe, state, list, define	Analyze, explain, connect, interpret, diagnose, look for patterns, discuss insights	Improve, change, re-teach, build upon
Purpose	Gives the reader a picture of your classroom setting, students and procedures.	Reveals thought processes used during the course of teaching.

Provides significance for evidence submitted. | Informs and improves future teaching practice with this lesson and/or with these students. |
| **Characteristics** | Gives specific, accurate details and explanations of critical features.

Retells a sequence of events in a clear & logical manner | Based on student response(s) to the lesson.

Provides a rationale for decision-making, demonstrates the ability to determine student needs.

Makes meaning from concrete artifacts or descriptions of practice.

Deals with reasons, motivations and causative factors. | Based on the analysis of student response to the instruction, teacher reflects on the effectiveness of instruction.

Retrospective analysis of instructional decisions and results for the purpose of improving professional practice and student learning. |

Figure 23. Types of Writing.
Key words, purposes and characteristics of descriptive, analytical and reflective writing are shown.

for your reflection, as it is the heart of accomplished teaching and student teaching.

Reflection is such an important part of the assessment process that candidates are often encouraged to record daily reflections in personal journals, as these notes may help them develop evidence when writing portfolio entries. In the National Board Certification process, reflection is a tool to show how candidates continually improve their teaching.

Revealing your Instructional "Architecture"

Now we will take a look at the structure and nature of the prompts as we "walk" you through an entry. If you compare your entries, you will find the prompts given in each section are remarkably similar within and across certificate areas. As you may recall from Chapter 4: Starting at the Core, The Five Core Propositions are the building blocks of your *architecture of accomplished teaching*. Now we will revisit these propositions to show how clearly the entry prompts cue you to discuss them. Each question, if answered with sufficient detail and precision, will help you provide evidence of teaching to the Standards for your certificate area and demonstrate the architecture and alignment of your lesson components.

During our walk through this entry, follow along with one of your entries, compare the prompts, and note the similarities. As we look at each section, we will discuss the nature of the evidence you need to provide and the types of writing indicated by the prompts.

Answering the Questions

For our walk through we will review the prompts from the NBPTS Portfolio Instructions for the *Early Adolescence/Science Certificate*, Entry 2, 2006.[45] Remember, this entry is shown as a sample for discussion purposes only. You must follow the instructions and prompts given in your Portfolio Instructions, which may be quite different from those shown in our sample.

Before we begin, turn to the instructions for one of your classroom-based entries, find the section called **Format Specifications**, and look for this sentence: *"Your response will be scored based on the content of your analysis…"* Description is necessary to provide your reader with your context, but *analysis* is the essence of the Written Commentary. Keep this in mind as we examine the prompts from our sample entry, and we will revisit that statement at the end of this section.

Let us begin: According to the section called **What Do I Need to Do?** the entry requires a 20-minute videotape and an 11-page Written Commentary. The instructions state the lesson should focus on a whole-class discussion of a new concept in science.

The prompts for the entry are found in the section called **Composing My Written Commentary**. For the purposes of this discussion, we have placed the prompts in a template and emphasized key words and phrases with bold type and/or underlining not found in the original text. In the matrix, you will see the three types of writing listed to frame our discussion. As we proceed through each section of the Written Commentary, notice the suggested page lengths.

Instructional Context (1 page)

As shown in Figure 24, in the Instructional Context the teacher is asked to discuss the context of teaching, including knowledge of students. This relates to Core Proposition 1: *Teachers Are Committed to Students and Their Learning*. This first section typically calls primarily for *description*, as you demonstrate your understanding of your students—both as a class and as individuals—and their learning needs. As you talk about your planning and instruction in the sections that follow, you will show how your decision-making is responsive to the needs of your class and of the individual students you have featured in this section.

1. Instructional Context (1 page)	Describe	Analyze	Reflect
What are the number, ages and grades of the students in the class featured in this entry and subject matter of the class?	X		
What are the relevant characteristics of this <u>class</u> **that influenced** your instructional strategies for this sequence of instruction: ethnic, cultural, and linguistic diversity; the range of abilities of the students; the personality of the class?	X	X (Implied)	
What are the relevant characteristics of the <u>students with exceptional needs and abilities</u> **that influenced** your planning for this instruction (for example, the range of abilities and the cognitive, social/behavioral, attentional, sensory and/or physical challenges of your students?	X	X (Implied)	
What are the relevant features of your <u>teaching context</u> **that influenced** the selection of this instructional sequence?	X	X (Implied)	

Figure 24. Instructional Context Prompts.
Each prompt calls for one or more of the three types of writing. Example from NBPTS Portfolio Instructions EA/*Science*, Entry 2, 2006.

Your planning, analysis, and reflection will refer back to this context, so it is important that a clear description is given in response to each question. It is also important that you identify *specific* individual students, their learning characteristics and needs in response to the prompt that asks, "*What are the relevant characteristics of the students with exceptional needs and abilities…*" In this case "exceptional needs" need not refer exclusively to students identified for special education services. It is by describing and addressing unique needs of individual students throughout the entry that you will demonstrate your understanding of and response to issues of equity and diversity.

If you state that you have no students with unique needs, you may be indicating that you do not know your students very well, as it is most unlikely that you have a class full of students with identical learning abilities. Some portfolio entries require teachers to work with only one student, or with a small group, in which case the teacher will be prompted to describe the individual characteristics of the students. If you are working with a larger class, it will be to your benefit to identify two to three students in the instructional context who will be "featured" through out the entry as you discuss your teaching decisions.

2. Planning (2 pages)	Describe	Analyze	Reflect
What are the goals for this instructional sequence, including concepts, attitudes, process and skills you want students to develop? **Why** are these important learning goals for your students? **How** does this instructional sequence fit into the overall inquiry process?	X	X	
What <u>specific goals</u> do you have for the discussion seen on the videotape?	X		
Why is a group discussion an effective method for introducing this particular new concept?		X	

Figure 25. Planning Prompts.
Each prompt calls for one or more of the three types of writing. Example from NBPTS Portfolio Instructions, *EA/Science*, Entry 2, 2006.

Planning (2 pages)

The Planning section, shown in Figure 25, calls for evidence of Core Proposition 1, as well as Core Proposition 2: *Teachers Know the Subjects They Teach and How to Teach Those Subjects to Students*. The prompts generally require both *description and analysis*, as you explain your rationale for your selected goals and strategies, based on your knowledge of your content area and students' learning interests, characteristics, and needs as explained in the previous section.

You may also need to explain how the featured lesson fits into the broader scope of learning in the content area. You might also refer to your scope and sequence of instruction for the school year, or to the development of content understanding over different grade levels. Remember, your specific goals for the lesson should be clear and assessable, as you will be asked to analyze and reflect on student learning in reference to these goals. Although students may be learning or practicing multiple concepts and skills, select a few specific goals as the focal point for your decision-making and discussion in the entry.

3. Video Analysis (6 pages)	Describe	Analyze	Reflect
How does the videotape segment fit into this day's lesson as a whole? (i.e., what happened in the balance of the classroom time, either before or after the video was taken?)	X		
What common initial understandings and particular misconceptions did students express on the videotape when first introduced to this area of science? **How** did these understandings and misconceptions compare to what you had anticipated? **How** did you address the different levels of understandings that your students have?	X	X	
How did you elicit and probe students' ideas about relevant science concepts?	X	X	
Describe a specific example from this lesson as seen on the videotape that shows how you ensure fairness, equity, and access for students in your class.	X		
How effective was your learning environment with respect to fairness, equity, and access?		X	

Figure 26. Video Analysis Prompts.
Each prompt calls for one or more of the three types of writing. Example from NBPTS Portfolio Instructions, *EA/Science*, Entry 2, 2006.

Video Analysis (6 pages)

The next section of this entry is focused on analysis of the required video as shown in Figure 26. In other entries, the analysis section will focus on student work samples and/or instructional materials. These artifacts provide you with a focal point to analyze and discuss student responses to your instruction to demonstrate your evidence of Core Proposition 3: *Teachers Are Responsible for Managing and Monitoring Student Learning.*

The selected instructional strategies, organization of the specific lesson, and assessment methods are discussed in this section. You will be asked to justify the instructional approach you have selected and may also be asked to describe your assessment strategies in reference to student responses to your teaching.

Notice the first question in this section asks the writer to give the context, i.e., how the video recording fits into other parts of the lesson not shown. Again, context is important for analysis and reflection. Some entries may ask you to set the context by discussing the organization of the class environment and the routines that are part of your practice.

Other prompts in this section often ask the teacher to describe student responses and/or his or her teaching behavior as the basis for analytical questions that follow. As indicated by the second prompt, you must reveal your thinking during the course of instruction, especially when student responses are different than you had anticipated. You will explain how and why you adjusted instruction for certain students or for the whole class during the course of the lesson if student responses indicated they were not learning as expected. Whether the lesson calls for a video or student work samples, prompts will direct you to discuss specific evidence in the artifact. Do not assume anything in your artifacts is "obvious" or the viewer can "just see it." Your job is to identify the specific evidence and tell why it is significant.

Prompts such as these will encourage you to demonstrate that, as an accomplished teacher, you have a range of different strategies to draw upon in order to enhance students' learning, and you are able to assess student learning during the course of the lesson. Although not explicitly stated in this example, analysis should always discuss student performance in reference to the selected learning goals for the lesson. Notice the suggested page length, which indicates the importance of this section for the entry.

Fairness, Equity, and Access

The last two prompts in this section refer specifically to fairness, equity, and access to learning for all students. It is extremely important to address these issues in your entry, and to understand the terminology. Many teachers mistakenly think equity means treating every student exactly the same way. In fact, educational equity means providing maximum and equal learning opportunities for all students, which often means treating students differently.

The characteristics and needs of some students may require differentiation of goals, instruction, and/or assessments in order for them to have fair and equal access to learning. Teachers may employ technology, preferential seating, classroom assistance, or other strategies to ensure all children will learn to the best of their ability. Equity means that barriers to learning are overcome so that every child can be successful.

In order to provide equitable learning experiences, you must understand and appreciate diversity. In the past, many educators equated diversity with cultural appreciation and provided activities where food, music, and dress from different ethnic and cultural groups were shared. Today, the notion of diversity is much broader. It refers to the fact that each person is unique, with different experiences, interests, abilities, and personal qualities to bring to the learning situation. Diversity issues in the classroom may be related, but not limited, to any or all of the following: gender, ethnicity, language, socio-economic status, disabilities, religion, appearance, and/or sexual orientation.

Ensuring fairness, equity, and access to learning means the different qualities and abilities of individuals are recognized, appreciated, and addressed with meaningful learning experiences. It means a teacher holds high expectations for all students, provides varied resources, strategies, and assessments in a conscious effort to meet different learning needs, and addresses attitudes that may interfere with students' well-being and performance. The teacher strives to respond to the diverse needs of individual students in order to provide fair and equitable opportunities for all students to acquire content knowledge and skills.

Whole books have been written about multiple intelligences, individualization, differentiated instruction, and other topics that refer to fairness, equity, and access. However, when it comes to the portfolio entry, equity is most simply addressed in the demonstration of Core Proposition 1: *Teachers Are Committed to Students and Their Learning.*

If your teaching is student-centered, you are aware of students' individual characteristics and needs, and are committed to their success. Fairness, equity, and access will be intrinsic to your planning and instruction. Your challenge in the entry is to think and write about what you do to maximize the learning experience for all students.

This section may ask you to discuss a specific example showing how you ensure fairness, equity, and access in the featured lesson. It also allows you to discuss how you show an appreciation for individual differences as evidenced by the climate of your classroom. How do you encourage positive interactions among your students? Do you promote tolerance and respect for diverse opinions and perceptions? Do you honor all students' contributions to a large group discussion? How do you help every student feel a sense of belonging and self-worth so he or she participates comfortably? These are all aspects of fairness, equity, and access.

In this entry, notice the prompt that requires the writer to describe what he does to promote fairness, equity, and access; then to analyze the effectiveness of his strategies. Both parts of this prompt must be answered.

Reflection (2 pages)

The reflection section clearly refers to Core Proposition 4: *Teachers Think Systematically about Their Practice and Learn from Experience.* As shown in Figure 27, description, analysis, and reflection are called for by the prompts in this section, but the focus is on reflection—implications for future practice. Notice the section begins by asking the teacher to reflect on student learning with reference to the selected goals. You will be asked to think about the results of your instruction for the purpose of improving learning for your current students, as well as for those you might teach in the future.

4. Reflection (2 pages)	Describe	Analyze	Reflect
As you review the videotape, **what** parts of the discussion do you think are <u>particularly effective in terms of reaching your goals</u> with this group of students? **Why** do you think so? Cite specific examples.	X	X	X
In light of what you learned from your students, **what are the next steps** in this teaching sequence? **How** does your teaching respond to the understandings that the students bring with them to the classroom?	X	X	X
What would you do differently if you had the opportunity to introduce this same concept again with a different class? **Why?** If you would not change anything, explain why it was successful.	X	X	X

Figure 27. Reflection Prompts.
Each prompt calls for one or more of the three types of writing. Example from NBPTS Portfolio Instructions, *EA/Science*, Entry 2, 2006.

Your reflection should be balanced in terms of what went well in the lesson and what you might improve upon. Your reflection may speak to your need to seek more information about the subject, changes you would make to the lesson, or what your next steps would be based on the students' responses to the instructional sequence described in the entry.

Teachers waste valuable space when they respond with statements such as, "Everything went very well in this lesson. There is nothing I would do differently," or "The students really enjoyed this lesson and learned a lot." While we hope students enjoy learning and have the benefit of positive classroom climates, this is not a meaningful reflection. As an accomplished professional, you are asked to demonstrate that you continually seek to improve your teaching practices.

You are asked to think deeply about your ability to direct student learning. Did all students meet the stated goals? Did all learn equally well? What about those with special needs? Did every facet of the lesson go as planned? Are there additional resources you could bring to this lesson? How will the results of this lesson influence what you do next with these students? What will you do differently as a result of your thinking about this lesson?

> *Effective teachers accept responsibility for their students'*
> *learning—listening to students and watching them as instruction*
> *occurs and then later analyzing why things worked or didn't work.*
> *To improve student learning, teachers must consider both*
> *immediate and long-term consequences.*
>
> *-Corcoran and Leahy*[46]

Core Proposition 5: *Teachers are Members of Learning Communities* will be demonstrated when prompts ask you to describe resource materials or personnel employed to assist the class and/or assist individual students with special learning needs for the lesson. It also speaks to your desire to seek information from others in order to improve your effectiveness with students. This might come in at any point in the planning and instructional sequence. It might include your work with other teachers, counselors, paraprofessionals, parents, and/or community resources.

Summary: The Written Commentary in Classroom-Based Entries

We have shown you how The Five Core Propositions are connected to each part of the instructional sequence and how your responses to the prompts will help you demonstrate teaching to Standards. Accomplished teaching is made evident in the way you explain your decision-making, in the way you analyze and respond to the needs of your students, and through your reflection on your teaching effectiveness.

As you develop the Written Commentary for each entry, it is important you focus on the question—and only the question. Do not distract your reader and waste your space by diverging into other topics or aspects of your teaching. As assessors have told us over and over again—JUST answer the question!!

To this phrase, we would like to add, "...and answer the whole question!" Candidates often answer the "what" part of the question, (What are the goals for this instructional sequence...), but fail to answer the "why" part of the question (Why are these important learning goals for your students?). Remember the sentence "Your response will be scored based on the content of your <u>analysis</u>..." found in the **Format Specifications** section? The "why" is the analysis portion of your response. In your analysis, you will demonstrate and synthesize the first three propositions and lay the foundation for the fourth: You will demonstrate that you know and are committed to the learning of the student, that you know your subject matter and how to teach it, and that you manage and monitor student learning. This analysis will help you reflect effectively on your teaching to demonstrate that you *think systematically about your practice and learn from your experiences.*

I could not believe that I had actually forgotten parts of questions, whole questions. I was writing and I thought I did the entry, but when I look back now I see what I did not include. There was so much to do that I was not even aware of it.

- Wendy Smith, NBCT, New Jersey

Did you look at the number of pages assigned to each section in the sample entry? The Instructional Context and Planning sections combined were approximately three pages, while the Videotape Analysis (six pages) and Reflection (two pages) sections total eight pages. Analysis and reflection are highly valued in your entry. The description provides the subject matter for the analysis however, if you use six pages to discuss planning and only three pages to discuss your analysis, your entry may not score well. Even with the page lengths you are given, your writing must be concise to provide a rich body of evidence of accomplished teaching.

If you have not already done so, review the prompting questions in your first entry. You may find it useful to locate and highlight each prompt or part of a prompt that calls for an analytical response as indicated by words such as "Why," "How," "Explain," etc. You may wish to review the key words used for analysis shown in Figure 23 (Types of Writing), and follow a similar process with the prompts in each of your classroom-based entries.

Key Points for Candidate Support Providers

No matter how much preparation and information a candidate has, it is different once he "gets in the driver's seat." Candidate support providers should be prepared to work candidates through the message of this chapter, *Thinking and Writing about Your Teaching*, knowing that the writing process itself is a learning process within the task of certification. Many candidates feel overwhelmed when they consider the levels of writing required for the task, and CSPs need to be prepared to assure candidates that they can learn to write for the portfolio exercises when they reach this point.

When CSPs work with candidates as they are thinking and writing about their teaching, the Standards should be a resource at their fingertips. Good teaching practice is described in the Standards for each certificate. Refer candidates to the Standards as a way to showcase good teaching strategies and methods.

- As they begin to think and write about their teaching, remind candidates that the writing process is an important tool for growth in the process of certification. Help them get started by focusing initially on just one aspect of their entry work.

- Candidates often read and respond to the entry prompts without more than a cursory reading of their Standards. Through exercises at support sessions, teach candidates to match examples of their practices to descriptions of accomplished teaching in the Standards. The Standards describe best teaching strategies and methods for the certificate area, and will provide support for candidates who keep it at their fingertips as a resource.

- Help candidates understand the architecture of accomplished teaching, and connect this framework for teaching to the sections of the portfolio instructions and to the specific prompts of one of their own entries. Encourage them to compare the requirements to each of their classroom-based entries and find the similarities and differences between them. When candidates can see the commonalities in the entry formats and understand how this format helps them demonstrate The Five Core Propositions, the task ahead will become much clearer.

9

Reflective Practice

W e have discussed reflective practice at several points throughout the text but, in this chapter, we will emphasize how integral it is to your work on the National Board portfolio entries and to the continuing development of your professional practices. *Core Proposition 4: Teachers Think about Their Practices and Learn from Experience* describes essential attributes of accomplished teachers. The intent to improve your practices must be readily apparent in each of your portfolio entries.

The importance of reflective practice in education is widely noted in the professional literature. In *The Life Cycle of a Career Teacher*, authors Steffy and Wolfe advocate that "... teachers must develop through progressive phases to sustain a career-long standard of excellence." They describe six possible stages in the continuum of a teaching career, and explain the critical role that reflection plays to help teachers progress from one phase to the next:

> *The reflection-and-renewal process both impels development across the phases and serves as an intervention against withdrawal. Though the growth process changes—over time, across individuals, and through the phases—the processes of reflection and renewal remain constant and operate as the mechanism through which growth occurs.*
>
> *-Steffy and Wolfe* [47]

Constant reflection on one's teaching practices is a necessity for effectiveness in the classroom, and is the source of sustenance and rejuvenation throughout one's teaching career. It is a signature characteristic of teachers who focus on student learning as the driving force in their classroom practices.

In the National Board Certification process, your reflection is multi-faceted. You must reflect on:

1. <u>The National Board Teaching Standards:</u>
   What do I know about the practices of accomplished teachers in my certificate area?

2. <u>Your teaching:</u>
   How well do my own practices align with those described in the National Board Teaching Standards?

3. <u>Your evidence in the entry:</u>
   How can I provide proof of my accomplished practices as I write about my teaching in this entry?

Reflection on the Standards

In previous chapters we have emphasized the Core Propositions as the lens through which to view your teaching practices. The Core Propositions and the Standards are closely related, but not synonymous. The Five Core Propositions are the underlying principles for all certificate areas. Based on these core principles, a set of specific Standards for each area describes accomplished teaching for that certificate. In effect, when you reflect on The Five Core Propositions, you are studying the broad concepts behind your Standards. However, the Standards will provide you with a more detailed picture of what it looks like to implement The Five Core Propositions for your specific area of teaching. The Standards for a given certificate area include an understanding of developmental needs and characteristics of students in addition to knowledge of subject matter and pedagogy.

Just as you analyzed each of The Five Core Propositions in Chapter 4, you will need to study, analyze, and reflect on each of your Standards. As you work on your portfolio entries, specific examples of your practices will help to provide evidence that you have met each of the Standards for accomplished teaching in your field.

As you study, you should be able to recognize that The Five Core Propositions are imbedded in each of your Standards. While a single Standard may contain elements of all Five Core Propositions, some will have a stronger presence than others. You will also find areas in which the Standards overlap, as similar practices will appear in the text of more than one Standard.

For example, though it may appear under different titles, every certificate area has a Standard relating to reflective practice. Clearly, this Standard is directly related to Core Proposition 4: *Teachers think systematically about their practice and learn from experience.* While Core Proposition 4 describes reflective practice in general terms, the Standard will describe it within the context of the specific certificate area.

Elements of reflective practice will also appear in other Standards for the certificate area. In order to respond appropriately to students, make adjustments to lessons, and assess student learning, all teachers will need to apply reflective practice as part of instruction and assessment.

The relationship between The Five Core Propositions and Standards becomes clearer when we look at Standards relating to instructional techniques. Although every teacher must "...*know the subjects they teach and how to teach those subjects to students*" (from Core Proposition 2) appropriate instructional strategies for the *Early Childhood Generalist* will look quite different from those of an *Early Adolescence Mathematics* teacher. The core proposition is the same, but the Standards for each certificate will describe the specific behaviors appropriate for the teacher of the given age group and content area.

If you completed Exercise 4-3 (Analyzing Practice), you composed evidence-rich statements based on The Five Core Propositions. As you read your Standards, you will find that these examples, based on your teaching in the certificate area, are actually examples of teaching to your Standards. You will probably find that some pieces of evidence relate to more than one Standard.

Reflection on Teaching

> ...*effective teachers need to recognize what they value and what their practice says about themselves as educators.*
>
> *- Corcoran and Leahy* [48]

To some degree, all good teachers reflect as naturally as they breathe, making instantaneous decisions in the classroom based on student responses to instruction. In fact, sometimes very experienced teachers work so intuitively that they have difficulty analyzing exactly what they do. For the purposes of National Board Certification, you are asked to engage in conscious reflection—to become aware of your thought processes as you work with students, and to explain the connection between your thoughts and actions to your reader.

It is this kind of reflection that redefines the art of teaching from a service to a profession. Professional learning communities and candidate support groups help teachers think more deeply about their teaching contexts and the needs of their students. They encourage teachers to share their thinking processes aloud, rationalize and justify their decisions to others, and think more critically about what they do and why they do it. Professional dialogue moves teachers beyond description, into analysis, toward consideration of new practices, and along the continuum of professional growth.

As you discuss a recently taught lesson with other professionals, you will have new insights on both positive and negative aspects of your practices. You may hear new ideas from others and will consider improvements you could make in your teaching. Regularly writing about your teaching and talking about your entries will help you clarify and explain your Standards-based teaching practices.

I re-read the Standards for second time, more slowly, more thoughtfully, and found reassurance that I do engage in many of these best practices, but do so unconsciously, without being analytical enough or perhaps observant enough to give enough depth to my reflections and maximize effective revisions to my entries.

-Nina Garcia, Pre-candidate, Hawaii 2006

Reflection on Evidence

Over and over, you will be instructed to provide "evidence" of accomplished teaching through descriptions of your classroom practices. What does "evidence" mean? Is it your personal philosophy of teaching? How is it tied to student work samples? Can it be provided by descriptive writing alone?

Writing and Reflection

If you are a candidate for National Board Certification, it is vital that you begin to write about your teaching early in the certification process. The writing itself is the tool which will help you grow as you consider how best to describe your instructional practices. You will find yourself weighing your words as you struggle to fit your discussion within the suggested limits for each section of the Written Commentary, and must often make choices about what is most important to include.

Writing supports your thinking processes and allows you to examine and evaluate how you have expressed your thoughts. When you return to a piece you have written, you may find yourself asking "What *did* I mean by that?" as you re-examine a section that seemed clear to you when you poured your words onto the paper a few days previously. In the process of writing, reading, and revising, you will distill the most essential aspects of your teaching, and may discover new perspectives, patterns, and implications of your practice.

The portfolio development process requires two levels of reflection. At the first level, you reflect *on your teaching practices*. For most experienced teachers, many practices have become automatic and intuitive. Now, you must stop, think, and deconstruct your thoughts and actions with regard to your planning, teaching, and assessment. You must explain not just what you do when working with students, but why you do it, and how it is an example of teaching to your Standards.

You will read and respond to each of the prompts in an entry as you describe an instructional sequence, ending with a reflection on the effectiveness of your teaching in the lesson. Writing about your teaching will help you capture your thoughts, examine them, and expand on them to compose an accurate picture for your reader.

Once you have composed a draft of your entry, you will need to step to the second level of reflection. Now, you will need to reflect *on your writing* in the entry. You will need to examine how precisely you have answered each of the questions, how thoroughly you have provided evidence required by your Level 4 Rubric, and how well you have addressed the overall intent of the entry. To reflect on your writing, you may wish to consider questions such as these:

1. Have I answered each and every prompt clearly and completely?

2. Have I provided ample evidence for each of the scoring criteria (Level 4 Rubric)?

3. Have I provided clear, convincing, and consistent evidence of meeting my Standards through multiple examples that focus on my specific practices with individuals as well as with groups of students?

4. Are my goals for students clearly stated, specific, and assessable? Have I described exactly what students should know and be able to do as a result of my teaching in this instructional sequence?

5. Is my architecture of accomplished teaching clearly visible? Have I aligned:
   • my contextual information to my goals for students?
   • my strategies to my selected goals?
   • my assessments to my selected goals?
   • my analysis of student learning to my selected goals?
   • AND have I provided a thoughtful reflection on my teaching in this instructional sequence?

6. Have I captured "the big picture" of this entry as described by the introductory pages for the entry in my Portfolio Instructions?

Little did I know just how deep this process would take me. It was like peeling away the layers of an artichoke. Every time I got through another layer, someone would ask me to clarify what I said or to provide evidence that would support what I said. Then, it was as though a thunderbolt struck. Essentially I realized that it wasn't enough to just state what I did unless I provided the evidence that would support it. I had to examine every detail of what I did, why I did it, and how I would do it again if I had the chance. I had to examine the students in my classes, what they did, why they did it and how I was going to help them reach their goals. As the leaves of the artichoke came off one by one, the heart of National Board became clearer—through questioning myself and my practice.

-Ingrid Williams, NBCT, New Jersey

When you begin the writing process early, you can share your work with an experienced reader. Your reader may prompt you to provide more detail, explain more clearly, or give other feedback to help you provide evidence of meeting your Standards. See Chapter 2: Support Systems for more information about readers.

Your writing is the tool that enables you to grow through the assessment process. As you continue the journey, your understanding of the architecture of accomplished teaching and your ability to reflect on your work will deepen. You will develop the ability to critique your own work through the lens of the NBPTS assessment materials, using questions such as those listed above. It is important that you become the reflective practitioner who can and does think about your teaching critically, and that you become less reliant on candidate support providers to read for you. Ultimately, you are responsible for the choices you make in presenting your evidence and demonstrating the reflective capabilities of an accomplished teacher.

Research and Reflection

Professional literature is replete with journal articles on reflective practice, and several researchers have coined new phrases and described new systems for utilizing reflection. Here, we will discuss two models that may be helpful for identifying layers of reflection within the NBPTS certification process.

In the book, *The Three-Minute Classroom Walk-through: Changing School Supervisory Practice One Teacher at a Time*, Steffy et al describe reflection as a process used by supervisors to prompt teachers' thinking. They differentiate types of reflection as direct, indirect, and collaborative.

Direct Reflection occurs when teachers examine specific attributes of an instructional sequence: The teaching context, curricular or instructional choices, decision-making, and student impact. When teachers respond to the prompts in a portfolio entry, they engage in direct reflection. The entry questions of the certification process invite direct reflection. It is important to read the questions carefully and answer each directly and completely.

Indirect Reflection is demonstrated when teachers respond to broad, open-ended questions. The reflection section at the end of each portfolio entry invites this type of reflection. Teachers are asked to think about whether or how they would change the lesson, and the emphasis is on the "what next" of the teacher's practice. Teachers are asked to think ahead, to project possibilities for teaching that have not yet occurred, and imagine the improvements to be made in their instruction.

Collaborative Reflection is evident when peers work together to think critically about their practices for the purpose of improvement. This type of reflection, used as a tool for processing information and opening doors for new insights, is commonly employed in candidate support groups for the National Board Certification process. Steffy et. al describe three necessary conditions for effective collaborative reflection:
  1) Trust among participants for honest sharing and support;
  2) Understanding about how to look for evidence; and
  3) Time to talk together and develop deeper levels of reflection.

  The reflective question is a gift – It's planting a seed for future growth. Its purpose is to enhance a person's thinking on the journey and quest to learn how he or she makes particular decisions and choices.

  - Steffy [49]

In the National Board Certification process, teachers engage in direct reflection when they answer the multi-layered questions of the entry; indirect reflection as they consider where and how the standards are embedded in their teaching tasks; and collaborative reflection when they dialogue with others about the choices they have made in their teaching and writing. Through professional dialogue at all three levels, candidates realize that there is no single, correct response to the prompts. Accomplished teaching is demonstrated in many ways, and entries submitted by candidates with very different teaching styles can be equally rich in evidence.

Authors Taggart and Wilson also describe reflection in terms of layers in which the practitioner moves from classroom-based concerns to broader issues of teaching, learning, and collaborative dialogue.[50] At the first level, reflection is primarily technical in nature as teachers plan their classroom instruction and management based on past experiences and challenges.

As they become more experienced, reflection is more critical in nature. Practitioners begin to consider moral and ethical issues directly or indirectly related to teaching practices, including underlying assumptions about teaching and learning. At this level examples of pedagogy, such as those described by the National Board Teaching Standards, help teachers utilize self-reflection to interpret and inform their practices. Understanding and improvement of the technical aspects of classroom practice are ongoing when teachers form habits of critical reflection.   Again, collegial dialogue is an important aspect of reflection at this level, providing a bridge across concepts, theories, and practices.

As forums for such conversations, support groups for National Board candidates are important tools for growth, prompting critical reflection as participants discuss teaching practices to meet the diverse needs of individual students. When reflection is viewed as a skill to develop, candidate support providers and/or more experienced colleagues can have a significant impact on the growth and development of less-practiced teachers.

Readers of professional literature will find many more perspectives on reflective practice but, regardless of labels, common themes are that 1) reflection is multi-dimensional, and 2) teachers reach deeper levels of understanding and improve their ability to positively impact student learning when they form habits of reflection including collegial dialogue. Addressing both of these themes, the National Board Certification process is an effective tool for developing teachers' capacities to think critically about their teaching.

Understanding Evidence

Helping candidates understand the level of detail required for "evidence" is one of the most challenging tasks faced by candidates support providers. We have found it helpful to discuss evidence in terms of three levels or "tiers" of responses that commonly appear in the way teachers write about their work. One example is shown below, and others may be found on your CD. These tiers are identified as follows:

Tier 1: Global
A candidate writes a global, often philosophical response that addresses students or education in general. The response is not specific to students as individuals or to a particular group of students. In many cases a teacher's thoughts seem vague, as they are expressed without reference to any specific instructional practices.

> *Example: I believe that students learn best when they have*
> *opportunities to dialogue and exchange opinions about issues.*

In statements such as this, no rationale or basis for the teacher's belief is provided. As a stand-alone statement, there is no evidence that the teacher "walks the talk" by applying beliefs and assumptions to actual classroom practice, nor that she is able to substantiate a positive impact on student learning.

Tier 2: General

This type of response describes the teacher's practice in general terms, and may be specific to a particular class or student. However, the response lacks details. The reader cannot determine exactly how the strategy or practice is implemented, and/or the nature of individual students' participation in the activity.

> *Example: In this class, I assign my students to discussion groups to share their opinions and suggest solutions to various community issues. Students are very engaged and gain many insights.*

Although the Tier 2 response could be used as an introductory or transition statement, if unaccompanied by supporting details it provides no evidence.

Tier 3: Specific

The response provides a clear picture of the teacher's specific practices. The description is enhanced by details and examples that may include, but are not limited to, any of the following:

- Description of an interaction between the teacher and individual students, or between one student and another.
- Identification and discussion of teaching strategies or learning significance demonstrated in student work samples or interactions on the video that accompanies the entry.
- Evidence that the teacher has considered and addressed the specific learning needs of one or more students.

Example:
In the discussion group shown on the video, the topic was the new shopping center proposed for our community. I asked students to use the "placemat activity" as a graphic organizer to insure each student first wrote an individual reflection before sharing, discussing, and writing the group's summary of ideas.

This is the third time I have had the students use this strategy, and it has been very effective for students like Jason, the boy in the blue shirt in the first group. Jason is a quiet student and, in the past, he seldom offered opinions in his group. He readily participated after I gave him just a little encouragement, "What do you think, Jason?" In the video, he can be seen writing his ideas on his side of the group chart in the middle of the table and taking part in the discussion as each student shares what they have written. He remains engaged and offers his opinion, "I think there will be too much traffic" as the group agrees on the main ideas for the center of their "placemat."

As shown on the video, my lesson design allowed me to circulate and help prompt or clarify ideas for students like Jason, while informally assessing each student's knowledge of the subject, ability to generate ideas, and participation in the discussion.

In contrast to the Tier 2 example, the Tier 3 response supports and illustrates the statement "in action." It features the responses of individual students in the lesson as examples of the teacher's purposeful work with students.

In the example above, the teacher references her video, identifies specific students engaged in the activity as shown in the video, and describes how student learning was impacted by the selected strategy. She has provided evidence of her knowledge and commitment to students in her description of Jason and his learning needs; of her subject matter in the topic for the lesson; and of managing and monitoring the learning of her students in her discussion of the strategy and her ability to informally assess her students during the session. This response allows her to discuss both her strategies for the whole class, as well as her attention to the learning needs of an individual student. When viewed by an assessor the video recording will verify what she has described in her commentary.

The Tier 3 response provides rich evidence by giving a picture of the teacher's work with students. To provide evidence, responses must go beyond describing a teacher's general practices to describing *specific instances* that demonstrate the *application* of the teacher's practices in working with *these students, at this time, in this place.*

Some teachers may find it helpful to think about these tiers in terms of the format for a written composition. The Tier 1 response is similar to the overall theme of the composition introduced by the title or in the introductory paragraph. Tier 2 responses correspond to main idea sentences for the paragraphs that follow, while Tier 3 responses provide the supporting details that are necessary for an effective written piece. At this level, specific details and real-life examples are provided. In a research review, for example, Tier 3 responses would most likely include descriptions and citations of specific research studies. Without such supporting details, the composition fails to establish a compelling purpose. It is neither clear nor convincing and, if it engages the reader at all, it simply leaves him with more questions than answers.

In a portfolio entry, the "theme" is already identified by the description and instructions for the entry, and Tier 1 statements are seldom desirable or necessary. As in any composition, Tier 2 statements provide clarity and continuity to the writing as they introduce main ideas and facilitate transitions between ideas. Candidates often use Tier 2 statements when they reword the language of the prompting questions to introduce their responses. The substance of the Written Commentary, however, lies in Tier 3 details and examples. As shown in Figure 28 (Reader Feedback on Levels of Response), Tier 1 and 2 responses tend to generate questions in the reader's mind, while Tier 3 responses answer such questions. You will find more examples of tiered responses in the Chapter 9 files on your CD.

In the following exercise, we will encourage you to make the connection from your scoring criteria for a particular entry, the language of the Standards, and your specific practices that provide evidence of these Standards for the entry.

Exercise 9-1: Meeting the Standards for an Entry

As the requirements for Entry 4: Documented Accomplishments are similar for all certificates we will use this entry again to discuss how to analyze your practice against the Standards. This time, our sample is based on the Entry 4 requirements for the *Early Childhood Generalist* certificate. Please note that we will be referring back to the entry maps described in Exercise 5-1.

Reader Feedback on Level of Response		
Tier 1 **Global**	**Tier 2** **General**	**Tier 3** **Specific**
Global: "Every student should…" **Philosophical:** "I believe…" **Vague:** "Opportunities should be provided…"	Statements of general practices and routines: "I always ask my students to…"	"As shown in the video… " "As seen in this student work sample…"
Reader's Reply How do you address these ideas in your teaching?	**Reader's Reply** What does this look like in your classroom? How and why do you do things this way?	**Reader's Reply** I can see specific strategies and examples of your thinking and teaching behaviors in this lesson.

Figure 28: Reader Feedback on Levels of Response.
Experienced readers often use questions to help candidates provide specific details in their entries. The candidate's goal should be to anticipate such questions, and write with sufficient detail that the reader can clearly see examples of the teacher's thoughtful and deliberate teaching practices.

To use Exercise 9-1, locate the template at the end of the chapter, and refer to Figure 29. The template contains three columns. As columns are filled from left to right, the scoring criteria from the entry directions are linked to more detailed descriptions of practice found in the Standards document, and finally to the teacher's personal examples of such practices. Completing this exercise may help make the Standards "real" to you, as you are prompted to provide details of your practice as evidence for this entry.

Column 1: Scoring Criteria.
In the first column of the sample, you should recognize some of the scoring criteria from Box 4 of our Exercise 5-1 Entry Map. As you recall, these were paraphrased from the bulleted list under the heading **How Will My Response Be Scored?** in the Portfolio Instructions for Entry 4. Remember, these criteria are drawn directly from the Level 4 rubric that is used to score your entry.

Column 2: Standards: Key Words and Phrases.
In this column, the general statements of the scoring criteria for Entry 4 are matched with the specific behavior and actions of an accomplished teacher as described in the Standards. To complete this column, you may refer to your own Standards, find descriptors that correspond to the scoring criteria for the entry, and list them in the second column of the exercise sheet.

Column 3: Evidence.
The third column is intended to help you reflect on the work you have done or plan to do for this entry. Under the title "Evidence in My Entry," you may note your specific activities that are similar to those described in your Standards for the entry. It can be very effective to describe specific situational examples from your teaching practice as possible sources of evidence.

In our sample, specific examples of communication with parents are described to provide evidence of the Standards and scoring criteria. A routine applying to all families is described, as well as a problem-solving situation with one parent and child. In both cases, sample pages from the teacher's communication log could be used to document and substantiate this evidence. Note that a single example of authentic practice often addresses more than one of the scoring criteria. You will need multiple examples of Standards-based practice in each entry to demonstrate *...clear, convincing, and consistent evidence.*

This exercise may provide you with a "mental map" of the connections between your scoring criteria, Standards, and practices, or may be used as a tool for writing and reflection. If you choose to use it, enter the scoring criteria listed in the entry directions under **How Will My Response Be Scored** for the first column, find corresponding key words and phrases

Sample: Exercise 9-1: Meeting the Standards for an Entry

Scoring Criteria (Level 4 Rubric) ➡	Standards: Key Words & Phrases ➡	Evidence in My Entry
Treat parents and other interested adults as valued partners in students' development and education;	...eager to listen to and learn from parents, because parents are especially knowledgeable about the past development and present attributes of their children.	I make a point of making a positive phone call to each child's family at least once a month. This helps me build good relationships, give updates on class activities and the child's progress, and find out if parents have any questions or concerns.
Use thoughtfully chosen, appropriate strategies that may or may not be original, but are effective in engaging parents and other adults in two-way communication focused primarily on substantive teaching and learning issues and individual student progress	...place a priority on regular communication with parents about each child's progress.	I call Judy's mother weekly, as she is concerned about Judy's dependency, and we have been working together to build her self-confidence. For example....
	...honest in communicating with families, telling them what goes on in the classroom.	
	...encourage and assist parents in sharpening their ability to observe and understand their child's behavior and discourse.	

Figure 29. Sample: Exercise 9-1: Meeting the Standards for an Entry.
In this sample, scoring criteria and phrases from the Standards for the *Early Childhood Generalist certificate* are shown with an example of evidence provided by the candidate for Entry 4: Documented Accomplishments.

from your Standards for the second column, and notate the evidence you can provide to meet the Standards for this entry in the third column. If you completed The Five Core Propositions Exercises 4-2 and 4-3, you will find that many of the examples you provided there can now appropriately be used as evidence of Standards.

Completing these exercises is time-consuming, and some candidates may find it too tedious for their taste. Others will find that writing down the key points described in Standards and matching those to actual classroom practices will help them internalize and make personal meaning from the Standards document. In any case, we believe that the visual map provided by this exercise may help candidates understand the task and the meaning of "evidence." By highlighting the Standards that you can meet, you will also be able to see the areas for which you do not have evidence. The Standards are your most important reference tool for each entry, as they describe the specific behaviors of an accomplished teacher in the certificate area.

As you analyze and personalize each of the Standards, you will undoubtedly find areas of your teaching that are in need of improvement. This is very common for candidates and does not mean that you are not ready for National Board Certification. The process is expected to help you develop professionally as you strive to meet each of the Standards.

From Standards to Scoring

In Exercise 5-1 (Entry Mapping), scoring criteria from the Level 4 Rubric were listed. These criteria are drawn directly from the Standards for the entry. Figure 30 (Building a Case for Accomplished Teaching), illustrates the relationships between the various components we have mentioned: The Five Core Propositions, the Standards, the scoring criteria (Level 4 Rubric), and evidence provided by a candidate.

The Standards for each certificate area are based on The Five Core Propositions. The scoring criteria from **How Will My Response Be Scored?** in the Portfolio Instructions are drawn directly from the Level 4 Rubric for the certificate area, and both are drawn from the Standards. The rubrics are applied to the evidence provided by the candidate, and the resulting score indicates whether or not accomplished teaching according to the Standards has been demonstrated. Each of the scoring criteria must be addressed with multiple examples and sources of evidence to meet the Level 4 descriptor for consistency. To meet the requirement for accomplished teaching, your evidence must correspond to the Level 3 or Level 4 Rubric descriptors. See Chapter 14 for more information about the scoring process.

Often, new candidates struggle to understand what is expected in the National Board Certification task. The requirements are simple but not easy. Reading Figure 30 from the bottom up, the architecture of accomplished teaching is based on The Five Core Propositions. All five must be evident in the featured lesson for the candidate's entry. The Standards for the certificate area are based on The Five Core Propositions, however, they are more specific, as they describe the behavior of the accomplished teacher with reference to the content area and developmental level of the students. Candidates need to learn to answer prompts with both The Five Core Propositions and the Standards in mind.

The scoring criteria listed under **How Will My Response Be Scored?** help candidates focus on the most important aspects of the Standards for the entry. Candidates must be sure to give evidence that corresponds to the scoring criteria as they answer each prompting question in the Portfolio Instructions. The prompts for the entry are carefully constructed to elicit the required evidence of the Standards.

Candidates may need to revise their writing many times to ensure that adequate evidence has been provided in response to each aspect of each prompt. Rich, detailed evidence of Standards and alignment of lesson components as described in The Five Core Propositions are necessary for an accomplished entry. The nature of the required evidence is described in the scoring rubric used by the assessor and a score is assigned based on the quantity and quality of the evidence submitted by the candidate.

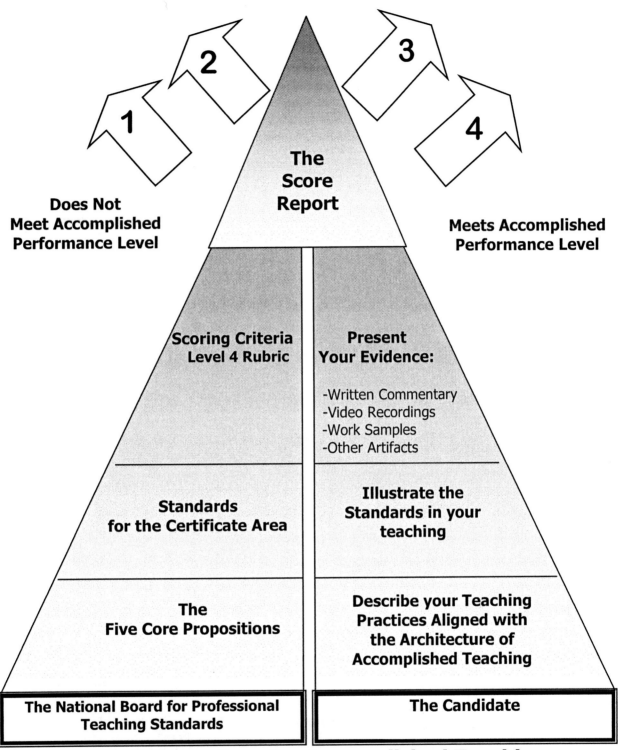

Building a Case for Accomplished Teaching

Figure 30. Building a Case for Accomplished Teaching.
The Standards describe teaching practices specific to the subject and developmental level of students, and the Level 4 Rubric specifies what is valued in the entry. The candidate must provide evidence specific to the Standards and the rubric will be applied to determine the candidate's level of performance. The resulting score indicates whether or not accomplished teaching has been demonstrated.

Key Points for Candidate Support Providers

- Scaffold reflective thinking and writing through exercises conducted over a series of support sessions. Few teachers are accustomed to thinking critically about their work, and you do not want to overwhelm candidates by asking too much too fast. Help them to understand the connection of The Five Core Propositions to the Standards, and provide opportunities for reflection and dialogue about teaching practices that demonstrate the Standards. As candidates begin to write, use the Levels of Response materials to help them understand the necessity for rich descriptions of these practices as evidence in the entries.

- Ownership and responsibility for the portfolio entries belongs to the candidate alone, and it is important to keep emphasizing this. When candidates ask you to read their work, they may be seeking validation and reassurance that the entry will receive a passing score from NBPTS. It is neither ethical nor wise to make such a judgment. You do a greater service to candidates by asking questions that clarify, summarize, or extend their thinking. By doing so, you help build their capacities to reflect and improve on their own work.

- Avoid the use of evaluative words such as "Good," "I like this," or "This is not right." Instead, keep comments to statements such as "Your details give me a clear picture." or use questions. This will help the candidate develop independence in reading his or her own work for evidence.

- Candidates will often ask the CSP to tell them if the lesson they have selected is good for the entry, or will want to see samples to show them how to write about a lesson. Resist showing samples and encourage candidates to find examples in their own writing, or in that of their fellow candidates. (Refer to the NBPTS Ethics Policy for more information on use of sample materials.).

- Help candidates identify and improve the level of response in their entry draft by using the Level of Response examples from the CD as a reference. Ask them to use different colored highlighters to identify Level 1, 2, and 3 responses in their own writing. If Level 1 responses are identified, ask candidates to explain how (or if) these support the evidence in the entry. Most candidates will find they have a preponderance of Level 2 responses, and they need to increase their details to reach Level 3.

Exercise 9-1: Meeting the Standards for an Entry

Entry_____

Scoring Criteria (Level 4 Rubric)	Standards: Key Words & Phrases	Evidence in My Entry

Directions: In the first column, the scoring criteria (Level 4 Rubric) for the entry from your Portfolio Instructions may be listed. Choose one Standard. As you read, list key words and phrases from the text in the middle column, noting how they correspond to the scoring criteria. In the last column, describe teaching behaviors and examples you can use to provide evidence. Several copies of this sheet may be needed to thoroughly analyze each Standard.

10

Contributions to Student Learning

<u>Core Proposition 5:</u>

Teachers are Members of Learning Communities

$\mathbb{E}$ ntry 4, Documented Accomplishments, will ask you to go beyond the walls of your classroom to describe a different dimension of your professional work. In this entry, the focus is primarily on your work with other adults to create opportunities and supports that enhance student learning. These might involve activities at your school, in the larger community, at the state level, or beyond. You are asked to provide evidence of three types of professional roles: 1) as a leader or collaborator, 2) as a learner, and 3) as a partner with families and others to support the learning of individual students.

It is important that early in the year of their candidacy, teachers read the requirements of this entry and identify accomplishments that will provide the evidence they need. Many candidates find they lack such evidence in one or more of the three areas, and need to develop activities and accomplishments that address these areas before submitting the portfolio. As each accomplishment should be accompanied by supporting documentation, teachers also need time to gather and write about the selected documentation in the Written Commentary for the entry.

Your Portfolio Instructions include diagrams and charts to help you think about the activities you might include in this entry. It is important to choose your activities carefully to meet the evidence requirements listed under **How Will My Response Be Scored**. You will also find the section called **Making Good Choices** helpful in guiding your selection of accomplishments and documentation. In Entry 4 you will write a description and rationale for each of several accomplishments followed by a single reflective summary on the body of all your accomplishments taken together.

Candidates may submit separate accomplishments that address each of the three required areas, or accomplishments that address a combination of the three areas. However, as of the 2006–07 assessment cycle, no more than eight accomplishments may be submitted. Quality is more important than quantity, as it is difficult to provide the detail needed for "evidence" if you try to discuss too many different accomplishments.

Most importantly, as your instructions will tell you, *your accomplishments must demonstrate an impact (direct or indirect) on student learning.* You must carefully select and write about accomplishments that clearly contribute to student learning. While eight accomplishments is the maximum, you may choose to write about fewer activities if you wish, as long as you are able to provide *clear, convincing, and consistent* evidence for each required area that meets the descriptors of the Level 4 Rubric for the entry.

Thinking About Your Accomplishments

The first step for Entry 4 is to develop a list of many accomplishments so that you can select those that best match the requirements of the entry. We encourage candidates to start by writing down everything they can think of, as sometimes several "smaller" activities can be grouped as parts of a larger accomplishment.

Many teachers' first response to Entry 4 is "But I really haven't done anything that important!" Some of the most dedicated teachers are often very humble about their efforts outside of the classroom, and do not easily take credit for what they have done. Most teachers will need a bit of prompting to develop an initial list of possible accomplishments.

I worked with a young teacher who taught special education students. She was very concerned about Entry 4, as she felt she had no accomplishments to write about. As I spoke to her about her work with students, she hesitantly mentioned that she provided after school tutoring for two teenagers with special needs on a regular basis. Then she mentioned that she had taken a course on brain-injured children to help her better understand how to work with one of her students. As an afterthought, she added that she had requested and received assistance from a state specialist, who had shown her strategies for working with the same student during the previous school year. These were all activities worthy of consideration for her entry.

-Bess

We encourage candidates to work together and brainstorm to create such lists, and then share out "round-robin" style in small groups. This is very helpful for several reasons: 1) As participants hear about one another's activities, they are prompted to consider similar activities of their own; 2) when candidates realize they are weak in one or more areas, they will hear several ideas for activities they might engage in to build evidence for this entry, and 3) it is often very inspiring to hear about what teachers do to enhance student learning! As always, sharing invites feedback, which helps teachers consider new perspectives and gain insights on their practices.

In Figure 31 (Defining Your Entry 4 Accomplishments), we have shown an example of how the brainstorming process encourages a candidate to move from the identification of several discrete activities, to defining significant accomplishments. While sharing of student portfolios, parent newsletters, a class website, a weekly communication system, and a parent volunteer program are all valuable activities, it might be difficult for a teacher to develop each as one of her eight accomplishments. When she identifies the same activities as components of a bigger idea: "Parent Engagement" they contribute to the greater significance of a single accomplishment. Similarly, leading the language arts committee and taking classes to improve delivery of instruction might be grouped under the larger idea of "Literacy Instruction Leadership"; however, the teacher must clearly describe how each of the component activities has contributed to this larger goal.

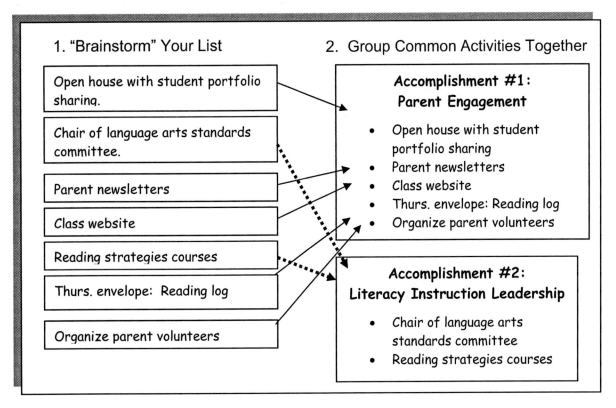

Figure 31: Defining Your Entry 4 Accomplishments.
Brainstorming a list may reveal that several items can be described within the context of a single, more significant accomplishment consisting of several component activities.

Simply taking classes does not provide evidence of leadership or instructional improvement. Candidates must describe how the information gained from coursework is *applied* to improve teaching and learning.

Because the number of accomplishments is limited, candidates must maximize the opportunities for evidence in each one. Sometimes related accomplishments can be legitimately combined, but it is not wise to "lump" activities together that do not contribute to a cohesive goal to impact student learning. You will find a discussion of this issue in your Portfolio Instructions.

Good Choices

Candidates often want to know what kind of accomplishments are the right ones to send in as a part of this entry. There is no easy answer to this, and candidates must ultimately determine the combination of accomplishments which best provide the evidence needed in the entry. Exercise 10-1: Analyzing Accomplishments may be used as a tool to help you think about your choices, the degree of evidence that can be provided by each, and the overall consistency of evidence you provide for each required category.

Exercise 10-1: Analyzing Accomplishments

To use Exercise 10-1: Write the scoring criteria (Level 4 Rubric) from the entry instructions **How Will My Response Be Scored?** in the left column, as shown in the provided template. For most candidates, the criteria shown in our template are accurate, as these are identical for many certificate areas. However, you must compare your Entry 4 Scoring Criteria to be certain they match your requirements, as there are some exceptions. You will notice we have posed each criterion as a question on the worksheet.

The numbers 1–8 at the top of the sheet represent the number of your allowed accomplishments, which may be more than you choose to include. For each accomplishment, answer the rubric question in each row by marking an "X" for "yes," or "0" for "no." Alternatively, you might rate the strength of evidence provided by entering "1" for "minimal," "2" for "some," and "3' for "strong".

It is important that you read, understand, and respond honestly to each rubric question. Your evidence must clearly demonstrate what is asked of you. Do not try to justify activities that are "related" but do not clearly provide evidence. For example, one rubric question asks: *"Do you treat parents and other interested adults as valued partners in students' development and education?"* Think about what actions an accomplished teacher demonstrates to provide evidence of this, and read your Standards for further clarification. Is it evidence if you hold an Open House and give parents an "opportunity" to come to it? Or, does evidence consist of multiple conversations with a student's family and working together to resolve issues of concern for the student's learning and well-being? Which one provides stronger evidence of treating parents as valued partners? In general, simply giving parents or students "opportunities" is meaningless. Unless you can write about your interactions and outcomes, opportunities alone do not demonstrate that anything has been accomplished. Remember, the focus of this entry is Contributions to Student Learning. You must explicitly describe how each of your selected accomplishments has had, or will have, a positive impact on students in your certificate area.

By completing this exercise, you will create a bird's eye view or "wall of evidence" for the entry, and you will be able to identify areas of strength as well as areas that may need work. The "wall of evidence" will be described in more detail in Chapter 12: Reviewing and Submitting Your Portfolio.

Writing About Your Accomplishments

In writing about each accomplishment, you will be asked to describe what you did, why it was significant, and how it impacted the learning of students in your certificate area. If you are an Early Childhood Generalist, your work with high school aged students would not be appropriate, in most cases, for an Entry 4 accomplishment. However, there are exceptions. If a teacher develops a program in which at-risk high school students are trained as "reading buddies" for Kindergarten through sedcond grade students to improve their engagement in literature, this could be an equally valid accomplishment for a high school teacher or an early childhood teacher. Just remember, your accomplishments must be relevant to students in your selected certificate area.

"I" and Why

When you write about your selected accomplishments, it is important to use lots of **I** and **Why** statements. Often candidates have difficulty using a personal pronoun when writing, but it is very important that you clearly state your specific actions related to the accomplishment. "I..." statements that describe your contributions provide the evidence to substantiate your accomplishment. In collaborative work situations, it is especially important that you describe exactly what your roles, responsibilities, and contributions to the outcomes were. Being a member of a committee and describing the work of the committee will not yield evidence for you without these specific details, as the "committee" is not being assessed for National Board Certification—you are! "Why" statements give your rationale for engaging in the activity. They demonstrate your commitment to students through the purposeful engagement in the accomplishment.

In Entry 4, you must *dare to declare*. Candidates often have difficulty understanding that who they are and what they do must be the accomplishment. This entry is about *you* as a teacher who collaborates, *you* as a teacher who leads, *you* as a teacher who learns. Therefore, *dare to declare* what **you have done** as you describe your accomplishments. Stay focused on your evidence. Let the reader see you clearly in your featured accomplishment and be able to declare what you have done. Begin statements with "I…" followed by precise action words that describe you in the accomplishment. Read the Standards for your certificate to find vocabulary that describes accomplished teaching. Consider the following statements:

   a. My department met twice a month and worked on math assessments for our grade level.
   b. *I met* with other members of the math department twice a month. *I brought* student work samples and *(I) shared* my rubric with my colleagues.

As you can see, only statement "b" describes specific actions of the teacher. Statement "a" describes what the department did, and does not actually describe the writer as being present at the department meetings; yet such statements are quite commonly made by new candidates. The following exercises will help you develop your evidence of accomplished teaching as you reflect and write about each of your selections. Completing Exercise 10-2 will help you *dare to declare* your specific contributions to an activity; while Exercises 10-3 and 10-4 will help you format your response as required by the Portfolio Instructions for Entry 4.

Exercise 10-2: From Actions to Evidence

This exercise may be used with each of your proposed accomplishments to help you clearly identify *your* specific contribution to one selected activity. To use the exercise, find the template provided at the end of the chapter, select one of the accomplishments you listed in Exercise 10-1, and write twenty statements about the accomplishment, **beginning with "I"** that include one or more action words. Underline your action words and phrases in each sentence.

   Examples:
      1. <u>I led meetings</u> with my department
      2. <u>I worked with my colleagues</u> to develop common assessments to better monitor student learning.

After completing Exercise 10-2, go on to Exercise 10-3 to outline a draft to meet the requirements of the entry. Each of your accomplishments must answer three essential questions:

1. What is the nature of the accomplishment? (description)
2. Why is it significant? (analysis)
3. How did it/will it impact student learning? (outcome)

Exercise 10-3: Outlining Your Accomplishments

Use Exercise 10-3 to help you develop a draft for each accomplishment. Locate the expandable exercise template on your CD and use the twenty "I" statements from Exercise 10-2 to draft the description section (the "What?") of this accomplishment. Clearly describe *your* contributions (underlined in the example below). Include a rationale for your actions (italicized in the example below).

> In conversation with the three other fourth grade teachers, I realized that our *delivery of the math curriculum was inconsistent.* I suggested that we work together to develop common assessments that would *allow us to track the progress of all students* in the grade level and *insure that all had a common math background* when they advanced to fifth grade.
>
> As a result, I met with my colleagues twice a week for eight weeks *to agree on what was essential for students to learn each quarter* and *how it would be assessed.* My colleagues and I brought work samples and suggested test questions. Based on our agreements at the meeting, I drafted sample tests for each quarter...

Continue to develop your description of the accomplishments on the provided template using the following information to assist you with each section:

1. *What* is the nature of this accomplishment?

This prompt calls for description. You need to provide specific detail about what you did. If you worked with a group or committee on a project, be sure to describe your personal contributions. This is not an assessment of your project; it is an assessment of your personal actions and contributions. If you describe only what the group did or what the project accomplished, there is no evidence of your own accomplishments. Be sure to provide descriptions of your Standards-based actions that meet the scoring criteria. Describe not only what you did, but also how you did it. Give a good picture of what it looked like for you to carry out this activity. Make explicit references to any accompanying artifacts or documents, explain what they are and how they support the evidence you have provided in your description. Answer questions such as: *What is the nature of this accomplishment? Describe what you did. What was it? How did you do it? Who did you do it with? Where? When? How Often? What artifacts have you included to support your description? Why have you selected these specific artifacts? How do they strengthen your evidence?*

2. *Why* is this accomplishment significant?

This prompt calls for analysis, which might also be reflective in nature. Tell why you worked on this accomplishment. Explain what student and/or family needs prompted you to take action. Answer questions such as: *In what way does this accomplishment demonstrate your leadership, your learning, partnerships, and/or collaboration with parents or colleagues? Why did you think it was worth your time and effort? Why did you do it? What did you hope to accomplish in terms of contributing to student learning? How did this accomplishment connect to the classroom? What did you learn about yourself through this effort? How did you grow professionally?*

3. *So What? How* has what you have described had an impact on student learning?

This prompt also calls for analysis, this time specifically in regard to the impact on student learning. You must explicitly connect your accomplishment to outcomes for students. Do not assume your reader will make the connection. Use specific examples wherever possible to make direct and specific connections from the activity to learning benefits for students. Answer questions such as: *How has this activity impacted (or how do you expect it to impact) student learning? Are there visible results? How can you tell it was worthwhile?*

After you think and write about your accomplishments in these initial drafts, you will select the pieces that can best provide the evidence called for by the scoring criteria, listed under **How Will My Response Be Scored?** Once you have made your selections, you will need to collect documentation to support your activity descriptions. There are strict page limits for your commentary and documentation, and it is especially important you write concisely in this entry and focus your writing on the essential questions and the evidence.

Titling Your Accomplishment

As you write your final drafts of each accomplishment, it is helpful to your reader to provide titles. A carefully composed title will cue your reader to look for specific evidence about *you*, and what *you did*. Emphasize your role or contribution, rather than simply naming a project or committee. Examples of accomplishment-focused titles are shown in Figure 32.

Examples: Titling Your Accomplishments

Instead of this... (subject cue)	Call it this... (role or contribution cue)
Language Arts Committee	Curriculum Leadership in Language Arts
Student Drama Club	Coordinator for Performing Arts
Recycling Project	Community Partnership: Recycling

Figure 32: Composing an Effective Title for Your Accomplishment.
Use your title to focus your reader on the contribution you have described in your entry.

The Reflective Summary

After answering the three essential questions about each of your accomplishments and assembling them with related documentation, you will be asked to write a separate reflective summary section on the entire group of accomplishments you chose to include in the entry. The key word is *reflective*. One of the common errors made by candidates is to simply reiterate information they have already provided in the description and analysis of the separate accomplishments. Reflection implies change, e.g., "What have I learned from the results of this work that will lead me to *make changes or continue my efforts* to improve learning for my students?" "How will I continue to demonstrate my work as a member of professional learning communities?" Review your body of accomplishments in terms of patterns and effectiveness. Think about what you have done, why it is significant, and what else you might do in the future. Be specific.

The National Board Certification process calls for metacognition, or thinking (and writing) about your thinking. You will be asked to respond specifically to the following prompts:

1. *In your work outside of the classroom, what was most effective in impacting student learning? Why?*

2. *Considering the patterns evident in all your accomplishments taken together, what is your plan to further impact student learning in the future?*

To identify patterns or themes in your accomplishments, try asking yourself these questions:

a. Which of the three roles (learner, leader or collaborator, or partner with families and community members) seems to predominate in my collection of accomplishments?

b. If I had to pick just one word to describe myself, what would it be?

c. If I had to pick two words to describe my collection of accomplishments, what would they be?

You may wish to ask a colleague to read your entry and answer the same questions. Do you or others see you as a communicator? As one who seeks new information? As a connector? As a researcher? Often a fresh set of eyes will help you identify traits and themes that appear throughout your writing and offer you a new way to reflect on your work as a member of different learning communities.

Do *not* use this section to simply review and summarize the activities you have already described. Your reflection should "dig deep" to provide a thoughtful self-examination of where you are in terms of your professional accomplishments and where you might go next. Remember— reflection always includes implications for future practice to improve student learning.   You must demonstrate that you reflect upon your work and learn from it as part of a continual process of professional growth and your commitment to students and their learning.

Exercise 10-4: Reflecting on Your Accomplishments

Exercise 10-4 has been provided to prompt your thinking and writing for the reflective summary on your body of work. Use it to identify the key points for this section of the entry. As you begin to write your summary, we recommend you write out each part of the prompt as a sentence starter to insure you give a complete response. You may remove all or part of the prompts later to save space. For example:

1. *In my work outside of the classroom, the most effective things I did to impact student learning were...*
2. *These were effective because...*
3. *With all my accomplishments taken together, the patterns I see are...*
4. *Considering my accomplishments thus far, my plan to further impact student learning in the future is...*

Many teachers work on the documented accomplishments entry at the beginning of their candidacy. If this is true for you, it is important to return and reflect on it again before you submit the portfolio. Your ability to analyze, reflect, and write about your teaching will develop and deepen throughout your candidacy. You may find you are able to give richer, more insightful responses to the questions above as you near the end of your portfolio work.

Exercise 10-5: Sources of Documentation

When selecting your accomplishments, make sure you can provide documentation to support the evidence in your Written Commentary. For each accomplishment you may have several different pieces of documentation.

On the worksheet provided for Exercise 10-5, it may help you to list the different artifacts and/or documents you can provide for each accomplishment, and briefly note how each relates to one or more of the three specified categories for Entry 4. This will assist you in organizing your material and selecting the best supporting evidence for the entry.

Evidence of Contributions to Student Learning

You will also want to review the scoring criteria for the entry, and be sure you have several sources of evidence for each of them. Your goal is to clearly, convincingly and consistently demonstrate that, taken as a whole, your accomplishments in this entry show you meet all the criteria, which are focused on student learning. As always, the criteria, **How Will My Response Be Scored?** are drawn directly from the Standards. By reading and re-reading the Standards for the entry, you will better understand how to select accomplishments that meet the criteria.

In particular, you must be sure to provide specific evidence of your work with the families and community of your students in the current school year. It is important to discuss your procedures for routine communications, as well as your work with parents and colleagues for students whose needs require extra support or attention.

Remember, your documentation and Written Commentary go hand in hand. In your commentary, you must refer to each piece of evidence included and explain how it relates to and supports the evidence for the accomplishment you are writing about.

The Communication Log

A communication log may or may not be required for your entry, but is strongly recommended as it is difficult to provide strong evidence of the interactive family communication requirement in any other way. Note the word "interactive." Teachers often communicate with families through notes and announcements of various types. However, your evidence must show *two-way communication*, as evidence you partner with families for the benefit of the student. In our experience, an entry that falls short in this requirement will NOT receive a passing score, even if it includes abundant evidence of meeting the other criteria.

When a communication log is included as an artifact, your commentary must discuss and explain the communications shown on the log. Refer to specific entries on your log, describe the communications, and explain why they are significant.

At the beginning of the school year, I established communication systems with families through e-mail and a website that shows the syllabus and assignments for each class. This has been very positive, as most families have computers and can communicate with me easily. I also send written information such as the invitation to Open House at the beginning of the school year (see parent responses in entries 1, 4), and progress reports which are sent to all parents at regular intervals (entry 9). If I cannot contact parents via e-mail or letter, I call them on the telephone.

RJ's father was ecstatic when I called to report on his child's progress, and it helped me to learn about RJ's home circumstances (12). RJ knows I am sympathetic to his situation, and he has continued to produce quality work in my class.

I called CK's mother to inform her that he was not performing up to his potential (3). When he did not improve after a few more weeks, I called again (13) and we discussed his previous math experiences. I learned that CK struggles in a large classroom environment, so I arranged for him to sit in the front row and to stay after school twice a week for tutoring with me until his grade improved. After I tutored CK for three weeks, his grade and understanding of concepts began to improve.

When I called KT's mother (2), to tell her that KT was experiencing difficulty in geometry, she told me KT has a habit of not completing her homework. KT's mother requested that I inform her weekly about her daughter's progress. Every Friday I sent a short e-mail indicating whether KT finished all of her assignments. As a result of our collaborative effort, KT's participation increased, and her grade improved. (5, 6, 7, 8, 10, 11)

1 9/04	AN's parents	In-email	Thank you for your introduction and your website address. We'll be there on September 12th. See you then!
2 9/15	KT's mother	Out-phone	KT has not been turning in her homework this week, and I wanted to enlist assistance from her mother in reminding KT to do her work. KT promptly turned in all of her work on Monday.
3 9/16	CK's Mother	Out-phone	Informed parent of CK's progress. Noticed some difficulties comprehending information. I reassured her that I will monitor CK's progress.
4 9/21	KT's mother	In-email	Thank-you for the introduction, and invitation. KT enjoys your class, and that is always a positive note to my husband and I. We look forward to any comments you may have, or any suggestions in how we may be of assistance to both you and our daughter during this school year.
5 9/21	KT's mother	Out-email	Replied to above, expressed concerns about homework.
6 9/22	KT's mother	In-email	Thank-you for your comments and updates. I have spoken with KT, and she assures me she will get caught up, and not let her work slide as she has. Could you please give me an update at the end of the week on her progress? I would hate for her to fall behind from the very beginning of the school year. I appreciate your time and concern.
7 9/22	KT's mother	Out-email	Replied to above, suggested weekly progress checks.
8 9/23	KT's mother	In-email	Thanks again. I look forward to hearing from you at the end of the week.
9 9/24	EVERY PARENT	Progress Report	Written report to inform all parents about their child's grade and any missing work during the first half of the 1st quarter
10 9/27	KT's Mother	Out-email	KT did not turn in her assignments yesterday. She may complete the assignments over the weekend.
11 9/30	KT's mother	In-email	Thanks for the update. Spoke w/KT, she claims she forgot. Not an acceptable answer. She assures me she will turn in her work tomorrow. Thank-you for keeping me informed.
12 10/3	RJ's father	Out-phone	Told RJ's father about his good grades and excellent focus in class. Father was very thankful. RJ's mother died over the summer and RJ has been going through drug rehabilitation.
13 10/4	CK's mother	Out-phone	I wanted more information on CK's previous math experiences, as he is still struggling in class. Mom wanted to know how CK can improve his performance in my class. We agreed that CK should come in for help at least twice a week to help him understand the assignments.

Figure 33. Sample Communication Log with Comments.
Adapted with permission from Loren Ayersman, high school mathematics teacher, Hawaii.

This is shown in Figure 33, with comments and examples from the communication log of a secondary teacher. In the comments, the teacher explains the significance of communications with different parents and how these communications helped him work more effectively with the students. A variety of communication venues are shown (invitation, reports, e-mail, phone calls) that provide parents access and opportunity to work in partnership with the teacher for the success of the student.

When teachers communicate regularly with parents, they show their concern for the students' well-being and their value for the family as an educational partner. Interactive communication may help teachers find successful instructional strategies for a particular child, and encourage parents to reinforce learning at home.

Exercise 10-6: Writing About Your Entry 4 Artifact

Use the Exercise 10-6 worksheet to help you think and write about each of your selected documents or other artifacts for Entry 4. This will help you clarify and explain your reasons for selecting each piece.

For example, if you took a class on teaching technology in the classroom, you could choose to include a certificate of completion as evidence. However, it might be much more effective to use a letter of verification from a colleague describing how you incorporated the use of technology in your lessons as a result of what you learned. The certificate looks nice, but provides very little evidence, while a letter of verification might enrich and confirm your written description about learning for the purpose of improving your instruction.

Every artifact that you choose to include in Entry 4 should be described and explained in your Written Commentary. The evidence should be clearly related to the scoring criteria for the entry, including how it impacts student learning.

Summary: Entry 4

In Entry 4 you will create a picture of your role as a professional outside of the classroom environment. This area of your practice may be very rich or somewhat limited, depending on your years of experience and on your personal initiative. In either case, use the thinking and writing process in Entry 4 to see how your professional work stretches into the larger picture of the school and learning community, into partnerships with students' homes and families, and back into the classroom to enhance learning experiences for the children you serve.

As you review your professional work to complete this entry, we hope you will seek further opportunities to connect your teaching to the community beyond your classroom. Perhaps answering that simple question, *"How does my teaching continue outside of the classroom?"* is the best place to begin to consider your role as a learner, a colleague, and a partner.

Key Points for Candidate Support Providers

- Many candidates hesitate to use the pronoun "I." Teachers are often humble people, and may have difficulty putting themselves in the forefront due to their upbringing or culture. Exercises like "Raise Your Hand" encourage an "I" statement and may be a way to open a support session. Invite teachers to *raise their hands* if the statement applies to them. Candidate support providers might be creative in providing sentence starters such as "I wrote a grant for my school" "I run a homework helper session" "I attend classes" "I write a newsletter" to prompt candidates to think of the "little things" that they are doing that might become accomplishments for this entry.

- Entry 4 is very similar for every certificate and can thus be used as a foundation for explanation of the certification process, responding directly to questions, and types of writing. Candidates can read one another's accomplishments for kinds of writing, for clarity and consistency, and can talk about similar issues. CSPs should keep in mind that the questions found in the classroom-based entries are more complex in nature, and require additional practice, and deeper reflection.

- Candidates often get deeply involved in Entry 4 and resist moving on. Candidate support providers should consider how and when they will move candidates from Entry 4 as they build their program agendas.

- Remember to build in a time to have candidates revisit Entry 4, since as they move through other entries, their thinking and writing will significantly change. This entry, often the first entry they write, needs to be revisited and edited as candidates near the end of the process.

- The Standards are often overlooked in this entry. Consider using the Standards as an intro lesson for support sessions as a way to encourage candidates to enrich their vocabulary, strengthen their word choice as they describe accomplishments, and spark thinking about their activities outside of the classroom as potential accomplishments. Since the entry is very similar for all candidates, this will also help build classroom community early in support sessions.

Exercise 10-1: Analyzing Accomplishments

Scoring Criteria: Level 4 Rubric	Accomplishments							
	1	2	3	4	5	6	7	8
In this accomplishment, do I:								
Treat parents and other interested adults as valued partners in students' development and education?								
Use thoughtfully chosen, appropriate strategies that may or may not be original, but are effective in engaging parents and other adults in two-way communication focused primarily on substantive teaching and learning issues and individual student progress?								
Facilitate ongoing, mutually beneficial interactions between the students and the wider community in a way that enhances teaching and learning?								
Engage in conscious and deliberate ongoing professional development to strengthen my knowledge, skills and abilities relevant to my teaching context?								
Work collaboratively with colleagues to improve teaching and learning within my school or in the wider professional community?								
Share my expertise in a leadership role with other educators through facilitating professional development of other teachers, improving instructional practices, or advocacy for positive change in educational policy?								
Accurately analyze and thoughtfully reflect on the significance of all my accomplishments taken together, and appropriately plan for future opportunities to impact student learning?								

Directions: As you read each statement with the pronoun "I," check the box if you can find evidence of this statement in your accomplishment. You may find it helpful to have a reader do this exercise and share the evidence with you.

Exercise 10-2: Actions of an Accomplished Teacher

Title of Accomplishment:	
Answer the question: <u>What did I do to impact student learning in this accomplishment?</u> **Start each statement with "I ..."**	
1	
2.	
3.	
4.	
5.	
6.	
7.	
8.	
9.	
10.	
11.	
12.	
13.	
14.	
15.	
16.	
17.	
18.	
19.	
20.	

Directions: Write twenty statements about the accomplishments **beginning with "I"** that include one or more action words. Underline your action words and phrases in each sentence.

Exercise 10-3: Outlining Your Accomplishments

The *"I"*:   Title of Accomplishment
The *"What"* **What** is the nature of this accomplishment? Describe what **you** did. What was it? How did you do it? Who did you do it with? Where? When? How Often? Provide details. Give your reader a good picture of the activity. Use "I..." plus action words to provide evidence.
The *"Why"* **Why** is this accomplishment significant? In what way does it involve your leadership, your learning, partnerships, and/or collaboration with parents or colleagues? Why did you do it?
The *"So What"* How has this activity impacted (or how do you expect it to impact) student learning?   What differences have you made through this activity?)Are there visible results? How can you tell it was worthwhile? **Make direct and specific connections from the activity to learning benefits for students.**

Directions: Beginning with the first statement you made in Exercise 10-2, give a more detailed description of each of your activities.   Provide specific details and examples to "prove" the underlined words and phrases in your statements. Continue to use "I" statements to identify *your* contributions, include the rationale for your actions and the impact on student learning. Use as many pages as you need to describe each accomplishment.

Exercise 10-4: Reflecting on Your Accomplishments

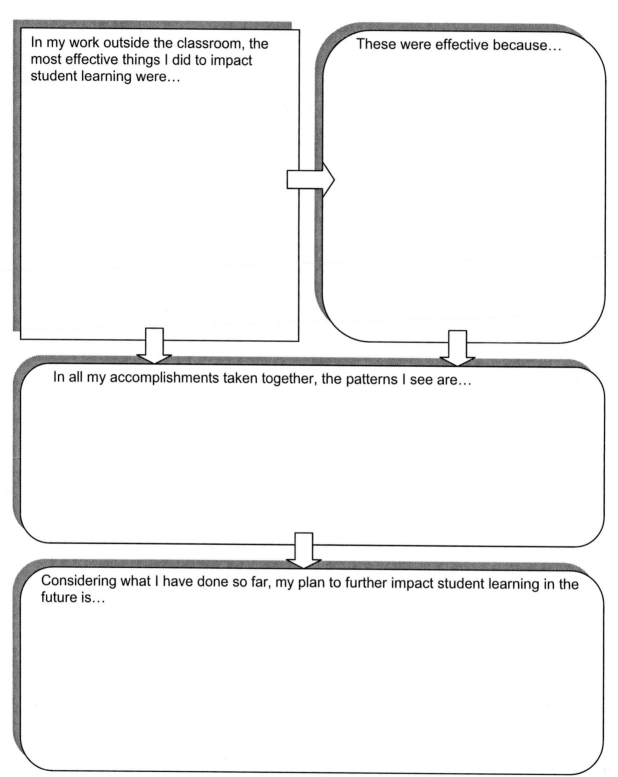

In my work outside the classroom, the most effective things I did to impact student learning were…

These were effective because…

In all my accomplishments taken together, the patterns I see are…

Considering what I have done so far, my plan to further impact student learning in the future is…

Directions: Review the collection of accomplishments you chose to describe and document for this entry, and respond to the questions above. Be *reflective*.

Exercise 10-5: Sources of Documentation

Accomplishment #	Document/Artifact	Evidence Provided		
		Work with Parents & Community	Learner	Leader/Collaborator W/ Colleagues

Directions: Record each artifact and/or document you can use to support your description of your accomplishments. Notate the accomplishment number it relates to and the nature of the evidence provided. Select your strongest sources of evidence to include in the entry.

Exercise 10-6: Writing About Your Entry 4 Artifact

Item:_____

What is this piece? How does it relate to the accomplishment you have described?

▽ **Evidence**

Which of the scoring criteria does it address?

How does it illustrate the impact (or potential impact) of your actions on student learning?

How does it support or add to the evidence in your Written Commentary?

Directions: Use the questions above to help you describe and explain your selection of a document or other artifact for Entry 4. Be sure you have chosen an artifact that adds to or enhances the other evidence in your entry to show how you have contributed to student learning.

11

Developing Your Evidence

Featured Resources:

- Portfolio Instructions
- Standards

You are going to court to be convicted of accomplished teaching. The prosecutor must provide evidence beyond a reasonable doubt that you deserve to be convicted. Does your teaching occur by accident or is it premeditated? What are the choices you make in the course of your teaching that reveal your intentions, your skill and knowledge, and your effect on your students? Do you live a life of accomplished teaching, or have you simply stumbled into a good lesson by accident? Whether to convict or convince, it is up to you to provide the evidence that you are, without a doubt, an accomplished teacher.

The assessment process is designed to provide you with different opportunities to present your evidence of the Standards in a manner that is *clear, convincing, and consistent.* Each of your sources—video recordings, tests of content knowledge, instructional materials, and student work samples—allows you to highlight various aspects of your knowledge and practice. Most importantly, your Written Commentary for each entry provides a powerful opportunity for you to provide evidence of accomplished teaching through your description, analysis, and reflection.

In this chapter, we will discuss how to best use your sources for evidence in the portfolio entries and we will provide you with some tools to help you review your finished entry pieces. The assessment center exercises will be addressed in Chapter 13: Preparing for the Assessment Center.

Do You "Get It"?

It is virtually impossible to make this question sound like the language of the profession, but it is, in fact, one of the commonly used expressions in the world of National Board Certification. It is hard to provide evidence if you do not understand the purpose of the task.

New candidates cry in frustration, "What do they want? I don't get it!" Candidate support providers ask one another, "Have they gotten it yet?" or "How can I help them get it?" Best of all are the moments when a candidate declares triumphantly, "I get it!!" The task of National Board Certification is simultaneously simple and rich. The candidate must reveal the structure of his or her teaching practice, as defined by The Five Core Propositions and as illustrated by the Standards for the certificate area.

> *What does it take to "get it"? You have to be ready to put your practice under a microscope and put the zoom on high power, examining every detail that you do and why you do it. You have to be willing to think harder and deeper about the decisions that you make every day. You have to be willing to ask, "What did I do?" "Why did I do it?" and "What will I do next?"*
>
> *- Ingrid Williams, NBCT New Jersey*

The task is not about implementing a fancy lesson plan or utilizing extraordinary resources—it is about good teaching practices based on knowledge of students, knowledge of subject, managing and monitoring learning, participating as a member of a learning community, and always reflecting on your work in an effort to improve student learning.

Candidates often spend an inordinate amount of time writing the first entry as they struggle through "getting it." When they understand what they need to do, it is as though a light has turned on, illuminating the path before them and highlighting the focal points for their thinking and writing. They are able to answer each question in an entry clearly and completely. Once candidates understand what they need to do, subsequent entries flow more easily. To be successful, candidates not only need to "get it," they need to "get it" soon enough in the process to apply their understanding toward quality work in each entry. The best way for them to do so is to read, think, discuss, and write about their teaching as soon as possible in the year of candidacy.

Sources of Evidence: Classroom-Based Entries

In Entries 1, 2, and 3 your possible sources of evidence are:

- The Written Commentary
- Video recordings
- Student work samples
- Instructional materials or other required artifacts

These sources are described thoroughly in your Portfolio Instructions: **Get Started** section. Review this section for more information on developing your writing, analyzing student work, and producing your videotapes. Each source of evidence must support the others, with the Written Commentary thoroughly explaining the evidence provided in the selected artifacts.

All sources taken together should represent your practice in the following respects:

- Consideration of multiple factors when planning a lesson, such as context, student background and abilities, knowledge of subject
- Connection/alignment between goals of the assignment, instruction, and assessment
- Philosophical basis of your teaching, e.g.: direct instruction, constructivist theory learning, universal design, etc.
- Nature of the relationship between student and teacher
- Awareness and attention to fairness, equity, and access for diverse learners
- Ability to communicate instruction effectively
- Degree of engagement between student and teacher
- Ability to adjust instruction based on students' responses
- Range and variety of assessments at different points in the instructional sequence to inform instruction and give feedback to students

As you consider the limited number of pages you have in which to provide your evidence, you can see that you must write concisely in order to provide rich evidence of the above in all areas.

> *A well-written portfolio entry is beautiful in its simplicity.*
>
> *- Sue Hovey, NBPTS Program Facilitator, University of Idaho*

Exercise 11-1: Sources of Evidence

Your entry must be rich with authentic evidence from your teaching practice. In each entry, you must review your scoring criteria, consider the sources of evidence you will be using, and determine where you can make the strongest case to provide evidence for each of the criteria. Your Written Commentary is your primary vehicle for evidence, but the case you make in writing is supported and strengthened through pictorial evidence in the form of student work samples, instructional materials, and

Scoring Criteria	Written Commentary	Student Work Samples	Instructional Materials	Videotape
Draw on your knowledge of child development and relationships with students to develop an informed approach to instruction;	X	N/A	X	X
Establish a theme, issue, or topic and related learning goals that are central to social studies/history, and justify the appropriateness for your students;	X	N/A	O	O
Plan and implement varied and effective strategies that engage and support student learning, understanding, and respect for a range of perspectives and give a rationale to support these strategies	X	N/A	X	X

Figure 34. Sample Exercise 11-1: Sources of Evidence.
Scoring criteria from the NBPTS Portfolio Instructions, *Middle Childhood Generalist, Entry 2, 2006–07* are shown with potential sources of evidence.

video recordings, or other artifacts required in the entry. When possible, you will want to use all sources of evidence and multiple examples to make your case for accomplished teaching.

Exercise 11-1: Sources of Evidence may help you evaluate your anticipated sources of evidence against the scoring criteria. To use this exercise, you will need a copy of the template for each entry. In the first column you will list the scoring criteria for the entry, from **How Will My Response Be Scored?** in your Portfolio Instructions, or from a previous exercise sheet such as Exercise 5-1 (Entry Mapping).

In the remaining columns, check off the sources you can use to provide clear and convincing evidence for each criterion. You will check off Written Commentary for each, as this is always your most important source. It has been included on this sheet to highlight criteria for which it is your *only* source of evidence. As you develop your entry, you will refer to this sheet to ensure you have used each available source to the greatest extent possible. When you are able to develop multiple sources of evidence for a given criterion, you will have the potential to fulfill the requirement in the Level 4 Rubric, which calls for *clear, convincing, **and consistent** evidence*.

A sample of Exercise 11-1 is shown in Figure 34. Three of the scoring criteria from the NBPTS Portfolio Instructions, *Middle Childhood Generalist 2006–07* Entry 2, certificate are shown.[51] This entry does not require student work samples, so this column is marked "N/A," for "not applicable."

The Written Commentary must be used to provide evidence for all criteria. It is essentially the only source for the second criteria listed, which asks the teacher to describe and justify the selected theme/issue/topic and learning goals. For the remaining criteria listed, the required instructional materials and video recordings can and should be used as supporting evidence for the Written Commentary discussion of the approach and strategies for instruction.

Providing Evidence Through Your Writing

The importance of your Written Commentary must not be underestimated. While you need not have the writing skills of a novelist, you *must* be able to articulate *why* you do what you do in your classroom. You must be able to provide details about your teaching and examples from your interactions with students that demonstrate the National Board Standards and your personal *architecture of accomplished teaching.*

An important aspect of this architecture is the consistency demonstrated in reference to the learning goals. All sections of the entry will connect to your selected instructional goals. Beginning with your foundation knowledge of your students and content, the context provides a basis for selection of high, worthwhile goals for the instructional sequence. You must select goals appropriate for your students, teach to those goals, analyze student learning of those goals, and reflect on your teaching with reference to the learning that occurred.

Potential Strengths and Weaknesses in an Entry

Often, in candidates' first drafts, alignment to the learning goals is missing. In Chapter 8: Thinking and Writing About Your Teaching, we discussed the types of writing—descriptive, analytic and reflective—alongside the prompts from a sample entry to see how they were related to The Five Core Propositions.

Now we will revisit The Five Core Propositions from the perspective of potential strengths and weaknesses in your Written Commentary. Remember, only certain Standards will be emphasized in each entry, and you will need to refer to the specified Standards and the **How Will My Response Be Scored** section of the instructions to determine what is most valued in a given entry. In Figure 35 (Contrast in the Architecture of Entries that Meet and Do Not Meet an Accomplished Performance), The Five Core Propositions are given as reference points for quality in an entry. Refer to Figure 35 as we discuss the following:

Core Proposition 1: Teachers are committed to students and their learning.

Accomplished: You demonstrate knowledge of students' abilities and experiences. You consider the needs of the group, and make suitable plans for individuals as needed. Clear, worthwhile goals are selected for the instructional sequence.

Lacking: No reference is made to students' abilities or past experiences. No rationale is given for selected goals. There is no discussion of the specific needs of individual students.

Core Proposition 2: Teachers know the subjects they teach and how to teach those subjects to students.

Accomplished: You have planned and selected instructional activities clearly designed to help students reach the selected goals. Your selected strategies refer to your knowledge of your students. Resources or strategies are used to accommodate the specific learning needs of individual students.

Lacking: Contextual information is not referenced; no rationale is given for the selected goals and strategies. Goals are not stated, too numerous, too vague/not clearly assessable, inappropriate, or seemingly unconnected to instructional methodology. Alignment among goals, instruction and assessment is not apparent.

Core Proposition 3: Teachers are responsible for managing and monitoring student learning.

Accomplished: You systematically plan and monitor student learning experiences. You structure activities for student success at reaching the selected goals and you are mindful of fairness, equity, and access for all students. You use a variety of assessment strategies, including those that inform your instruction on an on-going basis.

Lacking: Your system for managing and monitoring student learning is unclear. No accommodations or adjustments have been made to assist students with specific needs or diverse styles of learning. Assessment tools are very limited, infrequent, or not used to inform instruction. Evidence of student-to-student and/or student-to-teacher interaction is unclear. A positive learning climate and/or feedback to students is missing or unclear.

Meets an Accomplished Performance

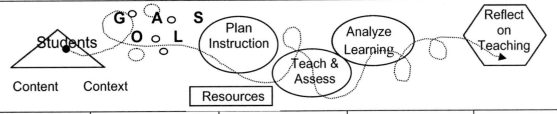

1. Knowledge of Students:	2. Knowledge of Subject:	3. Manages and monitors student learning:	4. Thinks systematically about practice and learns from experience:	5. Sees self as a member of a learning community:
Shows knowledge of students' attitudes, abilities, and experiences as individuals and as a group. Plans for the group as a whole and attends to individual needs. Context helps reader understand the teacher's decision-making in the commentary that follows.	Selects clear, specific goals for student learning. Demonstrates knowledge through selection of effective strategies for these students. Plans and implements thoughtfully selected instructional activities with reference to students, context, and selected goals for learning.	Activities are structured to help all students learn per the selected goals. Assessment of progress is on-going, and informs instruction. A variety of tools, both formal and informal are used for assessment.	Reflects on teaching: thinks about what has worked well, and what might be done differently for the purpose of improving instruction. Thinks about next steps for these students.	Uses all available resources to improve the learning experience for all students. Engages in two-way communication with parents. Shares information with colleagues, seeks new skills and strategies to help students learn.

Does Not Meet an Accomplished Performance

| Little or no reference is made to student knowledge, knowledge attitudes, or skills as a basis for the discussion to follow. Context provided does not add to understanding of the teacher's decision-making in the rest of the commentary. No rationale indicated for selection of goals. | Goals are not stated, not specific, or are too numerous. No clear rationale is given for the selected teaching activities; therefore, knowledge of content cannot be determined. Lacks clear alignment of context, goals, instruction and assessment methodologies. | Assessment tools are very limited, unrelated to goals, infrequent or not used to inform instruction. Lacks evidence of adjustments to instruction based on student responses. Lacks evidence of attention to the unique learning needs of individual students. | Reflection is minimal, too general, or one-sided (e.g., only negative). Does not reference stated goals. No evidence the teacher consciously thinks about how to improve practice, or build upon the learning that has occurred in this lesson. | Appears to work in isolation. No reference to parent involvement, colleagues, or resources. No indication the teacher knows how and when to access information or personnel in this lesson or in the future. No assistance indicated for students with unique needs. |

Figure 35. Contrast in the Architecture of Entries that Meet and Do Not Meet an Accomplished Performance

Core Proposition 4: Teachers think systematically about their practice and learn from experience.

Accomplished: You reflect on your teaching and consider what went well and what you might do differently in the future. You think about what you might do next with this group of students, as well as for individuals with unique needs.

Lacking: Your reflection is very general or one-sided (e.g., only negative). There is no indication that student learning will improve as a result of your consideration of your teaching in this lesson.

Core Proposition 5: Teachers are members of learning communities.

Accomplished: You show evidence of using outside resources to help improve student learning. You may involve parents, seek added support for individual students, use community resources, or seek new skills and strategies to bring to your classroom.

Lacking: You appear to work in isolation. No reference is made to parent involvement, colleagues, resource personnel, or access of information outside the classroom. There is no indication you seek to improve your teaching or student learning through your interactions with others.

Your Written Commentary tells the story of your teaching. Your artifacts and videos can support that story, but they cannot stand alone. You must use your Written Commentary to tell what happened, why it happened, and what you think about it.

Common Written Commentary "Pitfalls"

Your job in the Written Commentary is to present evidence that you are an accomplished teacher by describing, analyzing, and reflecting on specific aspects of your work with and about students. In their first encounter with the National Board Certification materials, candidates unaccustomed to thinking in this way often adopt one of the following ineffective roles when writing about their teaching.

The Soapbox Orator

Sometimes candidates err by using the commentary as a platform to express their personal views and/or frustrations about the profession. The writing may have the tone of a "doom and gloom" soapbox speech in which the candidate writes at length about why students do not learn. *Don't go there*!! Do not think of your Written Commentary as an opportunity to express your frustrations or give excuses. Teachers who use the commentary to suggest their student's learning is beyond their control due to social, economic, or other factors are wasting their words. Accomplished teachers do not whine; they maintain a "can do" attitude, and use every available resource to provide the best possible learning experiences for their students.

The Philosopher

Philosophical stances such as *"What all children need to learn....,"* *"The state of education today....,"* or *"I believe in differentiating instruction for all students...."* are generally irrelevant to the National Board Certification process.

In this process, the teacher's effectiveness is not measured by the teacher's general philosophy about education, but by specific evidence of teaching to the NBPTS Standards provided by descriptions, examples, analysis, and reflection on actual practices. It is not measured by students' placement on standardized tests, but rather by the teacher's ability to produce learning—to move students from point A to point B, whatever the teacher determines those points to be.

The Invisible Teacher

The following hypothetical passage illustrates one of the most common problems in written commentaries:

> *Students were introduced to the concept of multiplication as repeated addition. After a few problems were modeled and discussed to introduce the lesson, students were divided into small groups and provided with manipulative materials to help them solve a set of five problems.*

In this description, one is tempted to ask, *"Who was the teacher?"* The writer has described the lesson as though he or she was simply an observer rather than the teacher. Here is another example of a similar problem:

> *The students were seated in groups of four. First, they brainstormed and charted ideas to tackle the problem, and then they selected a specific strategy to use. Each group developed a plan and shared it when we met together at the end of the period.*
>
> *We discussed the pros and cons of each plan, then selected the one that we thought was most promising. We decided... We agreed to... Next, we... Then we...*

The biggest question in this sample is *"Where is the teacher?"* In this case, it seems the students are fully capable of making all decisions and plans regarding the instructional sequence. The writing is full of "they" did this, and "we" did that...Remember, your goal is to demonstrate that **you make a difference** in the learning progress of your students. Let us try rewriting the passage:

> *I assigned students to groups of four, with attention to diversity by mixing students' abilities, learning styles, and genders within a given group. I directed each group to brainstorm ideas for solving the problem, come to a consensus on one idea, and then discuss the pros and cons of the proposed solution. I asked that each group make a chart to share with the larger group at the end of the period. I also reminded students of our group rules to make sure everyone would participate equally in the process of developing and sharing the chart.*

> *The students are now very accustomed to this format that I established at the beginning of the year—working first in small groups, then sharing with the large group. This encourages quieter children to participate and builds their confidence as they work with others in different group situations. In this case, my intent was for the children to consider multiple perspectives by thinking about and discussing pros and cons of different solutions. When we met together at the end of the period, I asked each group to share their problem solution chart showing pros and cons. After the sharing, I asked students to think about each solution presented, then do a quick "pair and share" with someone next to them about the idea they would vote for and why. Then I passed out paper ballots and asked them to vote individually for one solution.*

The rewritten version contains lots of statements beginning with "I..."— and demonstrates the teacher's purposeful decision-making and rationale for instructional strategies. Many teachers feel it sounds like they are bragging when they begin every statement with "I."   If this true of you, you MUST get over it—you are required to describe your specific behaviors and thinking process to meet the Standards for accomplished teaching.

The Telepath

The telepath, like the invisible teacher, expects the assessor to connect the dots in the commentary and turn them into evidence. The telepath may be present and actively directing student learning in the entry, but does not adequately explain the thinking processes. These teachers think their reasons for what they do in the classroom are so obvious that no explanation is needed.

Telepaths are often veteran teachers who work so capably and intuitively with students, they do not consciously analyze the basis for their decision-making and reasoning. They have a tendency to think, "Everybody knows this!" and fail to provide adequate detail when writing about their teaching. They sometimes respond with annoyance when pressed by their support providers to explain and rationalize their teaching behaviors, and are often upset at the assessors when their entries do not score well.

Many candidates assume telepathic qualities when it comes to their student work samples, videos, or other artifacts. It is very important that you discuss each artifact, telling what the evidence is and why it is significant to your entry. Just attaching artifacts and assuming the assessor will "see" the evidence without explanation is a mistake. It is your job to present your evidence of accomplished teaching.

We have described the "pitfall" behaviors above in hopes that, if you recognize such tendencies in yourself, you will dispense with them early on and focus on the important aspects of your task. If we were to choose a role for you to emulate, it would be that of a lawyer whose job, like yours, is to present detailed, specific, and irrefutable evidence to make a case.

Video Evidence

> *Teaching is a complex endeavor that requires individuals to approach their work as both an art and a science... Videotaping, while not perfect, offers real-time evidence that ... [can be used] to deconstruct teaching from its most explicit to its most subtle nuance.*
>
> *- David Lussier, NBCT Massachusetts*[52]

When required by your entry instructions, your video recording is important for showing evidence that cannot be demonstrated in any other way, such as:

- The climate and quality of your classroom environment
- The characteristics and demographics of your students
- Your teaching behaviors that show fairness, equity and access for all learners
- **Interaction, interaction and interaction!**

Your video recording will help authenticate the high quality, interactive learning opportunities you create for students as described in your Written Commentary. The video recording also demonstrates your knowledge of the subject matter in the way you respond to spontaneous comments and questions from students.

Your video recording will allow you to show the quality of teacher-to-student and student-to-student interactions in terms of questioning strategies, thinking through issues, and student engagement in learning. It provides you with a unique opportunity to explain the nuances of your teaching behaviors as you use the Written Commentary to deconstruct your actions as seen on the recording.

Having said this, most former candidates have their "nightmare" stories, and the vast majority of them revolve around videos. Lack of equipment, technical problems, and student behavior are among the foremost problem areas so…start your video recording early!

It is critical to locate your equipment and practice with it very early in your candidacy. Make several practice recordings in order to work out the technical challenges and to help you and your students become accustomed to the camera. Many candidates set the camera up well in advance so that it becomes a part of the classroom environment. This way, students become accustomed to the presence of the camera and behave in a more natural way.

You must find a suitable microphone in which both your voice and the students' voices can be clearly heard. You may need to try out different camera placements to find the most effective camera angles. You will film an entire lesson, then select the best continuous segment to submit with your commentary. You must prepare your cameraperson(s) by explaining the key aspects of the recording for each entry, such as panning the room, or focusing on one small group at a time; and tell them over and over, "Don't stop the camera!" Unless your Portfolio Instructions tell you otherwise, you recording must be unedited and continuous. Letting the camera run accomplishes two things:

- It allows students to become comfortable with filming.
- It allows you to choose the segment in which Standards are most evident.

Remember, you can write about things that happen before and after the selected segment, so letting the camera run longer than the necessary time will give you an opportunity to choose the "best" part of the lesson in which teacher to student or student to student interaction is shown. As student responses are often unpredictable, it is important to have this degree of flexibility in the selection of your video segment. It is ideal to have several possible recordings for each entry.

Your selected segment must meet the specifications given in the Portfolio Instructions regarding the length of the segment and the nature of the instructional situation. Some entries will call for whole group lessons, others for small group lessons with a specified number of students. Even when the focus is on student interactions, you must be shown at least once on the recording so the assessor can verify your identity with your photo ID.

Promoting Interaction

The Portfolio Instructions: **Get Started** section will help you address the technical aspects of your video sessions. Equally important, as you plan your lesson, you will want to consider how to promote the interaction called for in your video entry. Whether you are working with your whole class or a small group, there are strategies you can use to enhance student interaction.

1. Provide a hands-on task to enhance student engagement. Younger students can carry out a science experiment or solve a math problem with appropriate manipulative objects, while groups of older students might work on a graph, an overhead transparency or other type of chart to display proposed solutions to a problem and generate discussion.

2. Promote interaction by preparing prompting questions for a discussion. If your entry calls for a whole class lesson, consider including a brief "Think, Pair, Share" section (teacher poses question, students share thoughts with a partner, then partner groups share ideas with the larger group). This promotes engagement, encourages even quieter students to interact, and increases the likelihood that students will respond to one another's comments in the larger group.

3. Be sure your discussion goes beyond simple recall of information. Your discussion should engage students in higher levels of thinking to show your goals are "high and worthwhile."

4. In your analysis, be sure to comment on the level of engagement and/or on-task behavior of students you described as "instructional challenges" in your Instructional Context section. If students are "challenging" rather than engaged as much as you would like, provide a rationale for how you chose to deal with them during the lesson and, in your reflection, what you might do next time.

Exercise 11-2: Video Analysis

It is easy to get attached to a specific recording for the wrong reasons, and you can avoid this by doing a careful analysis of one or more of your video selections. Be sure to refer to Portfolio Instructions: **Get Started**, which includes a helpful list of video analysis questions. You may use Exercise 11-2 to help you think about and select a video segment with multiple examples of evidence and interaction as shown in Figure 36.

In the first column, minutes are numbered for you. In the next section, "No Interaction," you can note if only one person is speaking. For example, teacher monologues often occur when directions for a lesson are being given, and student monologues may occur if a student is presenting information to a larger group. Monologues of any kind should be avoided as, by definition, there is no interaction. Rather than including monologues in your selected video segment, you will find in most cases teacher instructions or the content of student presentations can be easily summarized in the Written Commentary.

Your video recording should focus on the interactions that occur in the classroom, between teacher and students, or from one student to another. In the last two sections of the exercise sheet, you can note the type of interactions that are seen in your video, and take notes on where and how evidence of Standards can be discussed in your writing. It is important that you reference these specific examples of your evidence when you write your **Video Analysis** in the Written Commentary.

Video Interaction Analysis

Min	No Interaction		Interaction		Evidence Pertaining to Scoring Criteria
	Teacher Mono.	Student Mono.	Teacher to Student	Student to Student	
1:00	X				*T. Explained purpose of activity connected to previous lessons, big idea.*
2:00			X		*S. become engaged in experiments, making predictions, T. prompting students' thinking by asking questions.*
3:00			X		*Jordan uses term "hypothesis"*
4:00				X	*Sue tells Mary: "If you peel the orange, it will sink."* *Mary: "I think it will still float."*
5:00			X		*T: "What happened? Why do you think so?"* *Sue: "When we took the peel off the air got out." (Misconception)*
6:00			X	X	*T: more prompting—S. decided to test peel alone.*
7:00				X	*Pan of room—groups definitely engaged in experiments—lots of conversation, predictions.*

Figure 36. Sample: Exercise 11-2: Video Interaction Analysis.
The video is reviewed minute by minute; the nature of the interaction is recorded, with notes about incidents showing evidence of Standards.

To summarize, use Exercise 11-2: Video Analysis as follows:

1.   Do a minute-by-minute review of your video. Most recordings are no more than 15 minutes in length. Use the time display on

your recorder and make note of the interactions (or lack thereof) in each minute of your video. The more interaction, the better.

2. Refer to the scoring criteria for this entry, and notate where evidence is provided in your recording. You will want to include these examples in your Written Commentary discussion on the video analysis. Be sure to note student misconceptions where they occur and how you dealt with the learning process.

3. Some facilitators suggest viewing the video recording three times, each time for a different purpose:

   a) Watch once all the way through to verify you have captured the big idea of the lesson.

   b) Next, view it with the sound turned off and pay particular attention to body language and movements. Have you balanced your attention between different individuals and/or groups of students? Do you see evidence of student engagement? Does the video show a positive learning climate?

   c) Finally, with the sound on, focus on student responses to instruction. What do they say, what do they do that provides evidence of students' engagement and learning toward your stated goals?

4. Look for, and write about, the evidence of your architecture of accomplished teaching in the video, as demonstrated by teacher to student and student to student interactions.

Writing About Your Video

Do not expect your video recording to stand alone as a piece of evidence. The video itself is not scored, but contributes to the strength of your Written Commentary by showing your teaching behaviors and the nature and quality of interactions that take place in your classroom. You are expected to make specific references to your video in your entry, and as you read in Chapter 8: Thinking and Writing About Your Teaching, you will be prompted to do so in your Portfolio Instructions. Be thorough and analytic in this section. Help to orient your reader by describing the context, i.e., what occurs before and/or after the part of the lesson shown and what is happening as the video begins.

Use your Written Commentary to deconstruct and explain your teaching behaviors. Some behaviors will be explicit, such as your questioning strategies, while others will be subtle, such as the touch on a student's shoulder to bring his attention back to the task. Refer to specific occurrences; tell what you were thinking and why you responded to students as you did. The assessor may *see* the teacher utilizing the standards-based teaching behaviors, but for these behaviors to "count" as *clear, convincing, and consistent evidence*, the candidate must *explain his or her deliberate use* of such practices in the Written Commentary.

The Portfolio Instructions for these entries typically ask one or more questions that can *only* be answered in reference to your video recording, for example, "*Describe a specific example from this lesson as seen on the video that shows how you ensure fairness, equity, and access for students in your class.*" from NBPTS Portfolio Instructions *EA Science 2006–07, Entry 2,* that we reviewed in Chapter 8.

Likewise, you will often be asked to comment on students' levels of engagement during the lesson. Although some students may participate more actively than others, keep in mind that engagement can also be manifested as attentiveness, demonstrated by body posture, listening behaviors, and eye contact with the speaker.

Notice and describe any spontaneous adjustments you made to your instruction based on students' responses. Comment on your expectations for the lesson versus what actually happened, especially in regard to student misconceptions that were revealed. Point out examples that show you are demonstrating your Standards. You may find it helpful to do this with another reader. (See Chapter 2: Support Systems.) If your students' behavior is not perfect, do not worry about it. This can be used as an evidence opportunity as you talk about the challenges presented by individual students and how you deal with them.

Camera Anxiety: "Is That Really Me?"

If you are among the many people who have never spent time watching yourself on video before, be prepared to dislike the way you look and get over it. Assessors are trained to recognize and disregard their personal biases that may relate to style of dress, speech patterns, ethnicity, and other areas. There is no deficit scoring, so you will not lose points based on your appearance. Even so, it is wise to anticipate and provide an explanation for attire or behavior that might appear extremely unusual to your viewer.

At a candidate support presentation at the 2003 annual NBPTS Conference, NBCT Dr. Marlene Henriques gave the example of a video in which the teacher was dressed in a tank top and shorts, teaching a group of students who were only minimally responsive. Without knowing something more, a viewer might view her as unprofessional and ineffective. However, the teacher's Written Commentary explained that her classroom air-conditioning was broken and she was teaching during a heat wave of nearly 110 degrees. She had dressed appropriately for her circumstances and was doing her best to work with her group of perspiring, listless students under challenging circumstances.[53]

National Board Certification is not about presenting yourself as the "ideal" teacher, working in the "ideal" setting, with a group of "ideal" students. Rather, it is about what teachers "really" do in their classrooms. When faced with challenging students and challenging circumstances, how do you respond? When you try something that does not work, what do you learn from that? What do you do next? How do you plan for and conduct instruction for *your* students, in *your* class, under *your* teaching conditions?

Student Work Samples and Instructional Materials

The Glossary of Portfolio Related Terms in your Portfolio Instructions will provide you with guidelines for submitting different kinds of student work. We have underlined phrases from the original text as points of emphasis:

> *Student work samples that you have annotated provide assessors with evidence of your ability to pose meaningful assignments that elicit student understandings (and may possibly reveal misunderstandings) and of your ability to offer constructive feedback to your students.*

> *- NBPTS Portfolio Instructions (Underlines added)[54]*

Notice you are expected to annotate the student work samples with constructive feedback to students. The student work samples give you an opportunity to demonstrate accomplished teaching, especially in reference to the first two core propositions, knowledge of students and knowledge of subject. You must be able to both analyze and diagnose students' learning abilities and needs in the content area. The featured student(s) should be carefully selected for the purpose of allowing you to discuss the *range* of strategies you are able to utilize in addressing different kinds of needs. At the same time, the students' needs should not be so extreme that your accommodations are too distant from the stated learning goals.

Keep in mind that each piece of work allows you to analyze the student's learning and development. Details in the work sample will guide instructional decisions for this student and determine the nature of the feedback you provide. Your discussion of the work samples should reference the larger picture of learning in the content area and the student's learning of the intended goals as stated in the portfolio exercise.

The questions in the NBPTS entry instructions ask you to focus on these aspects:

> ➤ Planning and instruction for the individual:
> *What do you know about the student? How do you individualize instruction? To what extent is the student challenged?*

> ➤ Assessment of student growth during instruction:
> *How can you determine the student's growth? What will you use as indicators? How is this shown in the work sample?*

> ➤ Student's understanding of the subject area:
> *What does this work tell you about how well the student understands the key concepts of the subject area?*

> ➤ The quality of the work:
> *In what ways does this work meet, or fail to meet, the intended goals that were set for this student in the lesson? What is the evidence in the work?*

> ➤ Teaching practice:
> *What does the student's response indicate about the effectiveness of your instruction? What does it tell you about what to do next for this student?*

Selecting the Featured Students

In work-sample entries, two or more samples from at least two students are generally required. If you routinely have all your students keep portfolio collections of their work it will be to your advantage, as it is often easier to select your featured students at the end of your instructional sequence based on the nature of their responses.

- If you must determine your featured students prior to instruction, "select" more students than you need. If two featured students are required, you will want to have at least four students under serious consideration to ensure you do not find yourself facing catastrophe. Too often, a potential featured student moves or becomes ill before the teaching sequence is completed, or an entire collection of a child's work is lost due to unforeseen circumstances.

- Consider all the requirements of the entry. For example, if your work with a younger student or an exceptional needs student requires evidence of family involvement, then be sure to select a child whose family is supportive and easy to contact.

- Know the featured students well. For each selected student, you need to write an accurate description. You should know his or her interests, learning styles, and individual needs. You must be able to describe and analyze the unique needs of each selected student, and then describe and rationalize individualized methods or strategies that are particularly designed for *this student, at this time, in this setting.*

Here are some examples from a sixth grade language arts teacher:

1.   Student A is a quiet girl who seldom engages in classroom discussion. She is diagnosed as learning disabled and has an Individualized Education Plan (IEP). She has previously, but is not currently, receiving speech therapy services.

      Strategies from the teacher: *I was able to engage the student in more classroom communication by drawing upon her personal interests as the result of a parent interview. I observed her in different situations, including the classroom, lunchroom, and recess to find out about her interests and who her friends were, then made a point of pairing her with friends in small groups during class discussions.*

2.   Student B is at the center of all class discussions. Although she is an honors student, her written work shows she needs help in developing her writing vocabulary.

      Strategies from the teacher: *Student B was capable of independent learning, and I met with her to plan activities that would help her build and use her written vocabulary. We agreed she would take the initiative to use a thesaurus as a reference tool each time she wrote, and that she could opt to do the "Extended Learning" vocabulary exercises in our literature text rather than the comprehension exercises usually assigned to the class.*

3.   Student C, at the back of the room, seems capable but often fails to finish assignments because he "runs out of time."
      Student D works diligently, but is often off topic when his final draft is submitted.

      Strategies from the teacher: *For students C & D, I re-taught the use of a graphic organizer to plan their writing, and reviewed this with them before they began to draft. From that point, I kept them on-time and on-task by checking drafts more regularly, as well as increasing my proximity and task reminders.*

These examples, though typical in classrooms, are intended to show there is no single right answer for a given student. What is important is you demonstrate your ability to determine student needs and address them through a variety of different strategies. To be used in an entry, these examples would need to be described and analyzed in much greater detail, as you will see from the exercises below.

The Portfolio Instructions: **Get Started** section contains a focus chapter on analysis practice. Be sure to review this material in addition to practicing with the chapter exercises included here.

Selecting Student Work Samples

Entries that require student work samples have different specifications, so read the entry directions carefully to make sure your samples meet the requirements. For example, you may need to collect work samples over time, you may need to show multiple drafts of the same piece of work, or show the range of work created by a student. Once you are clear about requirements, select student work that will allow you to demonstrate and discuss the following:

- *Student performance directly related to the selected goals*
- *Documentation of your frequent and thorough feedback to students*
- *Multiple examples that demonstrate the range of your abilities to analyze students' abilities and needs based on their work*
- *Use the language of the Standards in your analysis and reflection on the work*
- *Analyze and reflect on the students' work specifically in reference to the stated goals*
- *Based on students' responses in the work, reflect on the effectiveness of your teaching to the stated goals. Suggest changes that would improve student learning of these goals*

- Sue Hovey[55]

Number each work sample you choose to use as evidence. This will make it easier to refer to the work samples as you discuss them in your Written Commentary. The exercises that follow are designed to assist you as you select and write about your students and their work.

Exercise 11-3: Student Work Analysis 1

This exercise will help you discuss an individual student's learning needs, and the strategies you have used to address them. A double column format is used to emphasize your use of descriptive (Column 1) and analytical (Column 2) thinking and writing. You will describe, then analyze each of the following:

- Student characteristics
- Instructional goals
- Selected strategies and materials

- Characteristics of the student's work
- Use of feedback

Finally, you will reflect on the student's progress and your next steps in teaching.

This exercise should be used to help you select the students to feature in the entry. When you have several students under consideration, doing the individual analysis exercise can help you determine the quality and quantity of evidence you have available to you on each of those students. You will want to select the student or students and work samples that allow you to demonstrate the range of your abilities as an aspect of your evidence.

When your entry calls for work by two or more students, completing a sheet for each student under consideration will help ensure you select students with different needs in order to show the range of your instructional abilities. You will examine, contrast, and discuss the needs of the selected students through the work samples you have selected to feature.

Exercise 11-4: Student Work Analysis 2

Student Work Analysis 2 will help you analyze the work of your selected student over time. Using one column per assignment, describe the assignment, how it demonstrates evidence of student progress toward the goals, and how your feedback to the student helps supports this progress.

Use the template to help you outline the key points for writing this section of your Written Commentary. Your goal is to demonstrate clearly that *you make a difference* in your classroom. Your analysis of the selected work samples must show how *your instruction* helped this student to improve over time.

Writing About Student Work Samples

The two exercises work together to help you make good choices in your selection of students and the specific work samples you feature in your entries. There are three parts to work-sample artifacts:

1.   The assignment or prompt that was given to the student(s) (this may include an instructional material as part of the given assignment).
2.   The student(s) response to that assignment or prompt.
3.   The teacher's feedback to the student regarding the response.

All three parts must be addressed in order to provide effective evidence. In your Written Commentary, you will describe the assignment, analyze the student's response, discuss the thinking processes that led to the feedback you gave to the student, and tell how the feedback impacted the student's learning.

Feedback to the student is an important aspect of the selected work sample. Research tells us feedback is most motivating for students when it is specific, descriptive, and immediate.[56] Students need and want to know what they are doing right. When their strengths are acknowledged and built upon, the student is motivated to find and address areas that need improvement. Comments such as "Good job!" or "Nice effort!" provide no specific information to students, do not motivate them and, in some cases, may have a negative effect on students' desire to learn. Such comments imply the teacher has judged the work against criteria that may not be clear to the student.

The graphic organizer shown in Figure 37 (Writing About Student Work Samples) may help you think and write about your student work samples. When multiple samples are collected over time, it is important for you to discuss how your feedback helped the student improve his or her work, and how your selected work samples provide evidence of the student's improvement.

Instructional Materials

Instructional Materials are required in many portfolios. The National Board defines them as follows:

> *An item used or produced during a teaching sequence that will help assessors better understand the activity featured in your video recording or Written Commentary. The item can represent an instructional resource that provides important background context for interpreting the discussion or work produced by students that was examined in or grew out of a class activity.[57]*

Teachers often make use of documents, objects, news items, etc. as part of instruction. Almost anything can be used as an instructional material. It would be impossible to provide a comprehensive list of such items, but here are examples of some things teachers might use:

- Video recordings
- Posters
- Photos
- Literary passages
- Newspaper or magazine articles
- TV commercials
- Websites
- Brochures
- Worksheets
- Student products

Background Information: Cover Sheets

Use the required cover sheets on student work samples and instructional materials to the fullest extent in order to provide additional evidence of your standards-based practices. These pages often invite you to provide information that will help your assessor better understand a featured assignment or instructional material. When they do so, cover sheets are "freebies" for more evidence building, and giving more details here can help strengthen your entry. In Exercise 11-5, we have provided questions to help you develop background information on your featured artifacts. With any artifact included in your entry, these questions may help guide your discussion whether in your Written Commentary, on the cover sheet, or both.

Exercise 11-5: Background Information: Selected Work Samples and Instructional Materials

Use Exercise 11-5 to help you describe, analyze, and reflect on your selection and use of student work samples and instructional materials. As you respond to the questions, you will have key points to draw upon when writing about the artifact in your Written Commentary or on the cover sheet for each of your featured selections.

Remember, the purpose of this information is to help the assessor better understand how the featured material was used during the instructional sequence, and how it helped students meet the goals for the lesson. Be sure to focus your discussion on what the assessor needs to know about the student work sample or instructional material you have chosen to feature. You will describe how the material was used and why you chose it, then analyze and reflect on the student learning that resulted.

Writing About Student Work Samples

Assignment:

What Did You Do?

- What were the goals?

- Why are these goals important?

- How will you determine student success of this assignment?

- What feedback did you give this student?

- Why did you choose to give this particular feedback?

- How does the student's original response to the assignment, as well as his/her response to your feedback, help to inform your instruction?

- What will you do next for this student?

What Did the Student Do?

- What was the student's response to the assignment?

- How does it compare to your expectations for this student?

- What did the student do correctly, or incorrectly?

- Are there patterns to this student's response(s) in an assignment of this nature?

- Does the response give you any new insights about this student?

- How did the student use your feedback?

- Was the feedback informative and motivating for the student?

- How did the feedback help the student make progress toward the goals?

Figure 37. Writing About Student Work Samples.
Use these questions to guide your analysis and reflection of the selected work samples in your Written Commentary.

The Whole Package

*Effective teachers accept responsibility for their students'
learning—listening to students and watching them as instruction
occurs and then later analyzing why things worked or didn't work.
To improve student learning, teachers must consider both
immediate and long-term consequences.*

- Corcoran and Leahy[58]

Your written entry with its accompanying artifacts and/or video recordings should provide a well constructed package that provides *clear, convincing, and consistent evidence* of accomplished teaching as described in a given portfolio entry. Explicit evidence must be provided in direct response to the prompts given in the entry instructions.

In each entry, your Written Commentary is the tool you will use to make your instructional decisions and artifacts meaningful. Your writing is the only way to make your thought processes about your practice visible to the assessor. Your description, analysis, and reflection must be unified by the selected goals for the lesson, and the student learning that resulted from teaching to those goals.

Unsuccessful entries often fall short because of the writing in the Written Commentary. They may lack detail, and/or fail to make adequate connections between the different sources of evidence. Candidates may unwittingly adopt the posture of the "Telepath" or "Invisible Teacher" and assume the assessor will see their evidence, even when they have not provided explicit responses to the given prompts in the Portfolio Instructions.

In this process, you must not assume your assessor will interpret your teaching practices as meeting the Standards. It is your responsibility to provide direct and explicit descriptions and explanations for the teaching decisions you make in your featured entry, and to explain how your actions demonstrate the Standards for your certificate area.

> *This process trained me to answer "why." "Getting It" is telling the **Why** of the question.*
>
> *-Wendy Smith, NBCT New Jersey*

This is accomplished teaching: Not just *how* you teach, but *how you think about* your teaching as you plan, while you are "in the moment," and afterwards as you reflect on your instruction and assessment. You must show both your knowledge and your capacity to guide student learning, as well as how you strive for continual improvement and effectiveness in your teaching. Your practice is demonstrated in how you talk about, think about, and write about your teaching.

Key Points for Group Facilitators

There are several areas of focus in this chapter, which can provide topics for discussion over several sessions. You may wish to have candidates bring drafts and focus on one or more of the following topics for revision during a single session:

- Candidates must "get it." The underlying architecture of The Five Core Propositions must be visible in the entry as a framework for evidence of the Standards. The structure rests on the alignment of goals, instruction, assessment, analysis, and reflection. When you read drafts for candidates, ask yourself this question first, "Can I see the architecture?"

- Candidates must provide evidence from multiple sources to meet the Level 4 Rubric for *consistency*. If evidence of a Standard is provided from only one source, consistency cannot be established.

- Candidates must make good choices in the evidence selected for the entry. They often select a video, a work sample, or a student for the wrong reasons (*"I really like this part of the lesson, I want them to see it....," "Jorge's writing piece is really humorous, I need to use it...."*) rather than focusing on evidence that best addresses the scoring criteria.

- The evidence must be of good quality. Details, thinking processes, and authentic examples from the classroom help to make the evidence *clear and convincing*. Encourage candidates to continually re-read the complete text of the Standards for each entry as a way to capture important details of their own practices. Continue to refer to the levels of response discussed in Chapter 9: Reflective Practice to help candidates understand the level of detail needed in their descriptions.

Exercise 11-1: Sources of Evidence

Entry_____

Scoring Criteria	Written Commentary	Student Work Samples	Instructional Materials	Video Recording

Directions: Select one classroom-based entry. In the first column, fill in the scoring criteria from **How Will My Response Be Scored?** Mark the sources that could be used to provide evidence of each criterion for the entry.

Exercise 11-2: Videotape Interaction Analysis

Entry_____

Minute	No Interaction		Interaction		Evidence Pertaining to Scoring Criteria
	Teacher Monologue	Student Monologue	Teacher to Student	Student to Student	
1:00					
2:00					
3:00					
4:00					
5:00					
6:00					
7:00					
8:00					
9:00					
10:00					
11:00					
12:00					
13:00					
14:00					
15:00					

Directions: View your videotape several times. First, record the type of interaction occurring during each minute of the tape. Next, watch and record evidence that can be discussed in your written commentary.

Exercise 11-3: Student Work Analysis 1

Describe	Analyze
Describe the featured student in terms of skills, interests, experiences, learning style, and/or barriers:	How does your knowledge of this student affect your expectations for this student and help you to analyze his/her work samples?
What are your instructional goals for this student?	Why did you select these goals?
What materials, strategies, and assignments did you use to help students accomplish the goals?	How do your selected materials, strategies and assignments help you explain/assess student performance in reference to the goals?
What characteristics of the selected work samples require the student to apply the relevant content, concepts, and skills?	What is your interpretation/explanation of the student's performance? How does this compare to your expectations for an acceptable performance from this student?
What mistakes, omissions, and/or misunderstandings did you see in the student's work? What feedback did you give to the student?	How did your assessment and feedback to the student help him/her make progress toward the goals?
Reflect: Given this student's responses, what will you do to build on the student's accomplishment? What new goals will you set?	**Reflect:** What strategies were most effective for this student? What might you do differently in the future?

Directions: Using a work sample from one student, answer each of the prompts to describe and analyze the instructional planning and student's response to the assignment.

Exercise 11-4: Student Work Analysis 2

Student:			
What are the characteristics of this student in terms of abilities, learning preferences, attitudes, and/or barriers to learning?			
	Assignment 1	**Assignment 2**	**Assignment 3**
What was the assignment? What was the learning goal (or goals)? What instructions were given to the student?			
Why was this assignment appropriate for this student at this time?			
What does the student's response indicate about his/her progress toward the stated goals? What mistakes, omissions, and/or misunderstandings did you see? Discuss specific examples that help you assess student learning.			
What feedback did you give the student?			
How will this feedback help the student make progress toward the stated learning goal(s)?			
What will you do next to build the skills and understandings of this student?			

Directions: Using selected work samples from one student, answer each of the prompts to describe and analyze the student's progress toward the stated goals. Your responses should demonstrate how **your instruction** helped this student to improve over time.

Exercise 11-5: Background Information:
Selected Work Samples and Instructional Materials

Material:_____

What is this piece?	**Description and Rationale**	How was it used in the course of instruction?
How will it help an assessor better understand the featured activity?		Why did you choose to use it?
What specific concepts did students need to know in order to complete the assignment (or to use this instructional material)? How did it help prompt their thinking?	**Analysis and Reflection**	How did it support student learning of the stated objectives?
If you are choosing student work samples over time, at which points are you sampling? Why did you choose these points?		What did you learn from the students' responses to this material or assignment?

Directions: The purpose of this information is to help the assessor better understand the context for the selected material. Use the questions above to help you describe and rationalize your use of an assignment or instructional material in the lesson sequence. Your responses in this exercise may help you develop information to use on the cover sheet for the featured material or in the written commentary.

12

Reviewing and Submitting Your Portfolio

Featured Resources:

- Portfolio Instructions
- Standards
- Scoring Guide

In the previous chapters, we have focused on the details necessary for producing evidence of teaching to the Standards. We discussed the different sources for your evidence and the importance of your Written Commentary for developing each source. Now, we will guide you through a review process to look at each entry from a holistic perspective.

Just as you might look through a magnifying glass, you will be looking at the structural integrity of your work to ensure you have demonstrated what is valued in each entry and have provided *clear, convincing, and consistent* evidence of the Standards for your certificate area. A single, superficial reference to a given activity does not provide such evidence.

In Part I of this chapter, we will lead you through a final review of your entries. Part II will provide you with information about submitting your portfolio for scoring by NBPTS.

Part I. Analyzing Your Evidence

The review process is done when the Written Commentary for an entry is in final draft form, but you still have time to make necessary revisions to strengthen your evidence. This means your teaching for the entry is finished, and your artifacts, such as the video or student work samples, have been selected and discussed in your commentary.

It will be of little value to do this review the day before you must mail your portfolio, as even if you find areas of need, you will not have time to revise your work at that point. You should be ready for the final review two to four weeks before your submission date. If possible, you should take a break from your entry before doing your final review so you are refreshed enough to look at it from a new perspective.

Before the final review and submittal of your portfolio, we hope you have asked at least one person to read your entries and give you feedback. At the end of this chapter you will find sample templates that may help you in communicating with your readers and seeking effective feedback. Responses from your readers should help you consider different aspects of your work; but remember, in the end you are the final judge of your submitted portfolio. You are responsible for understanding and providing sufficient evidence for the requirements and the Standards for each entry.

Reviewing Your Entry Against the Standards

Select an entry for review. You may find it helpful to refer to your entry map created in Chapter 5. For each entry we will ask you to re-read the introduction to the entry in the Portfolio Instructions, the Standards listed for the entry, and the Level 4 Rubric for the entry. You will ask yourself these questions:

1. Taken as a whole, is my entry a strong representation of the accomplished teaching described in the introductory section of the instructions for the entry?

2. Have I provided *clear, convincing, and consistent* evidence of the essential purpose for this entry, as stated in the summary statement?

3. Have I provided *clear, convincing, and consistent* evidence of teaching to each of the Standards specified for this entry?

4. Is my evidence of sufficient quantity and quality to meet the Level 4 Rubric for the entry?

By now, you know it is all about the evidence. You may understand what is meant by evidence that is *clear* and evidence that is *convincing*, but do you understand what is meant by evidence that is *consistent*? In facilitator training sessions, NBPTS has used "the Wall" as an analogy for determining the strength of an entry.[59] We will use this illustration to help you build a wall of your own that will help you understand how to provide *consistent* evidence

To build a wall of evidence for an entry, use the scoring criteria from the entry to represent the top row of bricks as shown in Figure 38 (Wall of Evidence Diagram). In the rows below, you will list your sources of

SOURCES OF EVIDENCE	SCORING CRITERIA: **How Will My Response Be Scored?**					
	Scoring Criterion 1	Scoring Criterion 2	Scoring Criterion 3	Scoring Criterion 4	Scoring Criterion 5	
Written Commentary		Evidence 1	Evidence 1	Evidence 1	Evidence 1	Evidence 1
Artifact A (Video)	Evidence 2	Evidence 2	Evidence 2	Evidence 2	Evidence 2	
Artifact B (Stud. Work)		Evidence 3	Evidence 3	Evidence 3	Evidence 3	Evidence 3
Artifact C (Inst. Materials)	Evidence 4	Evidence 4	Evidence 4	Evidence 4	Evidence 4	

Figure 38. Wall of Evidence Diagram.
Multiple sources of evidence are needed to demonstrate accomplished teaching of each scoring criterion.

evidence. The Written Commentary is always the primary source, with artifacts confirming and strengthening the description and analysis of evidence provided by the Written Commentary. For most certificate areas, artifacts for Entries 1, 2, and 3, will include student work samples, instructional materials, and/or video as required in the Portfolio Instructions for the entry.

In the resulting matrix, identify your evidence for each criterion. To build a strong wall of *consistent* evidence, provide your evidence in as many sources as possible. Like the components of the wall, your evidence must create a unified "whole" that meets the intent of the entry. The strength of the entry is dependent on the quality and quantity of the evidence provided. For an accomplished entry, you must build a sturdy structure, with interlocking "bricks" supporting each of the scoring criteria. In the next exercise we will show you how to create a Wall of Evidence using one of your entries.

Exercise 12-1: Creating Your Wall of Evidence

To build your Wall of Evidence, you will need the template shown at the end of the chapter and the materials listed below. You will need at least two template pages per entry to accommodate all your scoring criteria.

You will need:
1. Your entry
2. Your Portfolio Instructions
3. The Standards

We will walk you through this exercise using Entry 4: Documented Accomplishments as an example. Completing a similar matrix for each of your entries will help you determine if your evidence is *clear, convincing, and* *consistent*.

Turn to the Portfolio Instructions for Entry 4 and find the introductory section titled **How Will My Response Be Scored**? to locate your scoring criteria. It is important to re-read these criteria from the original text, as we tend to paraphrase when transferring the information to other documents, and may lose important details. You will fill in the scoring criteria for your Entry 4 as we have done in the example shown in Figure 39 (Example Exercise 12-1: Wall of Evidence for Entry 4). The example is shown for discussion purposes only. Only three of the seven criteria for Entry 4 are shown here.

Each row beneath the scoring criteria represents one source of evidence for the entry. The Written Commentary is always your most important source, as it is used to explain your decision-making as well as your analysis of and reflection on your work. In all entries, it is important you use your Written Commentary to explain why each selected artifact or document is important. You should also discuss how your selected artifact supports your written description.

For Entry 4, your sources of evidence are your Written Commentary and the supporting artifacts or documents you have chosen to include. In the empty blocks under each criterion, your goal is to note evidence of meeting the criterion in every available source of evidence, as shown in Figure 38. Each artifact or document should be listed separately, as it may provide evidence for more than one criterion. Exercise 12-1 should help you to consider your document from different perspectives in order to demonstrate all possible criteria.

I worked with 7 and 8 year olds, and chose to seek certification as an Early Childhood Generalist. One of my entries called for an integrated unit in social studies and the arts. I designed a multi-faceted unit with family involvement, community connections, hands on activities, and many other aspects of accomplished teaching. When I received my score report, I was stunned to find that this entry did not receive a passing score. When I revisited my work, I realized that I had not explicitly addressed some of the listed scoring criteria. Although there was nothing "wrong" with my teaching, I had worked harder than necessary to design a rather elaborate lesson instead of focusing on the specific evidence requirements for the entry.

- Bess

Sample – Exercise 12-1: Creating Your Wall of Evidence
Entry 4: Documented Accomplishments

SOURCES OF EVIDENCE	SCORING CRITERIA How Will My Response Be Scored?		
	Treat parents and other interested adults as valued partners in students' development and education	Use thoughtfully chosen strategies ... effective in engaging parents two-way communication focused on teaching and learning issues and student progress	Work collaboratively with colleagues to improve teaching and learning within my school or in the wider professional community
Written Commentary	*Explained how I share information about state standards and school expectations, as well as my concerns about individual students*	*Explained specific communications re student progress and concerns with individual students. Explained variety in types of communications*	*Explained my leadership role in my department for improvement in teaching to standards, project-based learning, family communications*
Artifact A Communication Log	*Showed how parent input influenced my strategies with CK; worked with parent to improve homework return from KT*	*Showed frequency and quality of info & direct contacts – phone, e-mail, web site, letters – including parent initiated conversations*	*Showed example of my communication log shared with others in my department who want to improve their communications with families*
Artifact B Website home page	*Shows access to current news, assignments*	*Shows web Q & A bulletin board used by parents to interact over questions about school or class concerns*	*Shows access to sample standards-based units I have taught*
Artifact C Standards-Based Teaching Committee Letter of Verification	*Confirmed that I explained to parents the purpose of standards-based teaching, the work of the committee, and my role*	*Confirmed informational parent meeting I held on standards-based teaching with Q & A*	*Showed my participation on the committee & verified the nature of the task*

Figure 39. Sample Exercise 12-1: Creating Your Wall of Evidence.
Selected scoring criteria from Entry 4 are shown with teacher comments notating how evidence of each criterion is provided through multiple sources.

For your entry to be judged as accomplished, you must be sure you have directly and thoroughly addressed each of the scoring criteria for the entry. We also recommend you re-read the complete text of the Standards that apply to the entry. The scoring criteria will help you focus on what is valued in the entry, but your Standards will give you a more vivid and detailed description of the nature of the evidence you need to provide.

In the National Board Facilitators' Institute, the Wall has been used as an analogy to show what entries "look like" at different levels of accomplishment. Figure 40 (The Wall – An Analogy for Applying the Rubric) demonstrates how the quality of your entry might be judged using the four-point scoring rubric (For more information on scoring, See Chapter 14: Scoring).

Like the walls shown at Levels 3 and 4, your entry must have structural integrity. These walls are composed of solid bricks. The Level 3 wall has a few more blemishes than the Level 4 wall, but both appear to be sturdy. Entries scored at Levels 3 or 4 need not be perfect, but must meet or exceed the evidence requirement using multiple sources.

Like the walls shown at Levels 1 and 2, an entry will receive a lower score when there are too many "holes" due to lack of evidence. An entry scored at Level 1 or 2, lacking structural integrity, does not meet the evidence requirement for an accomplished entry.

Completing a Wall of Evidence matrix for each portfolio entry will provide you with an overview of the quantity of evidence you have provided for each of the scoring criteria, but determining the quality of your evidence will require deep reflective analysis. You should re-read your Standards, review all your evidence for a given criterion, and then ask yourself how well you have described and supported this aspect of your teaching.

Have you "clearly" addressed each of the listed criteria? Are your descriptions and documentations "convincing"? Have you used evidence from several different sources to illuminate each of the scoring criteria? Do your pieces of documentation and your Written Commentary work together to demonstrate "consistency" in meeting them?

Reviewing Your Entry Against The Five Core Propositions

Throughout the text, we have used The Five Core Propositions as the guide to your work on your Portfolio Entries. Representing the *architecture of accomplished teaching*, they provide the organizing structure behind your Standards-based evidence in Entries 1, 2, and 3. Your architecture is revealed when you demonstrate the **connectivity and alignment** of the different parts of the entry.

For an accomplished performance, in addition to specific examples of your Standards-based teaching practices, you MUST demonstrate the presence of this organizing structure in each of your entries. The outline of the Portfolio Instructions for the entry and the prompts for each section

The Wall – An Analogy for Applying the Rubric

Level	The Wall	The Portfolio Entry
4		Provides *clear, convincing, and consistent* evidence of standards. Such evidence is found in every possible source (represented by the bricks in the wall). Though not necessarily perfect, the entry makes a strong case for teaching according to the standards for the certificate area.
3		Provides clear and convincing evidence. While there are a few areas where evidence could be more solid, overall the entry is sturdy and holds together well.
2		Some evidence is present, but it is simply not convincing and/or consistent. The wall has too many holes, and truly "accomplished teaching" cannot be determined with confidence.
1		Entry contains many gaps. Evidence of the specified standards is missing, incomplete, or unclear. Instructional decisions and practices may seem random, and the underlying structure appears unstable or is absent.

Figure 40. The Wall – An Analogy for Applying the Rubric.
Characteristics of entries at each level of the rubric are described using a brick wall as a visual analogy.

are designed to help you reveal the architecture of your teaching decisions in your featured instructional sequence.

Once again, we will ask you to revisit your work through the lens of The Five Core Propositions. Reflect on the statements and questions below in reference to each of your completed entries:

Core Proposition 1: *Teachers are committed to students and their learning.*

Accomplished teachers know the learning dispositions and needs of their students. In your contextual information sections (Contextual Information Sheet and Instructional Context or Student Profile) have you demonstrated your knowledge of the developmental characteristics and learning needs of your students, the social and cultural contexts that impact their learning dispositions, their past experiences and current levels of ability? Have you described individual students who can be featured throughout your entry to provide examples of your ability to address individual student needs? Will you refer to the characteristics of your class and of your featured individuals in the other sections of your entry and tell how this knowledge impacts your instructional decisions? *If the information in your contextual sections is not referenced in other parts of your entry, it is **not relevant**, and you should not include it.*

Core Proposition 2: *Teachers know the subjects they teach and how to teach those subjects to students.*

Accomplished teachers set high and worthwhile goals for their students and develop strategies to help students meet those goals. Have you demonstrated that you know the essential concepts and skills that *your* students need in the subject area? Based on your understanding of your students and their needs discussed in the contextual information sections described above, have you set high and worthwhile goals for *these* *students, at *this time,* and in *this setting*? Did you explain why these goals are appropriate for these students? Does your entry ask you to explain how these lesson goals are related to overarching or end year (or end course) targets for students? Are your selected goals for this instructional sequence clear, specific, and assessable? Are you able to effectively analyze and reflect on student learning toward these stated goals in other sections of the entry? Have you described instructional strategies that clearly help students make progress toward your selected goals? Have you described your strategies for featured individual students, as well as for the class as a whole? If your instructional sequence includes more than one lesson, have you described how your scaffolded lesson design helps move students toward the target goal?

Core Proposition 3: *Teachers are responsible for managing and monitoring student learning.*

Accomplished teachers are student-focused. They support all students in making progress toward the selected goals. Have you explained how your instructional strategies help students meet the goals of your lesson? Have you shown how you meet the learning needs of different students in your class? Have you described formative assessments that tell you *how well* your students are learning during the course of your instruction? Have you described any adjustments you made to your plans based on unanticipated student responses to the lesson? Do you continue to demonstrate your knowledge of your subject matter in your responses to students, as shown on your videos and in your feedback on student work samples? Have you demonstrated your commitment to student learning and your ability to identify and respond to student needs through thoughtful analysis of student products or performances?

Core Proposition 4: *Teachers think systematically about their practice and learn from experience.*

Accomplished teachers reflect continually on their work with students and strive to improve their practices to more effectively help students learn. At the conclusion of your instructional sequence did you reflect thoughtfully on your ability to help *all students* make progress toward the goals? Based on student products or performances, did you see areas that you could improve to be more effective in your work with students? Did you identify any issues or learning concerns that might be addressed in the next instructional sequence? Did you consider other resources that you could use to enhance student learning? Did you determine what you might do differently if you taught the lesson again? Did you explain what the next set of goals for these students will be and why?

Core Proposition 5: *Teachers are members of learning communities.*

Accomplished teachers seek and use resources to enhance student learning, including people, materials, and technology. Did you use particular resources to support the learning of the class or of individual students? Did you explain how your selected instructional materials support student learning? Did your support for individual students include other people, such as teacher assistants, counselors, or parents?

Reviewing Your Entry Using the Scoring Guide

Scoring Guides are made available to help candidates understand the process and criteria used to assess their portfolio entries and assessment center exercises. Access your Scoring Guide on the NBPTS website and study it to help you gain insight into the rubrics that will be used to score your entry or exercise. The guide not only describes each section of the assessment, it will show you the scoring process followed by the assessor who reads your work.

The Scoring Guide may be used as your final tool to insure that your entry meets the level of quality needed for an accomplished performance. It is specific to your area of National Board Certification and to your portfolio and assessment center requirements. We will discuss the guide in terms of your portfolio entries in this chapter, and will return to it in Chapter 13 to help you prepare for the assessment center exercises.

Scoring Guide Overview

The Scoring Guide contains four sections that 1) review the requirements for the assessment in your certificate area, 2) provide you with scoring materials that are used by assessors to score your entries and exercises, and 3) show you sample prompts for your assessment center exercises. We will review the Scoring Guide sections 1 and 2, pertaining to the portfolio entries, in this chapter.

Scoring Guide, Section 1: Background Information provides you with some general information about the NBPTS scoring system and an overview of all ten parts of the assessment for your certificate area, including the entries and assessment center exercises. The requirements given for an entry in the Scoring Guide will match those found in your Portfolio Instructions.

For example, here is the two-sentence description from the Scoring Guide for the *Adolescence and Young Adult Science Certificate*, Entry 1 – Teaching a Major Idea Over Time:

- You choose three instructional activities, related instructional materials, two student responses to each activity, a culminating assessment, and submit a Written Commentary.

- Your submission should demonstrate your strategies for linking instructional activities together to engage students in building conceptual understanding of one major idea in science.

From this simple description, you can see that the instructional activities in this entry must be linked together for the purpose of building conceptual understanding of a major idea in science. The candidate must demonstrate strategies that engage students and promote learning of the selected concept.

In previous chapters, we have explained that the selected activities, instructional materials, student responses, and culminating assessment must be purposefully described and analyzed in the Written Commentary to provide evidence of the candidate's ability to build students' conceptual understanding of the selected idea in science.

Every element of this description is important. If the candidate fails to demonstrate how activities are linked; if the discussion of strategies does not address student engagement; if the analysis of student responses and/or the culminating assessment is not focused on student learning of the selected goals; the entry may not meet the Standards for accomplished teaching required for this entry. As you read each entry overview in your Scoring Guide, we suggest that you underline or highlight the key words and phrases in each description; stop and reflect: "Have I clearly demonstrated this in my entry?"

Candidates' responses are often incomplete because they feel their thinking processes are obvious. Assessors do not give points for implied understandings. It is your responsibility to provide explicit evidence that you carefully select strategies and processes to enable student learning.

After reviewing the descriptions for your portfolio entries and exercises, read the remainder of the Scoring Guide, Section 1: Background Information for an Overview of the Assessment Scoring System. Using the Scoring Guide, Section 2: Scoring Materials for the Portfolio Entries, you will have an opportunity to review your entry using materials similar to those used by an assessor. In this section, a Level 4 Scoring Rubric and Note Taking Guide are provided for each entry.

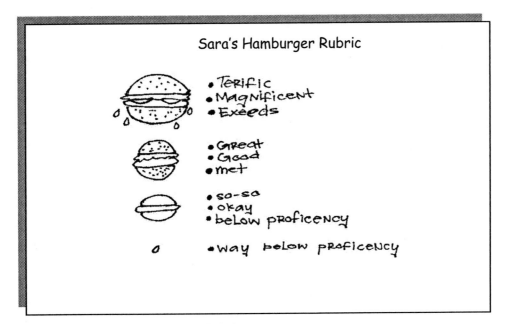

Figure 41: Sara's Hamburger Rubric.
Like a deluxe hamburger, your entry must contain multiple layers and details that demonstrate the dimensions of your thinking and teaching. Your description, analysis, and reflection on genuine examples from your teaching are the ingredients that make up these layers. Without them, the entry lacks the authentic flavor of purposeful practice.

Level 4 Rubric

Here are some suggested steps for reviewing and reflecting on your writing in each of your entries:

1. Locate the Level 4 Rubric for the entry. Read and underline key words and phrases. These should correspond to the scoring criteria in your Portfolio Instructions in the **How Will My Response Be Scored?** section. The scoring criteria provide focal points, but the rubric is the complete text used for scoring.

2. Reflect on the quantity and quality of evidence you have provided for each element of the rubric. Make a "Wall of Evidence" using your Scoring Criteria to insure your evidence is *clear, convincing, and consistent.*

3. Compare the Level 4 Rubric to the descriptors of Levels 3, 2, and 1 for the same entry. Can you clearly place yourself at Level 4, or are you uncertain of your place on the rubric? What is the difference between a Level 3 and Level 4 performance? Between a Level 2 and Level 3 performance?

Note-Taking Guide

Locate the Note-Taking Guide for the entry under review. The assessor uses this Note-Taking Guide as part of the scoring process. Begin by thinking about your entry in relation to the numbered prompts in the Scoring Guide, beginning with the Aspects of Teaching.

As you read the Aspects of Teaching for your classroom-based entries, you will notice the clear connection to The Five Core Propositions: *Knowledge of Students, Knowledge of Subject, Managing and Monitoring Student Learning, Reflective Practice, and the Teacher as a Member of a Learning Community.*

Each prompt in the Note-Taking Guide helps the assessor identify the architecture of your teaching and examine your entry for purposeful and clearly aligned planning, instruction, analysis, and reflection focused on the selected goals for student learning. Have you provided clear evidence that your teaching practices are systematic and aligned throughout a given sequence of instruction? Have you shown that your instruction has helped deepen students' understanding of substantive concepts in the content area? Have you provided a clear rationale, a thorough analysis, and a meaningful reflection based on your instructional decisions?

The Aspects of Teaching for Entry 4: Documented Accomplishments asks the assessor to seek evidence of the teacher as learner, as leader/collaborator, and as partner with families and community. The candidate must provide evidence of all three of these aspects. The remaining prompts in the Note-Taking Guide for this entry are focused on alignment and student learning.

Each portfolio has specific entry questions that target aspects of accomplished teaching that are specific to that certificate. Because of this, candidates should refer to their entries for their specific entry questions for Entries 1, 2, and 3.

We have asked you to revisit your entry requirements and reflect on your evidence over and over again. Although it seems repetitive, it is important to continually re-examine your work. Reflecting on and writing about your teaching is your tool for growth in the National Board Certification Process. Most candidates see a clear difference from their first entry drafts to their last, and often make significant revisions to early drafts to write more effectively about their teaching. The process is a journey, and your ability to analyze and reflect about your teaching is what the journey is all about. Your abilities will grow tremendously from the beginning to the end.

Scoring Guide Section 3: Scoring Materials for the Assessment Center Exercises, and Section 4: Selected Assessment Center Exercises, will be addressed in Chapter 13: Preparing for the Assessment Center.

Part II. Packing It Up

At this writing, your written portfolio entries must be returned in the box provided for this purpose. As with other aspects of the National Board Certification process, it is possible that future portfolios will be submitted electronically, but for now we will address the physical process of box-packing. No matter how your work is submitted, it will be a time-consuming process that requires your full concentration.

As candidates share their stories in the certification process, "horror stories" abound when it comes to the process of packing and submitting their work in time to meet the deadline. The key word here is "deadline," and you can avoid a lot of the stress associated with submission if you begin your work early, set a schedule, and stick to it.

Check the Website

Thoroughly read your Portfolio Instructions for detailed guidelines and packing information about submitting your entries. In addition, be sure to check the National Board website for any corrections that relate to your certificate. **Be sure to check this site before submitting your work, as there may be important corrections to documents, or other clarifications about entry requirements.**

Plan Ahead

Your deadline date is not a mailing date; it is the date by which NBPTS must *receive* your work. You must allow time for possible glitches in the transport system after the box leaves your hands.

NBPTS provides detailed portfolio packing and return instructions on your certificate area-specific web or CD Portfolio Instructions. Be sure to print these out and follow them exactly. NBPTS **will not** correct candidate packing errors that may lead to "non-scorable" entries.

When planning your schedule, you will want to have all entries finished a month before the deadline. This will give you time to do your final review, ask readers for feedback, and make any necessary revisions. You will also want to re-check each of your video recordings before packing to be sure you have correctly labeled the one you really want, and that your copy is technically acceptable.

Candidates consistently report that packing the box takes close to a full day. Schedule your box-packing day well ahead of time. Last minute candidates (this is most of us!) are often over-tired and over-pressured as they race to meet their deadlines for writing, packing, and mailing. It is clearly more desirable to be well rested and have time to spare. You will definitely want access to a copy machine. You should also have access to a computer, and have all your files on disk in case you need to make last-minute corrections to your text.

One of my organizational strategies was to create a "skeleton" portfolio. When I was too tired to think and write, I fastened my candidate ID stickers on the required pages and made extra copies of all cover sheets and forms. I kept the originals in file folders labeled for each entry, and used the copies for my skeleton. I punched the copies and put them into a binder with dividers for each entry. I put my copies of the required forms for each entry in the order specified by the Portfolio Instructions. I used colored pages behind cover sheets, with instructions about what to insert, e.g., "Insert Written Commentary," "Insert Student A Work Sample." Once I had the material, I replaced the colored sheet with a copy of the required materials. When it was time to pack and send my portfolio, I had my model in front of me. It went together easily because I was very familiar with all the pages, forms, and formats for assembling the entries.

- Bess

Make a Complete Copy

Be sure to make a duplicate copy of your completed portfolio just as it will be submitted, including forms, cover sheets, videos, student work samples, and other artifacts. If your box should be damaged during shipping, NBPTS may request another set of materials from you. For this reason, we recommend you retain your original video recordings and make copies to send in with your completed entries.

Follow Your Packing and Return Instructions

The National Board Packing and Return Instructions are very clear and specific. They are designed to ensure equity in the scoring process, and to ease the task of the assessor by establishing uniformity in the presentation of entries. Remember, submissions now number in the tens of thousands every year. You must meet the packing and return requirements, or risk having your work deemed "non-scorable."

The Packing and Return Instructions provide you with packing lists and diagrams to make sure nothing is left out of your box, and that your materials are packed in sequence. Follow your instructions! Many Candidate Support Providers recommend that you pack with a partner. Candidates can ask a well rested, non-candidate friend to sit next to them as they pack and crosscheck each item on the list as it goes into the box.

You must also be sure your entry is placed in the correct envelope, as this will direct it to the appropriate scoring location. An entry sent to the wrong location cannot be retrieved. It will be scored according to the rubric of the center to which it has been sent. As a generalist, for example, if you accidentally switch envelopes for a science entry and a social studies entry, your science entry will be scored against the social studies rubric and vice-versa. Do the assessors realize the mistake? Of course they do—but it simply is not feasible to re-route entries in order to correct errors made by candidates.

In addition to the envelopes containing your entries, you will be required to return a "Forms" envelope with specific required documents. Your portfolio will be marked "non-scorable" without them.

Sending the Portfolio

Call well ahead of time to determine which carrier you will use and find out their timelines for pick-up and delivery. Some carriers may advertise "Next Day Service," but may not actually be able to deliver within 24 hours. For example, candidates in Hawaii have learned that "Next Day" is more often two to three days due to distance and time zone differences.

When checking carriers, be sure to ask if your box can be sent without being X-rayed, as this may damage your videos. We have found certain carriers who will provide this service for you, but you must ask.

Request a return receipt that will let you know when your box has been received by NBPTS. Keep your paperwork as proof of mailing and track your box as it crosses the country to the scoring center. Check your NBRIC mailbox to verify it has been received on time and is logged in correctly.

Key Points for Group Facilitators

- It is important to prompt candidates to meet timelines that will help them finish entries well before the mailing deadline. When Exercise 12-1 is applied to the first completed entry early in the year of candidacy, it will help deepen the understanding of the writing task. Candidates who have skipped the exercises in previous chapters should be encouraged to complete Exercise 12-1, which addresses the consistency needed for a Level 4 performance.

- The final step of portfolio submission is stressful for candidates, who are often overly tired after last minute revisions. You may wish to arrange a special daylong meeting for candidates to pack their boxes. Meet in a location with plenty of table space, paper clips, a computer, and copier. Provide refreshments.

- Call local carriers to gather information about options and due dates for submitting packages to meet the deadline. Give each candidate a sheet that lists the options and phone numbers of carriers.

- Once candidates' portfolios have been sent, CELEBRATE! The completion of the portfolio is a tremendous accomplishment no matter how it is scored. Celebrating now helps to validate the hard work that has been done and may help candidates make a successful transition into Advanced Candidacy if they do not attain the threshold score in their first attempt at certification.

Exercise 12-1: Wall of Evidence

Entry #_____

Standards-Based Scoring Criteria			
Level 4 Rubric			
My Evidence of Meeting the Standards (Specific Examples)			
Evidence in the Written Commentary			
Evidence in Student Work Samples			
Evidence in the Instructional Context			
Evidence in the Video			

Directions: Make copies of this sheet and fill in the scoring criteria for each of your remaining entries. Complete a Wall of Evidence for each entry.

Exercise 12-1: Wall of Evidence
Entry 4: Documented Accomplishments

	Standards-Based Scoring Criteria: Page 1		
Level 4 Rubric Entry 4	Treat parents and other interested adults as valued partners in students' development and education;	Use thoughtfully chosen, appropriate strategies that are effective in engaging parents and other adults in substantive two-way communication;	Facilitate ongoing, mutually beneficial interactions between the students and the wider community in a way that enhances teaching and learning;
	My Evidence of Meeting the Standards (Specific Examples)		
Written Commentary			
Artifact A			
Artifact B			
Artifact C			

Directions: Use this 2-page form to complete your Wall of Evidence for Entry 4.

Wall of Evidence: Continued
Entry 4: Documented Accomplishments

Standards-Based Scoring Criteria: Page 2			
Engage in conscious and deliberate ongoing professional development to strengthen my knowledge, skills and abilities relevant to my teaching context;	Work collaboratively with colleagues to improve teaching and learning within my school or in the wider professional community;	Share my expertise in a leadership role with other educators thru facilitating professional development, improving instructional practices, or advocacy for positive change in educational policy;	Level 4 Rubric Entry 4
My Evidence of Meeting Standards (Specific Examples)			
			Written Commentary
			Artifact A
			Artifact B
			Artifact C

Directions: Use this 2-page form to complete your Wall of Evidence for Entry 4.

Reader's Response Guide

Name_____

Area of Certification: _____Entry: _____

Date Submitted: _____ Please Return By: _____

Thank you for agreeing to read my entry for National Board Certification. I have attached the following to assist you:

- ❏ An entry map: This shows an overview of the requirements for the entry.
- ❏ Entry Prompts Response Sheet: As you read my writing, please indicate if I have given a clear, complete response to each question by marking one of the columns on the right, "Yes," "Partial," or "No."
- ❏ Scoring Criteria Response Sheet: Please indicate if you see evidence for each of the statements.
- ❏ Standards for the entry: For your information only. The scoring criteria are based on these Standards. You may wish to refer to them for a more complete understanding of the entry requirements.

I would also appreciate your comments on the following aspects of my entry after you have read the entire piece:

1. Are the goals clearly relevant to the needs of these students, given the school and instructional context?

Directions: This cover sheet may be provided to your reader with attached documents to ensure a focused response to your work.

Sample: Entry Prompts Reader Response Sheet
Early Adolescent (EA) Science: Entry 2 (2004)

Have I given a complete, clear response to each question?

Instructional Context (~1 page)	Yes	Partial	No
What are the number, ages, and grades of the students in the class featured in this entry and the subject matter of the class?			
What are the relevant characteristics of this class that influenced your instructional strategies for this sequence of instruction: ethnic, cultural, and linguistic diversity; the range of abilities of the students; the personality of the class?			
What are the relevant characteristics of the students with exceptional needs and abilities that influenced your planning for this instruction (for example, the range of abilities and the cognitive, social/behavioral, attentional, sensory, and/or physical challenges of your students)?			
What are the relevant features of your teaching context that influenced the selection of this instructional sequence?			
Planning (~2 pages)	Yes	Partial	No
What are the goals for this instructional sequence, including concepts, attitudes, process and skills you want students to develop? Why are these important learning goals for your students? How does this instructional sequence fit into the overall inquiry process?			
What *specific goals* do you have for the discussion seen on the video?			
Why is a group discussion an effective method for introducing this particular *new concept*?			

Directions: Using this sample as a guide, you may wish to create similar matrices showing the prompts for your classroom-based entries to give to your readers.   p. 1/2

Adapted with permission from forms developed by Dr. Traci Bliss of Idaho State University and by the Hawaii Teacher Standards Board.

Video Analysis (~6 pages)	Yes	Partial	No
How does the video segment fit into this day's lesson as a whole? (i.e., what happened in the balance of the classroom time, either before or after the video was taken?)			
What common initial understandings and particular misconceptions did students express on the video when first introduced to this area of science? How did these understandings and misconceptions compare to what you had anticipated? How did you address the different levels of understandings that your students have?			
How did you elicit and probe students' ideas about relevant science concepts?			
Describe a specific example from this lesson as seen on the video that shows how you ensure fairness, equity, and access for students in your class.			
How effective was your learning environment with respect to fairness, equity, and access?			
Reflection (~ 2 pages)	Yes	Partial	No
As you review the video, what parts of the discussion do you think are particularly effective in terms of reaching your goals with this group of students? Why do you think so? Cite specific examples.			
In light of what you learned from your students, what are the next steps in this teaching sequence? How does your teaching respond to the understandings that the students bring with them to the classroom?			
What would you do differently if you had the opportunity to introduce this same concept again with a different class? Why? If you would not change anything, explain why it was successful.			

Directions: Using this sample as a guide, you may wish to create similar matrices showing the p. 2/2 prompts for your classroom-based entries to give to your readers.

Adapted with permission from forms developed by Dr. Traci Bliss of Idaho State University and by the Hawaii Teacher Standards Board.

Scoring Criteria Reader Response Sheet

Entry 4: Documented Accomplishments

Summary Statement for this Entry:			
I must provide clear, convincing, and consistent evidence of my ability to further student learning through my work with families and the community, with colleagues and other professionals, and as a learner.			
Have I provided evidence that my teaching meets each of the following scoring criteria?	Yes	Partial	No
• Treat parents and other interested adults as valued partners in students' development and education;			
• Use thoughtfully chosen, appropriate strategies that may or may not be original, but are effective in engaging parents and other adults in two-way communication focused primarily on substantive teaching and learning issues and individual student progress;			
• Facilitate ongoing, mutually beneficial interactions between the students and the wider community in a way that enhances teaching and learning;			
• Engage in conscious and deliberate ongoing professional development to strengthen my knowledge, skills, and abilities relevant to my teaching context;			
• Work collaboratively with colleagues to improve teaching and learning within my school or in the wider professional community;			
• Share my expertise in a leadership role with other educators through facilitating professional development of other teachers, improving instructional practices, or advocacy for positive change in educational policy;			
• Accurately analyze and thoughtfully reflect on the significance of all my accomplishments taken together, and appropriately plan for future opportunities to impact student learning.			

Directions: Using this sheet for Entry 4 as a guide, you may wish to create similar sheets showing the scoring criteria for your classroom-based entries to give to your readers.

13

Preparing for the
Assessment Center

Featured Resources:

- Standards
- Scoring Guide
- NBPTS Assessment Policies

The six assessment center exercises are designed to test your content knowledge across the range of your certificate area. You must identify this range and be sure that you prepare yourself accordingly. For example, a Middle Childhood Generalist must know all content areas for children aged 7 – 11 years, while an Exceptional Needs Specialist must know the field from 0 – 21+ years. A high school math teacher may have taught only algebra and geometry for several years, but must also demonstrate content knowledge of discrete mathematics, calculus, statistics and data analysis, as well as technology and manipulatives.

In this chapter, we will give you some tips on preparing for your assessment center experience. We will also show you how to locate and analyze your exercise descriptions. Finally, we will show you a sample prompt and its relationship to an analysis exercise we have provided for you.

Scheduling

Check the NBPTS calendar to determine the testing "window" for your assessment center exercises. NBPTS states that candidates may choose to take their assessment center exercises before or after submitting the portfolio, and are at no disadvantage in either case.

Many support group facilitators feel strongly that the candidate should complete the portfolio work first, and that by doing so he or she is better prepared for the assessment center. We tend to agree. There is no doubt the portfolio process is the catalyst for tremendous professional development. Candidates become well versed in their Standards and improve their writing skills, learning how to provide evidence with specificity as they describe, analyze, and reflect about teaching.

Whatever you decide about scheduling, your assessment center appointment should be made well in advance to ensure that you are able to test at the time that is best for you. Be sure to allow generous time to research current material in your field and study for your content area exercises before your appointment.

Assessment Center Resources

Assessment center preparation information may be found in the candidate section of the NBPTS website. It includes the Guide to National Board Certification, the Assessment Center Orientation Policy and Guidelines, and the NBPTS Assessment Policies. Carefully review these resources so you are well aware of requirements and recommendations from NBPTS. Here are few additional notes based on our experiences with candidates:

1. **Review the Website assessment center information.**
   Details are given for first-time candidates, retake candidates and those who are in need of nonstandard testing accommodations. Be sure to read through all parts of the assessment center information on the website. You may want to print out some of the material that is especially relevant for you.

2. **View exercise descriptions.**
   You will find these on the website and in the NBPTS Scoring Guide for your area. A link to this document is provided on the website. Print your exercise descriptions from both locations, and, if they differ, determine which is most current.

3. **Locate the assessment center(s) in your area.**
   The NBPTS assessment center information will provide you with contact information and a list of authorized testing centers. Determine if you have more than one center available to you in case you are not able to get your preferred appointment date and time at the first place you call.

   Be aware that testing centers handle assessments for a variety of professions and purposes. Some centers are busier than others, and some may have seasons in which they are especially busy. In some areas, the NBPTS assessment is relatively new and testing center personnel may be less familiar with it than with other tests that they give throughout the year.

4. Make an appointment.

Your entire application fee must be paid to NBPTS before you will be permitted to schedule an appointment at the assessment center. Be sure to schedule an appointment well ahead of time, and *do not* book yourself for the last possible appointment in your window.

You want to give yourself some leeway in the event of a personal disaster such as illness or accident, or a natural disaster such as a fire or storm. Fees will be charged if you need to change the appointment, but this is minor compared to losing your opportunity to take your assessment center exercises altogether. Consider the day of the week and time of day that you will be at your best.

5. Study for your assessment center exercises.

Use the analysis of your exercise descriptions, discussed later in this chapter, to guide your study. Confer with a content mentor or fellow teacher to locate helpful resources. Research current practices through content area journals or websites. If you feel especially unclear about your ability to respond to one or more exercises, locate an NBCT in your area from the NBPTS Directory on the website who can direct you to specific resources.

For some certificate areas, NBPTS may provide test materials to candidates ahead of time. If you receive such preparatory information, take time to study it. You may be able to apply the analysis process in the next section to these materials.

For secondary teachers, retired Advanced Placement (AP) test prompts in the content area can be a useful tool to practice test-taking skills. Like the NBPTS prompts, they are often structured as multi-step questions.

6. Use the tutorial.

Many candidates skip this resource and regret it. The format and tools used in the computer-based exercises are unique to the NBPTS assessment. Although you will be given some practice at the assessment center before beginning your exercises, this should be a review rather than your first contact. Even though the exercises provided on the tutorial may not match your certificate area, it is very important for every candidate to practice with the assessment center tutorial for the following purposes:

- Most current navigation and word processing functions
- Timed response (30 min)
- Scrolling to find different parts of the prompt

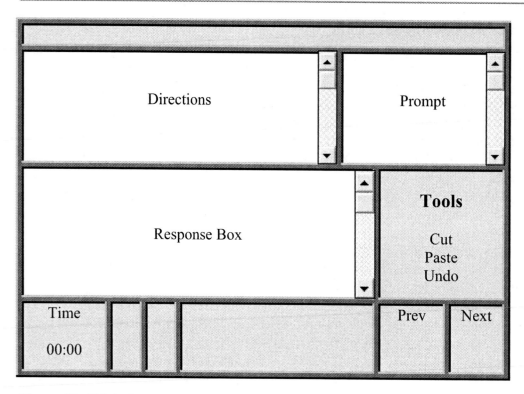

Figure 42. Triple Screen Format.
At this time, the assessment center exercises are completed on a computer screen, formatted as shown above.

The system currently used is a triple-screen format; similar to the diagram shown in Figure 42, which allows the candidate to view the directions, prompt information, and the response area simultaneously. Each screen can be scrolled separately. You will need to become accustomed to this format in order to navigate successfully within and between screens in a timely manner. You will also want to locate and be comfortable with tools that you may be able to use for cutting, copying and pasting sections of text into different areas. It is *not* like other word processing programs.

Use the tutorial to practice answering a question (or series of questions in one exercise) within 30 minutes. Your screen will display a timer that counts down the minutes and seconds for you. When your time is up, your screen shuts off. You may be amazed to find out how quickly 30 minutes goes by when you try to provide a thoughtful response to a given prompt. Practice responding to a prompt with bulleted phrases, rather than composing whole sentences.

Remember to "scroll first!" at the assessment center to locate all parts of each exercise as it is presented. Many candidates have had the unfortunate experience of using 30 minutes to respond to a prompt; only to find out the question had a second part that did not show until they scrolled the screen down. On the tutorial, practice scrolling to locate all parts of a given prompt. One question may have two or three parts.

Scroll the entire screen to locate all parts of the prompt question, and time yourself on each part accordingly. For example, if the question has three parts, give yourself approximately 10 minutes per section, using the timer as your guide. This will ensure that you do not neglect to answer a whole chunk of one exercise.

Practice with the tutorial several times, so that you are completely familiar with the program. Your practice at the assessment center will provide you with a quick review, and you will begin the testing process confidently without the distraction, frustration, and loss of time due to using unfamiliar tools to complete the task.

7. **Visit the assessment center before your test date if at all possible.**

Be sure you know how to get to your assessment center, and know how much time to allow for traffic delays and other unexpected occurrences. Find out where to park.

If possible, view the seating area where you will test. Note conditions including furniture, lighting, heating, and air conditioning that may affect your comfort and clothing choices.

Review your guidelines for items you may bring with you. Check to see if there is a secure area in which to store your personal items, such as a wallet or purse, while you are in the testing area. Locate the bathroom.

Ask about the paperwork that you will need to fill out at the center before you test, and how much time you should allow for this before your appointment. Find out what procedures to use in the event of an equipment failure or other disruption during a timed test segment.

8. **Call to confirm your appointment at least a week ahead of time.**

Centers can have their own disasters, including communication problems, equipment failures or unanticipated closures that can result in schedule changes. Be sure to verify your appointment shortly before your testing date.

9. **Prepare for test day.**

Set yourself up for success by planning your schedule carefully in the few days preceding your appointment. Make sure you eat well, exercise moderately, and get plenty of rest. You will want at be at your best for your testing session.

Arrange family commitments to minimize stress. Make plans for the care and supervision of your children on test day. Select comfortable clothing and have it ready. Pack some healthy snacks and beverages. Plan your schedule so that you will arrive at the testing center at least an hour prior to your appointment time. You will spend at least four hours there, with preparation activities and one allowed break between your exercises.

10. Test day.

Although you may have to travel a significant distance to get to your testing center, do not make the mistake of turning it into a family outing. You may wish to have an adult friend or spouse accompany you on the ride for personal support and company, but you will not want to be preoccupied with the needs of your children on this occasion.

If you *must* bring your family with you, make sure you have another adult along to care for children, and arrange to be dropped off extra early at the testing center so that you can relax, complete paperwork, use the bathroom, and otherwise prepare yourself with plenty of time to spare.

Eat a decent meal before your appointment so that you will not become uncomfortably hungry in the midst of your testing. You may be able to refresh yourself with snacks between exercises.

Be sure to bring your Authorization to Test, your picture IDs, and any other materials listed by NBPTS. Bring a jacket or sweater to ensure your comfort in air-conditioned spaces.

Remember to use the thinking and writing skills you have been practicing throughout this process: Be confident that you have the knowledge to analyze the given prompt, then describe what you are asked to do. If appropriate to the prompt, analyze student needs based on the information you are given and reflect on best practices for *...these students, at this time, and in this setting*, using the information presented in the prompt. Respond directly to each part of the question.

Analyzing Your Exercise Descriptions

The exercise descriptions for your assessment center appointment can be found on the website, Assessment Center Orientation, and in the Scoring Guide. In Figure 43 (NBPTS Assessment Center Exercise Descriptions), the exercise descriptions for the *Early Adolescence Social Studies - History Certificate* are shown as an example of the information available to you. Note the range of subject matter required for this certificate. The candidate must demonstrate knowledge of geography, U.S. and world history, economics, and political science. You must be similarly prepared for the range required for your certificate by obtaining the descriptions for your assessment center exercises.

For each exercise, the description will give you information about the content area focus and the task requirements. Locate your exercise descriptions and print them out, along with the Level 4 Rubric and any sample prompts provided in the Scoring Guide.

Exercise 13-1, below, will help you analyze your exercises in order to direct your course of study for the assessment center. As an example, we will show you how to deconstruct your exercise description with an analysis from the *AYA Social Studies - History Certificate*.

AYA Social Studies - History (2006) Assessment Center Exercise Descriptions	
Exercise 1: Documents *(U.S. History and Political Science)*	Teachers will identify the topic of an historical document, explain issues relevant to the creation of the document, explain the motivation of the author(s) for creating the document, and explain an opposing point of view from the same time period about the topic addressed in the document.
Exercise 2: Population *(Movements, Geography, and World History)*	Teachers will describe the motivation for a specific population movement, the identified region before the population movement occurred, then analyze the impact of the population movement on the identified region.
Exercise 3: Systems *(Economics and Political Science)*	Teachers will define a political and economic system, explain the relevance of specific principles of these systems, and provide an example of the political or economic principle.
Exercise 4: Social Movements *(Political Science and U.S. or World History)*	Teachers will explain historical circumstances precipitating a specific social movement, identify a specific strategy and how it was used to draw attention to the social movement and/or effect change, and analyze societal changes resulting from the movement.
Exercise 5: Resources *(Geography and Economics)*	Teachers will interpret a graphical display of data displaying a trend relating to the use of natural resources in a region outside the United States, explain reasons for the occurrence of the trend, and analyze an economic and geographic impact of the trend on the region identified.
Exercise 6: Conflict (from the perspective of one of the disciplines)	Teachers will analyze the causes and consequences of a particular conflict in society from the perspective of one of the disciplines comprising the domain of Social Studies-History as identified in the Standards document. The teacher will show his/her in-depth of knowledge in the discipline of choice: U.S. History, World History, Economics, Geography, or Political Science.

Figure 43. NBPTS Assessment Center Exercise Descriptions.
From the Scoring Guide, *AYA Social Studies - History Certificate, 2006.*[60]

Exercise 13-1: Assessment Center Exercise Description Analysis

To complete this exercise, you will need your assessment center exercise descriptions and a copy of the Exercise 13-1 template. We will demonstrate the analysis using the descriptions shown in Figure 43 (NBPTS Assessment Center Exercise Descriptions). As shown in these examples, the content areas are clearly stated. In Exercise 1, the candidate will demonstrate knowledge of U.S. History and Political Science; in Exercise 2, Geography and World History will be tested. Additional information about each exercise is given in paragraph form.

We have deconstructed the paragraph descriptions for the two exercises on the sample sheet for Exercise 13-1: Assessment Center Description Analysis shown in Figure 44. Key words and phrases from each exercise are placed in the matrix to highlight the most important aspects of each task.

In this analysis the type of prompt material, the action required of the candidate, and the key points that must be made are clearly defined. Based on knowledge of potential prompt materials, the candidate can anticipate the nature of the response that must be given in the testing situation and prepare accordingly. For example, to prepare for Exercise 1 in this certificate area, the teacher must be familiar with all major documents

Sample - Exercise 13-1: Analyzing the Assessment Center Exercises				
#	Content Area	Prompt Material	Action Words	Task
1	U.S. History Political Science	An historical document	Explain	Knowledge of: • issues relevant to the creation of the document • motivation of the author(s) • opposing point of view from same time period
2	Geography World History	A specific population movement	Describe	• motivation for the population movement • the identified region before the population movement occurred
			Analyze	• impact of the population movement on the identified region

Figure 44. Sample: Exercise 13-1: Assessment Center Exercise Description Analysis.
Key words and phrases from two EA Social Studies Exercises are placed in a matrix to highlight the most important aspects of the tasks.

normally discussed in U.S. History at this level of student development, as well as the time period, social climate, and issues that influenced the development of such documents. The action word is "explain." The teacher must be familiar with the motivations of the author(s) of the document and be prepared to discuss opposing views on relevant issues held by others in the same time period.

In Exercise 2, the candidate must "describe and analyze" a population movement. He or she must be knowledgeable about significant population movements in World History and be able to discuss motivations and impacts of such movements.

Sample Prompts

For many certificate areas, the NBPTS Scoring Guide provides example questions taken from retired prompts. You can and should use these examples to simulate testing by performing a timed response to the question(s). It can also be very valuable to try creating your own "tutorials" by practicing responses to the prompts based on your knowledge of your subject area. Members of certificate-alike candidate study groups can create such practice prompts and exchange with one another for practice purposes.

For the NBPTS *EA Social Studies - History Certificate*, the Scoring Guide provides a sample prompt for Exercise 1: Documents. This example shows us the information that is provided for this exercise when it opens on the computer screen at the assessment center. We will review the entire prompt, and you may use it as a practice test if you would like to do so.

Remember as soon as the screen opens for this exercise, the timer will start running. The more you understand about what you will need to do in this exercise by analyzing the description given in the Scoring Guide, the less time you will need to absorb the instructions in the testing situation. You will see how similar they are to the analysis we did in Figure 44 (Sample: Exercise 13-1: Assessment Center Exercise Description Analysis).

Please note: We have abbreviated the exercise description slightly as noted for the purpose of this discussion. If you would like to time yourself in this practice test, you will have 30 minutes to respond to the information that follows. Use a computer to simulate assessment center conditions.

Practice prompt begins here.
Start your timer, turn the page, and BEGIN.

Sample assessment center exercise begins here – Start timer.

Exercise 1: Documents

30 minutes

Introduction

In this exercise, you will use your knowledge of U.S. History and Political Science to analyze an excerpt from an historical document. You will be asked to respond to three prompts.

Criteria for Scoring

To satisfy the highest level of the scoring rubric, your responses must provide *clear, convincing, and consistent evidence* of the following:

- an accurate identification of the topic addressed in the historical document, and a detailed explanation of historical issues relevant to the creation of the document;

- an insightful explanation of the motivation of the author(s) for creating this document; and

- an in-depth explanation of an opposing point of view from the same time period about the topic addressed in the document.

Directions

(Brief directions are given here about navigating on the computer screen)

Stimulus

> *"...That on the first day of January, in the year of our Lord one thousand eight hundred and sixty-three, all persons held as slaves within any State or designated part of a State, the people whereof shall then be in rebellion against the United States, shall be then, thenceforward, and forever free; and the Executive Government of the United States, including the military and naval authority thereof, will recognize and maintain the freedom of such persons and will do no act or acts to repress such persons, or any of them, in any efforts they may make for their actual freedom....*
>
> *And I further declare and make known that such persons of suitable condition will be received into the armed Service of the United States..."*
>
> -excerpt from the Emancipation Proclamation

Prompts

1. Identify the topic addressed in this excerpt and explain the historical issues relevant to the creation of the document from which this excerpt was taken.

2. Explain the motivation of the author(s) for creating this document.

3. Explain an opposing point of view from the same time period about the topic addressed in this document.

*Sample assessment center exercise ends here.– **End timer***

I took the test yesterday and I am glad it is over. It is amazing how quickly the time went by for each section. One thing the assessment center did for me was to show me how students feel in a timed situation when time is almost up... I can empathize with them even more now.

-Tonya Uibel NBCT - NJ

The analysis of the prompt for Exercise 1 shown in Figure 44 helped to clarify what we could expect to see in this exercise, and would help the candidate prepare to give an appropriate response. The key phrases we identified in the "task" section of the analysis were, in fact, the three prompts given at the assessment center. The only "unknown" was the particular historical document that would be presented for discussion.

Compare the Criteria for Scoring given in the sample exercise to the Level 4 Rubric found in the Scoring Guide. You will find they are nearly identical. Both include adjective phrases such as, "accurate," "fully explain in detail," and "rich and insightful." You may wish to add this Level 4 Rubric information to each of your assessment center exercise description analyses in Exercise 13-1 to further prepare yourself. The more information you have ahead of time, the less time you will need to read and process during your 30-minute test.

Analyzing your assessment center exercises will help you identify potential subject matter for the prompts and understand the type of response you will need to give in each case. At the assessment center, you can give your full attention to your response as you will already know what you need to do with the prompt material and how your response will be scored.

On the exercise sheet provided, analyze your exercise descriptions and use the information to develop a study plan that will help you prepare for your assessment center experience. Be sure to look for sample prompts to use for timed practice, and review the Level 4 Rubric for each exercise in your Scoring Guide. With the information from your exercise description analysis, you can easily develop your own practice tests to simulate each task.

Abundant practice with practice tests and the tutorial will help you prepare for a successful experience at the assessment center. You will be able to describe, analyze, and respond to each exercise with confidence as a result of your thorough understanding of the task.

Scoring of Assessment Center Exercises

In Chapter 14, we will discuss the scoring process used by NBPTS to determine an accomplished performance by the candidate. A four-point rubric is generally used on each part of the portfolio; however, because some assessment center exercises have multiple prompts, shorter, simpler rubrics may be used to assess the response to each prompt in a given exercise. Once these individual prompts have been scored, the cumulative results for each exercise are converted to the regularly used score scale. You must read the Scoring Guide for your certificate area to see how your exercises will be scored.

Key Points for Group Facilitators

Encourage candidates to complete Exercise 13-1, and then create sample prompts that match one or more of their assessment center descriptions. If the sample prompt requires any material, such as an historical document, the candidate should supply a copy of this as well. Candidates in the same certificate area can exchange the sample prompts for practice.

Generally, candidates do not take advantage of the tutorial exercises. Most intend to, but never quite get around to it. They simply do not want to take the time to respond to a prompt that, in most cases, is not from their own certificate area. Here are two things you can do to ensure they get valuable practice for the assessment center experience:

- Hold a support session at a school or university computer lab. Have your group go online together to locate the tutorial and practice navigating on the testing screen simulation.

- Create (or ask candidates to create) practice prompts based on the assessment center exercise descriptions for each teacher's certificate area. Write them on separate cards. At a support session, simulate the timed test situation: Place the appropriate prompt card face down on each person's desk, give a "start" signal at which everyone turns over the card and begins writing. Have them do their best to give a complete response in 15 – 20 minutes. Afterward, debrief and discuss. Do this at least three times, giving a different prompt on each occasion. They will learn to focus in quickly on the key parts of the prompt, and build confidence in their ability to respond within the time limit (30 minutes will seem generous if all your practices are 15 – 20 minutes). They may also be motivated to study more on their own, and anticipate questions in the test situation.

Candidates and facilitators must use extreme caution when discussing the assessment center experience. Those who test early will want to share about the experience, which is fine as long as they do not discuss the prompts themselves. Candidates must be directed not to ask one another about the test information, and not to tell about it themselves. Candidates are asked to sign a statement of confidentiality at the assessment center, and should know that NBPTS is very serious about any breach of ethics involving the National Board Certification process.

Exercise 13-1: Analyzing the Assessment Center Exercises

#	Content Area	Prompt Material	Action Words	Task
1				
2				
3				
4				
5				
6				

Directions: Using your assessment center exercise descriptions from the Assessment Center Orientation or the Scoring Guide, deconstruct each by locating key words and phrases as shown in the chapter.

Scoring

Featured Resources:

- Standards
- Portfolio Instructions
- Scoring Guide

I f you are like most candidates, you have skipped ahead to read this chapter. Even before you begin to write, you would like to know who will read your work, how it will be evaluated, what information you will receive, and how to interpret your scores. An overview on scoring can be found in your Portfolio Instructions, Section 1: Overview, How Assessments Are Scored.

The National Board Assessment consists of ten parts: Four portfolio entries and six assessment center exercises. Each of these parts will receive a separate score. At different locations, each will be read by at least one assessor trained on the specific piece. In other words, a different person will score each part of your assessment. No single person will review your entire portfolio or all of your assessment center responses.

Scoring Centers

NBPTS has established national scoring centers to address different certificate areas. At these centers, groups of teachers trained by a NBPTS Scoring Team evaluate just one portfolio entry or assessment center exercise. Selected through an application process, assessors are not necessarily National Board Certified Teachers (NBCTs). However, they are experienced teachers working in the classroom with students of the same age and in the same content area that they will assess. Part of their training to assess includes an orientation so they will understand the depth and breadth of the process of National Board Certification.

Assessors

Assessor training includes learning the background of NBPTS, developing a scoring rubric based on the given prompt, calibrating scores on benchmark entries, and learning to identify biases that might affect scoring. Although they might not have had the experience of a candidate, all assessors will have an idea of the time and effort required, and will have an appreciation of the writing they will assess.

Guided by an experienced scoring director, each group of trainees spends time developing a deep understanding of the prompt and developing the rubric for a given entry. An entire room of teachers works on the rubric for the one entry they will assess and score. They define best practice, discuss developmentally appropriate teaching, define some of the thought processes involved in the prompt, and take time to dissect it thoroughly. In some groups assessors may even answer the question on their own to get a feel for the work. They often make big charts of the rubric to post around the room as references during the scoring period.

After defining the rubric, trainees are given benchmark cases to practice their scoring skills. These cases are reliable examples of the scoring points on the rubric and give assessors an experience of interpreting the nuances of the rubric before scoring real portfolio entries. Throughout the process, trainers double check the assessors' judgments and make sure their scores calibrate with those of the benchmark pieces.

> *As a candidate, I thought of the assessors as faceless people who would do their best to find fault with my work. The first time I met assessors at a National Board function, I was impressed with the attitude of respect each of them held for the work of the candidates. They seemed to work hard to find evidence in order to give an entry the best possible score, but at the same time they maintained a deep sense of responsibility for the integrity of the rubric and the necessity for the evidence to be sufficient for the given score.*
>
> *- Bess*

Scorers are taught to look for specific information within the written response or video entry that can be used as evidence to define a score for a candidate. They are advised to give as much credit as possible to a candidate, not taking off for spelling or grammar while reading the entry. Finally, assessors are required to give evidence of the score they assign to an entry on an "Exercise Scoring Record" (ESR). Supervisors review this evidence to ensure each score has been responsibly awarded.

Assessors also receive bias training. They learn to identify their own "triggers," such as wordy phrases, bad spelling or grammar, poor or rich vocabulary, etc. that might influence their attitude toward the writing piece or the teacher shown in the video. They learn to guard against such biases, whether positive or negative, in order to fairly score each entry against the standards-based rubric. When assessors are away from the process for any length of time, such as a weekend, they will be retrained on benchmark cases to ensure reliability in the scoring process.

A room of assessors may be responsible for reading thousands of entries over a period of two to three weeks. Scoring is mentally and physically demanding. During the scoring process, assessors are fed well, and are encouraged to take breaks and to refresh themselves regularly. Overall, NBPTS takes steps to ensure the integrity and consistency in the scoring process.

As I entered the room where scoring would be held for the next two weeks, I realized that I would be among the few National Board Certified Teachers in the group. I knew that many of these teachers had simply come to make some extra money for a few days of work during their vacation time, and I listened as a few wondered out loud about what kind of teacher in her right mind would go through this process. Over the next few days, as we talked about teaching, students, the big ideas of National Board, and how they were infused in what we all did in classrooms, there was a noticeable shift in attitude. As my fellow assessors practiced their responses to the prompt and scored accomplished and unaccomplished entries, they began to talk about becoming candidates. All of them got to know their own teaching better by reading and scoring entries. When I met up with two of the teachers in a scoring session the following year, they told me how the assessment process had helped them improve their own teaching.

- MaryAnn

The Scoring Process

We have already talked about the four-point rubric that is developed for scoring purposes, and you know that the scoring criteria given in your entry directions describe a Level 4 performance in which the candidate provides *clear, convincing, and consistent evidence* of meeting the standards for the entry. It is important to note that slight but significant changes in language differentiate each level of the rubric. All levels refer to the same important aspects of the entry, but describe different levels of quality in the evidence provided. The actual range of possible scores for an entry is 4.25 – .75, so let us talk about how the assessor determines a given score.

The rubric defines four levels of performance, with Level 1 the lowest, and Level 4 the highest. The level of performance is determined on the basis of the stated scoring criteria as shown in Figure 45 (The Language of the Rubric). An accomplished performance is determined both by quantity— "*little or no evidence*," "*limited*"; and quality— "*clear*," "*clear, convincing, and consistent*."

Meets Accomplished Performance	Level 4: *"Evidence is clear, convincing and consistent…"*
	Level 3: *"Evidence is clear…"*
Does Not Meet Accomplished Performance	Level 2: *"Evidence is limited…"*
	Level 1: *"Little or no evidence…"*

Figure 45. The Language of the Rubric.
At each level, the language of the rubric defines the quality of the evidence necessary to achieve the score.

After reading an entry and using the rubric to document the evidence provided in that entry, the first question that the assessor must answer is, "Has this candidate provided adequate evidence of an accomplished performance, or not?" The answer to this question will determine whether the entry is placed as Level 2 or below (does not meet an accomplished performance), or as Level 3 and above (meets an accomplished performance).

From that point, the assessor will further refine his or her judgment by committing to the level the entry matches most closely. Then, within a given level or "family," three different scores are possible, as shown in Figure 46 (Scoring Families). The assessor will determine a strong, weak, or average performance for the given level, and will adjust the score accordingly in .25 increments. An entry placed in the "3" family would be scored as 3.0 if "average," as 2.75 if "below average," or as 3.25 if "above average." Figure 45 shows you the possible scores for an entry, ranging from 4.25 to .75. You can also see why a score of 2.75 is the minimum for an "accomplished" performance.

To ensure reliability, a percentage of all the entry pieces at each scoring center will be double scored. This means a piece is scored separately by two different assessors. If different scores are given within the same family, the piece will receive the average of the two scores. If the two scores are too far apart, a third, more experienced reader will score the same entry and will contribute 50% toward the final score for the piece.[61] Every precaution is taken to ensure a fair judgment of the portfolio entry.

Meets an Accomplished Performance						Does Not Meet an Accomplished Performance					
Level 4			Level 3			Level 2			Level 1		
+	4.0	–	+	3.0	–	+	2.0	–	+	1.0	–
4.25		3.75	3.25		2.75	2.25		1.75	1.25		.75

Figure 46. Scoring Families.
There are four scoring "families" as defined by the rubrics. Within each family, one of three possible scores may be awarded.

Training and scoring as a National Board assessor is a professional development experience in and of itself. This has been recognized at some universities, where college credits are awarded to participating teachers. Interested teachers will find more information about how to become an assessor on the National Board website, but you should know that a teacher cannot be a candidate and an assessor during the same year. Some teachers train as assessors before becoming candidates to gain a better understanding of the National Board Certification process.

How is Certification Determined?

Candidates often wonder if they will need to achieve the minimum score of 2.75 in each of the ten sections of the assessment in order to achieve National Board Certification. The answer to this question is "no"—the process is intended to recognize that all teachers are not equally strong in all areas, and a non-passing score in one or more areas will not necessarily prevent a candidate from becoming certified.

National Board Certification is determined by the total of the candidate's scores for all sections combined. If a candidate has low scores on one or more sections, high scores on other sections can help achieve the minimum total points of 275.

It is important for candidates to know that all sections are not equal when it comes to scoring. "Weights" are assigned to different parts of the assessment, giving some sections more impact on the final score than others. The "weight" comes in the form of a multiplier. The weights are currently assigned as follows:

Portfolio Entries
Entry 1, 2, 3 : Each score is multiplied by 16
Entry 4: The score is multiplied by 12

Assessment Center Exercises
Each exercise is multiplied by 6.67

Portfolio Entries (60%)	Weights	x	Score	=	Points	
Entry #1	16	x	4.0	=	64	
Entry #2	16	x	4.0	=	64	
Entry #3	16	x	4.0	=	64	
Entry #4: Documented Accomplishments	12	x	4.0	=	48	
Subtotal Portfolio						240
Assessment Center Exercises (40%)	Weights	x	Score	=	Points	
Exercise 1	6.67	x	4.0	=	26.67	
Exercise 2	6.67	x	4.0	=	26.67	
Exercise 3	6.67	x	4.0	=	26.67	
Exercise 4	6.67	x	4.0	=	26.67	
Exercise 5	6.67	x	4.0	=	26.67	
Exercise 6	6.67	x	4.0	=	26.67	
Subtotal Assessment Center						160
TOTAL: LEVEL 4 PERFORMANCE						400

Figure 47. Possible Points on the National Board Assessment.
The relative values of different parts of the assessment are shown given "perfect" 4.0 scores on each section.

The result is that the candidate's portfolio entries will count for 60% of his or her final points, while the total of the assessment center scores will count for 40%. Figure 47 (Possible Points on the National Board Assessment) will show you the theoretical possibility if all sections received a score of 4.0, and will allow you to compare the relative values of the different sections of the assessment. As a note to our readers experienced with the NBPTS scoring process, we have purposely omitted any in depth discussion of the Universal Constant. Suffice to say, this is an additional factor added to a candidate's score report. Mathematically derived, and based on testing criteria, the Universal Constant ensures scoring accuracy and validity. It does not affect the scoring review, but is constant and applied to every candidate portfolio.

When candidates understand this system of "weighting," they can see how important it is that they turn in a strong portfolio. The candidate has complete control over these entries. There are abundant resources available to help them, from support session facilitators, to fellow colleagues, to NBCTs, to professional mentors, and other candidates.

Theoretically, a candidate who earned a score of 4.0 on each of the portfolio pieces would be only 35 points away from certification, and could be successful even if their assessment center scores were relatively low. Of course, Level 4 scores are not common, and no one should count on universally high scores. However, it would be especially foolish to turn in a poorly composed portfolio and expect to achieve success on the basis of one's assessment center scores. While every candidate should strive for the best performance possible on every section, it is a MUST to provide strong evidence of the Standards in your portfolio entries.

It should be noted that, while it is possible for a candidate to earn as much as 4.25 on an entry, this is extremely rare. Assessors report that even scores of 4.0 are not common. Most entries will be scored in the family of 3 or the family of 2. The difference between a performance that "meets" and "does not meet" the Standards is often a fine line.

The Score Report

When you finally receive your score report, what will it tell you? Will the assessors tell you which parts of your entry were strong, and which areas were not? If you receive some low scores, will they tell you how you to improve your pieces? Although you might like to have this kind of feedback, you will get only two pieces of information:

1. whether you have achieved certification or not
2. the numerical score assigned to each individual piece of the assessment

In Figure 48 (Sample Score Reports), three sample reports show different outcomes for candidates. In the first example, Candidate #1 has achieved National Board Certification, even though five out of the ten scores are below the minimum score established for an accomplished performance. Stronger scores on the portfolio sections, with their heavier weight, helped the candidate earn the needed points for National Board Certification. Look at Entry 3, which is scored at 4.25. With the multiplier "weight" of 16, this entry alone earned 68 points for the candidate. Even Entries 2 and 4, though not scored as accomplished, were close at 2.50 and yielded more points than a Level 4 performance on an assessment center exercise.

Candidate #2 did not achieve certification even though every scored section is at an accomplished level and the point total is adequate. Candidates must complete all ten sections of the assessment in order to be eligible for National Board Certification. This candidate may have failed to turn in a piece for Entry 3 or may have turned in an entry that was incomplete in some respect. Because Entry 3 is marked NS for "Not Scorable" the candidate is ineligible for National Board Certification on the basis of this score report. The candidate's scores will be "banked." Entry 3 may be re-done and submitted for scoring during the next cycle.

Candidate # 1				
	Score		Weight	Total
Entry 1	3.00	x	16.00	48.0
Entry 2	2.50	x	16.00	40.0
Entry 3	4.25	x	16.00	68.0
Entry 4	2.50	x	12.00	30.0
Exercise 1	3.00	x	6.67	20.0
Exercise 2	4.00	x	6.67	26.7
Exercise 3	1.00	x	6.67	6.7
Exercise 4	2.00	x	6.67	13.3
Exercise 5	1.00	x	6.67	6.7
Exercise 6	3.00	x	6.67	20.0
TOTAL				**279.4**

Comments

Candidate #1 has achieved certification, even though five out of the ten scores were below the minimum score established for an accomplished performance. Stronger scores on the portfolio sections, with their heavier weight, helped the candidate earn the needed points to pass the 275-point threshold.

Candidate # 2				
	Score		Weight	Total
Entry 1	3.50	x	16.00	56.0
Entry 2	2.75	x	16.00	44.0
Entry 3	NS	x	16.00	-----
Entry 4	4.00	x	12.00	48.0
Exercise 1	2.75	x	6.67	18.3
Exercise 2	4.00	x	6.67	26.7
Exercise 3	3.00	x	6.67	20.0
Exercise 4	3.00	x	6.67	20.0
Exercise 5	3.50	x	6.67	23.4
Exercise 6	3.00	x	6.67	20.0
TOTAL				**276.4**

Comments

At first glance, it appears that Candidate #2 has also achieved certification. However, even though the point total is adequate, this candidate did not turn in a scorable piece for Entry #3 and is therefore ineligible for certification on the basis of this report.

Candidate # 3				
	Score		Weight	Total
Entry 1	2.75	x	16.00	44.0
Entry 2	2.50	x	16.00	40.0
Entry 3	3.25	x	16.00	52.0
Entry 4	2.50	x	12.00	30.0
Exercise 1	1.00	x	6.67	6.7
Exercise 2	2.50	x	6.67	16.7
Exercise 3	2.75	x	6.67	18.3
Exercise 4	1.00	x	6.67	6.7
Exercise 5	3.00	x	6.67	20.0
Exercise 6	4.00	x	6.67	26.7
TOTAL				**272.7**

Comments

Candidate #3 did not achieve the minimum number of points needed for certification. The candidate may bank this score report and retake one or more of the sections that scored less than 2.75. New scores, higher or lower, will replace the older scores.

Figure 48. Sample Score Reports.
Adapted with permission from Sue Hovey, NBPTS Program Facilitator, University of Idaho

Candidate #3 did not achieve the minimum number of points needed for National Board Certification. Again, the scores are automatically "banked" and the candidate can choose to retake one or more of the sections that scored less than 2.75. In this case, fewer than 3 points are needed for National Board Certification, so it is unlikely the candidate will retake more than one section. He or she can choose from Entry 2, Entry 4, Exercise 1 or Exercise 2.

If you successfully achieve National Board Certification, perhaps you will not be too concerned with your individual scores, but if you are not successful, you will want to study your scores from the perspective of an advanced candidate who will continue the certification process for another year or two.

Receiving your scores is an elating experience if you find that you have achieved National Board Certification, and may be devastating if you have not. Candidates who are not successful will have many questions about their pieces that scored less than 2.75. Should you be in this position, locate a candidate support provider who can read the entry and take time to discuss it with you. Return to the Scoring Guide discussion in Chapter 12 to review your entry and determine the areas in which you may need to improve.

Appealing a Score

Each year when scores are released, many candidates will feel sure a mistake has been made when they find their attempts at National Board Certification have not been successful. Some will consider requesting that one or more scores be reviewed under the NBPTS score appeal process. Before proceeding with a score appeal request, here are some things you should know:

The scoring process has built in safeguards to insure that assessors award a valid score to each entry or exercise. All assessors are teachers of the subject area in which they score. They are trained to identify their personal biases, and to look carefully for evidence in the candidate's response. They practice on anchor pieces, and are checked for reliability during their training. During the scoring process, entries are intermittently double-scored to verify reliability among assessors. Due to these safeguards, when a score is appealed, the entry itself will *not* be re-scored.

In the score appeal process, NBPTS will only examine procedural issues that could have impacted the entry or exercise when it was submitted for scoring. If the correct procedures were followed, the score will stand.

For this reason, it is important that candidates are attentive to procedural issues, that they contact NBPTS immediately to report any concerns, and that they secure documentation if an irregularity occurs. There have been incidences, for example, when a candidate's assessment center exercise was interrupted by a power failure or a computer glitch. In another situation, a candidate's instructions permitted the use of a calculator for a math subtest, but the test center personnel mistakenly denied it. These are valid reasons to report the situation to NBPTS, as they negatively impacted the candidate's ability to respond to the prompt.

If you experience a problem and report it promptly, NBPTS may allow the testing session to be rescheduled. If not, documentation of the incident may help you if you want to appeal the score received on the exercise. Irregularities during a test should be reported immediately to the testing center personnel. The report should be made to NBPTS as soon as the session is completed.

As disappointing as it may be, if you are unhappy with a score and feel that your work was not assessed accurately, the score appeal process will not help you unless a procedural issue is involved. It will be more productive to work with an experienced support provider to improve your work and resubmit the exercise or entry in the next cycle.

Moving Into Advanced Candidacy

Certification is the ultimate goal of the National Board candidate, but there are smaller accomplishments along the way that should be savored and celebrated. NBPTS allows unsuccessful candidates to "bank" initial scores for up to two years in order to retake selected sections. Formerly referred to as "retake candidates" or "bankers," candidates in their second or third year are now called "advanced candidates." Many NBCTs have achieved their certification as advanced candidates, and have found their second or third year of candidacy to be deeply rewarding.

Many candidates will not achieve National Board Certification in their first year, and it is important to emphasize that a non-passing score report does not imply that the candidate is not a competent teacher. The notion of providing "evidence" of our teaching practices is new for many of us, and we may need to learn new skills in order to do so. If you are not successful in your first attempt at National Board Certification, it simply means that the evidence you provided was not *clear, convincing, and consistent* enough for assessors to make a determination of accomplished teaching according to the National Board Standards.

The NBPTS website contains a section about retake procedures for advanced candidates. Check this section for answers to your questions, deadlines, and current procedures regarding advanced candidacy.

Analyzing Your Scores

You are able to retake any piece of the portfolio that was scored less than 2.75, which is the minimum score for an accomplished teaching performance. There are a variety of factors that may influence your decision about retaking. The first is to see how many points you need to achieve an overall total of 275, then to look at the sections you could retake. Small improvements on portfolio entries, with their greater weight, may yield more points than great improvement on assessment center exercises. However, portfolio entries require a greater investment of time and a teaching situation that is within your original certification area. Remember, you cannot simply rewrite your original entry and resubmit it. The new entry must be based on a new teaching sequence in a classroom appropriate for the same certificate.

Assessment center exercises, if retaken, require some time to study before going to the testing appointment. As you do not know exactly what prompt material will be presented to you, there is less control over your performance. Some candidates may feel they do not perform especially well in the timed testing situation.

Whether you are resubmitting an entry or an exercise, you may want to consider taking time for a related class at a local college or other study on specific areas to improve your scores. There is also a cost factor to consider, as you will pay a fee for each section that you retake. You will not want to retake more sections than necessary, but neither should you do just the minimum, as you cannot expect to earn perfect scores.

For more information on how to read and interpret score to determine retake entries, refer to Chapter 15.

Exercise 14-1: Score Report Retake Analysis

Exercise 14-1 is provided to help you make good choices in retaking sections of the assessment. You may access a similar electronic exercise provided by NBPTS through the web or your candidate CD that will perform the calculations for you. [62]

On the exercise sheet, enter and calculate your retake score potential for each of your eligible entries. Figure 49 (Comparative Retake Analysis) provides you with an example, and shows you the difference in the point gain between a portfolio piece and an assessment center exercise when raised one full level.

Eligible Entries or Exercises (Scored less than 2.75)	Score	x	Weight	=	Points	
Current Score: Entry 1	2.25	x	16	=	36	
Retake Expectation:	3.25	x	16	=	52	
Points Gained:						16
Current Score: Exercise 3	2.25	x	6.67	=	15	
Retake Expectation:	3.25	x	6.67	=	21.7	
Points Gained:						6.7

Figure 49. Comparative Retake Analysis

Raising your score from 1.25 to 3.25 would yield 32 additional points on a portfolio entry, and only 13.4 points on an assessment center exercise.

Analyzing Your Performance

In addition to determining the potential points to be gained by retaking different sections, you will also need to take into consideration your personal strengths and potential for improvement in each section. It is important to determine if your weakness lies in your understanding of the content and Standards for the area, or if your understanding is strong, but your response was weak. A score in the Level 1 family, for example, may indicate that you did not respond appropriately to the prompt. Plan to spend some time in reflection and analysis of your retake possibilities.

Make sure you have the most recent NBPTS Scoring Guide for your certificate area, which provides you with information on how each of your portfolio entries and assessment exercises was scored. See Chapter 12 for more information on using the information from the Scoring Guide to review each of your entries.

You will need to revisit the portfolio entry instructions to determine what was required in the task, and the scoring criteria that were used to assess the entry. You should also reread the Standards for the entry and ask yourself why your evidence was not sufficient. Perhaps you need help from a candidate support provider in learning how to describe good quality evidence. Likewise, review the descriptions given for your assessment center prompts and ask yourself if you need further study of the content area. As you review your materials, ask yourself the following:

- What is lacking in the entry?
- Did I fully understand the question? Did I fully answer all parts of the question?
- Did my answer stay on the topic that was valued?
- Were there any "holes," i.e., important aspects of the Standards in the Level 4 Rubric for the entry that I did not address?
- Did my entry demonstrate clear connections from students to goals, goals to instruction, goals to analysis and reflection?
- Do I understand what I need to do to earn an accomplished score?
- How would my response look different if it was scored as accomplished?
- Do I have the skills I need to improve my performance?
- If not, how will I acquire them? How can I further my growth and development in the area in order to demonstrate accomplished teaching?

It is important to note that when re-submitting an entry or exercise, the newer score will replace the former. In a worst-case scenario, it is possible for a candidate's score to go down rather than up. Also, when retaking an entry you must re-do the entry with a new teaching sequence. You may not simply rewrite and resubmit the original lesson.

You should use every available resource to study, analyze, and plan for your re-submittal. Review your Scoring Guide for each entry or exercise and re-read the Level 4 Rubric. Study the Note Taking Guide for portfolio entries, and review the sample prompts for assessment center exercises.

The difference between a candidate who successfully becomes certified and one who does not may literally be only one or two points. In truth, many teachers will become certified without really knowing how they did it. The advanced candidate must analyze the entry that did not receive a passing score and understand what is needed to produce and submit an accomplished entry in its place. In doing so, the second or third year candidate often experiences even greater depth of understanding.

The process of retaking entries requires hard thinking about your strengths and weaknesses as a teacher and requires you to think about how your journey toward National Board Certification has influenced your teaching thus far. As an advanced candidate, you can focus on a particular entry or area of study without the pressure of completing the whole assessment. Even so, it is important that you establish a schedule and devote yourself to your task. Most importantly, use the support available to you. Seek help from readers, support groups, and content mentors. To provide evidence of Standards you must teach, think, and write like an accomplished teacher. Remember, it is all about the evidence!

National Board Certification is a journey of professional development. If your first attempt is not successful, you have an opportunity to reflect, analyze, and focus on an area of need that will make you a stronger teacher in the end. If you are a candidate who is still in the process toward certification, you are to be commended. You know the rigors of the process, and you are committed to continuing your professional journey.

Key Points for Group Facilitators

- Many candidates need to be assured that scoring is done in a controlled setting and assessors are carefully trained on exemplar pieces to accurately identify performances at each level of the rubric. Without this understanding, some candidates, (especially those who do not score well) may regard the process as highly subjective, and feel that National Board Certification is a matter of luck rather than performance.

- Assessors tell us there are few pieces scored in the "1" family, and few pieces scored in the "4" family. The vast majority of candidate entries and exercises will score in the "2" or "3" families. This is a critical point, as the threshold between "meets an accomplished performance" and "does not meet an accomplished performance" lies between these two families. The evidence must be of sufficient quantity and quality to cross this threshold.

- Capable teachers may be upset if they fail to achieve as expected, and must be reminded that this process of thinking and writing about teaching requires new skills from most who attempt it. In Chapter 8, we gave you a section on providing support for advanced candidates, and we hope you followed our advice. You must begin your support for advanced candidates at your first session, long before you know who they are. The announcement of scores will "make or break" many candidates. Some simply will not continue if they do not successfully certify in the first year. You must help candidates cross the bridge into advanced candidacy by laying the groundwork for the transition well ahead of time.

- Offer to help advanced candidates analyze the score report and decide on retakes. Offer to read and conference with candidates over the entries chosen for resubmission. Most importantly, if candidates have been reluctant to share their work in the past, urge them to get past this and make use of readers and mentors as they go forward.

Exercise 14-1: Score Report Retake Analysis

Score Needed: **275**

My Score:_____

Difference:_____ = Additional Points Needed

Eligible Entries or Exercises (Scored less than 2.75)	Score	x	Weight	=	Points
1. Current:		x		=	
Retake Expectation:		x		=	
Possible Point Gain					
2. Current:		x		=	
Retake Expectation:		x		=	
Possible Point Gain					
3. Current:		x		=	
Retake Expectation:		x		=	
Possible Point Gain					
4. Current:		x		=	
Retake Expectation:		x		=	
Possible Point Gain					
5. Current:		x		=	
Retake Expectation:		x		=	
Possible Point Gain					
TOTAL POINT DIFFERENCE					

Directions: Using Figure 42 Comparative Retake Analysis as a reference, enter current scores for potential retake entries and exercises. Calculate the potential point gain for each, based on raising the score to 2.75 or more.   Use this information, along with reflection on your areas of strength, to help you select entries or exercises to retake.

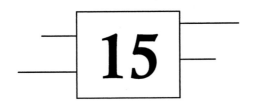

Advanced Candidacy

Featured Resources:

- Portfolio Instructions
- Standards

Most candidates are well aware that National Board Certification is considered a three-year process, and that many applicants will not be successful in the first year of candidacy. Nonetheless, when candidates are informed that they were not successful in their first attempt, most feel devastated.

In this chapter, we will discuss the feelings and issues faced by advanced candidates, and provide tools that may help you determine how to improve your performance when retaking one or more sections of the assessment.

Facing the Score that is Below 275

All candidates hope they are capable of achieving certification in the first year. When scores are released and they are faced with a score of less than 275, disappointment may make it seem impossible to read the score from the perspective of identifying areas for improvement. By doing so, however, candidates may acquire an informed perspective on the reasons for not achieving certification, and be empowered to make the necessary adjustments to their teaching or writing.

Although the NBPTS does not provide you with descriptive feedback on how to improve an entry, some conclusions can be drawn from reading your scores carefully, especially when coupled with a careful analytic review of your written work. The truth is that the score must be used as a tool or self-assessment if a candidate is to improve his score in the next certification cycle. When scores do not add up to the 275 that is the threshold for certification, it may be difficult to "read" a single score, or know how to approach the retake decision.

First, a candidate should see a score below 2.75 on a given section of the assessment as a potential area of improvement in the next year of the process. The score prompts you to re-read the standards, the core propositions, and the instructions for the entry.

In the previous chapter, we provided a chart to help you calculate which sections of the assessment might be retaken or resubmitted, but your decision really involves your understanding of how to teach and write to the entry to demonstrate evidence of the Standards. We recommend that you discuss your choices with your candidate support provider, who may be able to help you identify other considerations given your personal situation and areas of strength in your content area. Your decision involves much more than "doing the math" of the scores.

Before we ask you to look more critically at your work, let us first address the emotional aspects of your experience. The score report said simply that you did not provide sufficient evidence of accomplished teaching. It did not that your teaching is inadequate but, all the same, it feels like you have failed.

Dealing with a Sense of Failure

> *One November night, Michael Jordan and I found ourselves alone, and he told me about being cut as a sophomore from his high-school basketball team in Wilmington, NC "The day the cut list was going up, a friend—Leroy Smith—and I went to the gym to look together," Jordan recalled, "If your name was on the list, you made the team. Leroy's name was there, and mine wasn't. I went through the day numb. After school, I hurried home, closed the door to my room and cried so hard. It was all I wanted—to play on that team."*
>
> *- Bob Green, From Failure to Famous* [63]

Yes—we know! We say that the process alone is a worthwhile professional development experience, but when you find you have not (made the team) there is an inevitable sense of failure. It is particularly difficult when, among colleagues working together, some achieve and others do not. Most candidates feel confident about their teaching and many are high achievers who are accustomed to success at most anything they do. When they do not achieve National Board Certification in their first year, they may be so devastated that they distance themselves from the process completely. Hopefully, this does not describe you. It is natural and understandable to feel a sense of loss, but you can re-coup, regroup, and resume your journey. We hope you will think about the students in your classroom who struggle every day, that you will give yourself some time to recover from your sense of loss, and then return to the journey.

Because certification is a high-stakes venture, it is not unusual for unsuccessful candidates to experience an overwhelming sense of grief. Author and psychiatrist Elisabeth Kubler-Ross [64] has identified five stages of grief that can be applied to the advanced candidate's experience to help them better understand the process of coping with their feelings.

Stage One: Denial (this isn't happening to *me!*)

Candidates typically move through the stage of denial very quickly. Since you know that the score is a result of your work, this stage of grief is directly associated with your performance. Remember the feeling of putting the BOX in the mail? After months of work, you packed up pages of your reflective writing with videos, work samples, and other artifacts and shipped them off. It may have been hard to let go, because it felt like a piece of you was going with it. Maybe you struggled when the shipper asked to put a value on the box because to you, its value was beyond any price tag. When you received the unhappy news, and found your work was judged as less than accomplished, you may have felt that your very identity was found wanting. It is hard not to take the score report as a judgment of one's personal worth. Your candidate support provider will acknowledge your feelings while helping you move beyond your emotional response to see the score for what it is—a simple statement of fact.

Stage Two: Anger (*why* is this happening to me?)

In this stage, you might compare yourself to others who did achieve. You mentally sum up your individual talents, your writing abilities, and perhaps your students' achievements and look for reasons why you did not achieve certification when others did.

Support providers can remind you of your strengths and help you find those strengths in the entries that scored well. This stage is easiest (but not easy) when you and your candidate support provider have established a comfortable relationship. Candidates who try to navigate this phase alone may find it tough, as it is easy to be drawn into a downward spiral of self-doubt. If you have become involved in a new candidate support session before the score results are announced, it may help you prevent the feelings of isolation that often come with this stage. By building relationships with new candidates you may be already engaged in the professional dialogue that will ease you through this stage.

Stage Three: Bargaining (Just *tell me* what to do...)

In Stage Three, candidates often "bargain" by seeking validation or exemplars to show them what their work should look like to meet an accomplished performance. You may want your candidate support provider to judge and even attempt to score your writing to find an easy answer for the score that you received. You maybe tempted to seek out peers who have achieved and ask to read through their entries. You do not mean to be unethical but, in essence, you want to find an explicit solution for reaching the magic score of 275. You may want your candidate support provider to tell you which entry to retake.

The decision regarding retake entries is a personal one. Your support provider can help you weigh your choices, but the decision is yours alone. It is especially important that copies of entries that have been sent to NBPTS are not shared, as this is a violation of ethical candidate support.

Stage Four: Depression (I don't care anymore)

Stage Four is probably the most surprising for candidate support providers and for candidates, as it is often seen after one has reentered the process of certification. As an advanced candidate, you may need to make the decision to retake within a month of seeing your scores. You may do so readily, or after encouragement from your CSP, but in many cases you are still grappling with feelings of failure. You may have progressed through the first three steps of grief rather quickly, and not realize you are working through it.

Some candidates vigorously get back to work but then hit a snag, overcome by feelings of hopelessness. If the work you are doing feels the same and you do not know how to make improvements for a higher score you may feel overwhelmed and want to withdraw. Give yourself a chance to rest, and talk through your feelings with your CSP.

Disappointment...that is a word that is hard to appreciate until you live it. I did not pass my certification test, and I was crushed. The feeling was overwhelming...it encompassed all my emotions and I was so sad. I could not believe it! I kept wondering, maybe I had not studied the right stuff; maybe they did not score one section...I started thinking about all the money and time I had invested; this was something I worked hard for! And then I realized there was nothing I could do but put one foot in front of the other and move forward. I made an appointment to take the test again. This time I knew that no matter what, I was putting 100% of my energy in this – this was my goal, my only goal, and I was going to make it.

- Abby Joseph, NJ Physical Therapist

Stage Five: Acceptance (*I'm ready* for whatever comes)

When you reach the stage of acceptance—you are on your way! You have come through the fire, and you are stronger. Often, you will find that you are able to talk about your first writing and how your second writing is different. You may be willing to acknowledge what you should have done the first time and are more ready to seek support. You want to share advice with first-year candidates and are willing to let go of your writing to receive support.

It should be said that there are candidates who never get to this stage. They remain in the stage of anger or depression and disengage completely from the certification process or face new scores from this negative perspective. When you can separate your sense of worth as a person from the process of certification you are prepared for a productive quest to improve your evidence.

> *OK – I am through with my pity party. I had a tough week; I could not write, but now I am ready to get back to it.*
>
> *Advanced Candidate - New Jersey*

Recognizing and preparing for the stages of grief can help disappointed candidates know their feelings are normal and that recovery will come as they progress through each of the stages.

Exercise 15-1: Advanced Candidate's Reflection

In this exercise, you are asked to reflect on your feelings as discussed above. Use the exercise to think about the experience you have had as a candidate thus far, and determine if, when, and how you are ready to move forward. Identify the stage of grief you are in, and acknowledge that you are moving through a process that, if completed, will allow you to feel a sense of closure. Think about how you will feel if you choose to go forward with your candidacy, and how you will feel if you don't. Looking back on the process in 5 years, where would you like to be? How would you like to feel about your experience in the certification process?

Support and Improvement

As an advanced candidate, you have different questions and concerns than those approaching the National Board certification process for the first time. You understand the process and specifications for National Board Certification, but one or more of your assessment pieces lacked sufficient evidence to be scored as accomplished. As a second or third-year candidate, you do not want to repeat the process with the same level of understanding you had in your first year. What will be different this time? What changes are you willing to make the second or third time you attempt this process? Honest self-reflection in the following areas will help you determine a course of action that will help you to be successful in your pursuit of certification:

1. In my past year(s) as a candidate, did I fully commit myself to the process?

Often candidates enter the National Board Certification process and expect to carry on all their usual "above and beyond" activities. They are still coaching, leading professional development groups at school, and still managing home, church, and/or community activities. Are you one of these candidates? What are you willing to give up in order to successfully become a National Board Certified Teacher? If you are not able to make it a top priority for the time being, you cannot expect success.

2. Do I understand what I need to do? Do I "get it?"

In most cases, when candidates achieve scores significantly lower than the National Board Certification threshold of 275 points, they simply do not understand what they need to do. You must be able to demonstrate your *architecture of accomplished teaching* through evidence of the Standards for your certificate area. If you do not know what that means, you must reflect, dialogue, and study your resources until you do. If you have an entry that scored well (3.0 or above), compare it to the entry that was less than accomplished. Look for the essential elements that set it apart. Perhaps there is an NBCT whose entries scored well who would conference with you about your work.

3. Am I willing to accept support?

Many candidates who do not achieve National Board Certification in the first year have attempted it without support. Are you willing to seek support? Are you willing to allow an experienced candidate support provider to read your work and give you feedback? Can you make the time to become a member of a learning community focused on National Board Certification?

4. Do I have the skills, experience, and understanding I need?

Do you understand how to produce evidence of Standards through your writing? Did you thoroughly respond to the "why" or "how" portion of each prompt? Do you believe you are an accomplished teacher? If your entry does not reflect accomplished practices as described in the certificate Standards, you may need to take classes to improve your understanding and teaching strategies before attempting to re-submit an entry or retake an assessment center exercise.

Core Issues for Improvement

When a score comes back to a candidate that is less than the passing score of 275, there are two necessary issues to deal with.

Understand What is Assessed. You may need time to rest with the heavy news that your score is below the threshold for an accomplished performance but, remember, it is not your teaching that has been assessed, but your presentation of the evidence. The Written Commentary and documentation that you submitted did not show enough evidence for an accomplished performance. With that in mind, your task is to increase the amount of evidence that you present for scoring.

Determine How You Can Improve Your Performance. Often candidates think that just redoing an entry will give them a chance at a better score. You need to know that, when re-submitting the first score is erased, and is replaced by the newer score, whether it is higher or lower. If you have not determined what was lacking in your performance, you will not necessarily do better on the second attempt. Retaking an entry should not be a gamble. Some candidates have retaken an entry without analyzing their work and scored lower than on the first attempt.

When I received my scores back from the National Board, one of the areas in which I did not earn an accomplished score was integration of math and science. As I considered retaking the entry the hard question for me was: "Can I really do better here? Is my teaching of science and math strong enough to reach a higher score?"

Advanced Candidate - New Jersey

Exercise 15-2: Reflection on Your Entry

The template provided for Exercise 15-2 may help you see more clearly what is assessed in an entry, and how you may be able to improve your performance. As you reflect on each of the questions provided, you will be prompted to consider different aspects of your thinking and writing about an entry, and may be able to determine why a submitted entry did not receive a passing score.

Also consider the following:
- Did you choose students who allowed you to showcase the range of your teaching abilities?
- Did the video help verify evidence of the scoring criteria?
- Did you follow the suggested page length for each section in your Written Commentary? The suggested page lengths are cues to help you understand when to be concise and when to provide details to enhance your evidence.

Selecting Your Retake Sections

While it is important to "do the math" to determine which sections you might retake and/or how to proceed as a year-two or year-three candidate, this is not a decision to be made simply on the basis of a mathematical equation. To do so would be an overly simplistic method to determine how you will proceed in your next year of candidacy. To improve your scores, you must identify and reflect on your choices for re-submittal, identify the areas in which you need to improve, and target those in which you *can* improve. The following discussion is designed to prompt your thinking in this process.

Assessment Center Exercises

Was your content knowledge sufficient to answer the questions?
The assessment center asks you to apply content knowledge to teaching scenarios. If you had difficulty with the content, you may need to spend time studying, or even take a class to improve your content knowledge. Remember your content area may include subjects that you do not normally teach. Review the range in subject matter and developmental levels of students to better prepare for your assessment center questions.

Did you have difficulty responding in the timed test situation?
If you feel confident about content, but had difficulty responding within the given time frame, study the descriptions of your assessment center exercises and use the available tutorial. Sample exercises found in your Scoring Guide will show you the typical format for each question, and the nature of the prompt material. Try anticipating what a prompt might look

like and even try creating a few of your own to match the exercise descriptions. Most importantly, set up several sessions for yourself to practice responding to sample prompts in a timed situation so you learn how to 1) focus on the question, 2) organize your thoughts and response strategy, and 3) write quickly and concisely to answer the question.

Portfolio Entries

Read your scores: For entries that did not meet an accomplished performance, see Chapter 14: Scoring and review the scoring families to find where the entry was placed on the rubric. If the entry is eligible for a retake, your score is either in the family of one or two.

The Family of One. Your score is between .75 and 1.74. This means there was little or no evidence of the Standards in your entry.

The Family of Two. Your score is between 1.75 and 2.74. This means that there was limited evidence of the standards in your entry, or that the evidence was not clear, or convincing, or consistent.

When your entry has scored in the level one or level two scoring families, the score suggests that one or more critical aspects for an accomplished performance were missing. Exercise 15-2: Reflecting on Your Entry may help you identify the area(s) in need of improvement, while Exercises 15-3 and 15-4 can be used to help you "zoom in" on your targeted areas to think about how to provide the evidence needed in these areas.

Exercise 15-3: Selecting the Retake Entry

Use Exercise 15-3 to help you analyze your responses to specific aspects of the Level 4 Rubric for an entry you may retake. On the exercise template, you will select criteria from the Level 4 Rubric for which you believe more evidence is needed. These will be entered in the first box labeled "Standards."

In the next box, "My Writing," notate the evidence from your entry that addressed your selected criteria. In the box labeled "My Teaching," consider examples from your teaching that could be added to enhance your evidence if you choose to retake this entry. Finally, reflect on what is needed to raise your score on the retake.

Exercise 15-4: Finding the Big Ideas

Exercise 15-4 prompts you to respond with an even greater degree of detail. In this exercise, you are encouraged to find the big ideas embedded in the introductory pages of your portfolio entry instructions and in the Level 4 Rubric, reread your standards for these ideas, and describe your specific teaching practices that would help you provide evidence in your entry. For example, you might find that your entry instructions describe evidence of "student engagement through dialogue," or "use of various assessment methodologies." Re-read your Standards to find keywords and phrases for more information about these big ideas, and then analyze your Written Commentary to find your evidence.

Exercise 15-4: Finding the Big Ideas

We encourage you to use the exercises from this chapter and all previous chapters to help you plan, think, write and develop evidence in your retake entry. While you may not wish to attend support sessions with new candidates, find a CSP who will work with you to help you determine and improve your areas of need. Chapter 17, Providing Candidate Support has been written for CSPs to assist them in their work with advanced candidates. You also might benefit from reading this chapter and reviewing Exercise 17-2: Talking with an Advanced Candidate.

When you clearly understand what is being assessed and how you can improve your performance on an entry, you will be able to resume your work with confidence. We encourage you to move through your feelings of grief to reach the stage of acceptance, and then *choose* your status as an advanced candidate to deepen your study and understanding of an accomplished teaching performance.

In closing, we would like to remind you that many very successful people have had to overcome experiences of failure to reach their goals. Do you want to be a National Board Certified Teacher? The score you received is not about *you*, it is about *your evidence*. There is a wealth of resources and supporters at hand who want to help you improve and submit successful retake entries. What do you want? The ball is in your court.

Key Tips for Candidate Support Providers

- Support for advanced candidates begins at your first meeting with a new group of candidates, when you explain that National Board Certification is a three-year process for many teachers. In any candidate group it is more than likely that some members will not succeed in the first year of candidacy, and that some may need up to three years to achieve success.

- Bring in a NBCT who is willing to talk about the experience of being an advanced candidate. It is important for candidates to have a model for the role in the event they, too, enter advanced candidacy. These NBCTs will often stress the value of working with mentors and readers and urge candidates to do so.

- Celebrate the completion of the assessment requirements with your candidate group before the scores are announced, emphasizing the tremendous accomplishment of completion alone.

- In the few weeks before scores are announced, make contact with all candidates to reassure them of your support whatever their results. Ask them to let you know about the results as soon as they can, as scores are released only to candidates. A public announcement naming the new NBCTs will be released after a few days.

- Recognize that for many teachers, the lack of success is a huge blow. Teachers who strive for National Board Certification expect to achieve it. They have usually experienced a high degree of success in the past. Some candidates will experience a series of emotions often associated with grieving—denial, anger, and self-doubt—before they are able to "regroup" and begin the work of advanced candidacy. Some will choose not to go forward.

- After the public release of new NBCTs, call or write to your potential advanced candidates to reiterate the value of the work they have done, and to reassure them of your continued support. Give them time to make a decision about going forward.

- Hold a meeting to "debrief" with the advanced candidate group. This provides an opportunity to vent feelings, see they are not alone, and re-establish a sense of camaraderie with their peers. Offer to meet with each of them to review the score report and help select entries and/or exercises to be retaken.

Exercise 15-1: Advanced Candidate's Reflection

We know this is a difficult time for you—that you have experienced a great disappointment, but through this exercise we hope to keep you invested in your teaching. When the time is right and you are ready to continue your journey toward accomplished teaching, this may help you determine where to begin.

Am I a better teacher now? What skills and resources have I developed as a result of this process?

Research has found that 97% of teachers who engage in the certification process felt that it made them better teachers, regardless of whether or not they certified.

When I look at my scores, in which sections of the assessment did I do well? Where did I provide evidence of accomplished teaching?

Refer to Chapter 14: Scoring

When I look at my scores, where do I need to show more evidence of accomplished teaching? Is this issue in my content knowledge? In the way I write about my teaching? In my lesson design?

Refer to Exercise 15-2 to help answer this question.

What is my next step? Think deeply. Will I continue my journey? What would it take for me to do so? What will it feel like if I do not continue?

Where Am I Now?
Stages of Grief

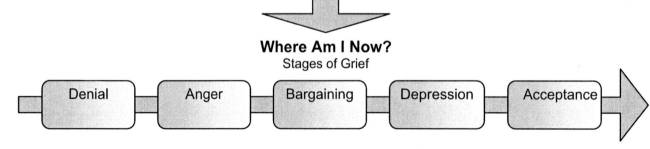

| Denial | Anger | Bargaining | Depression | Acceptance |

Directions: Use this exercise to think about the experience you have had as a candidate thus far, and determine if, when, and how you are ready to move forward.

Exercise 15-2: Reflection on the Entry

Entry #_____

Reflective Questions	Yes	Partially	No
1. Have I answered each and every prompt clearly and completely?			
2. Have I provided evidence for each of the scoring criteria (Level 4 Rubric)?			
3. Have I provided clear, convincing, and consistent evidence of meeting my Standards through multiple examples that focus on my specific practices on featured individuals as well as with groups of students?			
4. Are my goals for students clearly stated, specific, and assessable? Have I described exactly what students should know and be able to do as a result of my teaching in this instructional sequence?			
5. Is my architecture of accomplished teaching clearly visible? Have I aligned: • my contextual information to my goals for students? • my strategies to my selected goals? • my assessments to my selected goals? • my analysis of student learning to my selected goals? • AND have I provided a thoughtful reflection on my teaching in this instructional sequence?			
6. Have I captured "the big picture" of this entry as described by the introductory pages for the entry in my Portfolio Instructions?			

Directions: To determine where your original entry lacks evidence, reflect on and notate your level of response to each of the questions above. Identify the aspects of your writing that need to be improved for your next attempt at this entry.

Exercise 15-3: Selecting the Retake Entry

The Standards Select criteria from the Level 4 Rubric and list them here.	e.g., "Teacher prompts students' thinking"
My Writing *In my writing, I see…* Turn each aspect of the rubric into a question, and answer the question. This will help you to understand your score.	e.g., Where did I write about examples of how I prompt students' in my writing?
My Teaching *In my teaching, I do…* Ask yourself if there are things that you do, but did not include in your writing. This will help you to know if you can improve when re-writing this entry.	e.g. Do I prompt students' thinking when I teach? Did I miss an opportunity to write about a part of my teaching that I should have included? Think of a lesson, an example that is missing from your writing.
My Reflection On Retaking This Entry	☐ write more details of my teaching that are closer to the rubric ☐ think again about a better lesson that includes more examples of accomplished teaching as defined by the standards ☐ research the standards, talk to a content expert, find some articles, literature to better understand accomplished teaching through the eyes of the NBPTS. ☐ I know more about the standards than I included in my writing. ☐ I have seen that my writing did not include the evidence that was in my lesson. ☐ I have other lessons that I can do that are more evident of accomplished teaching.

Directions: Use this exercise to talk through an entry with an advanced candidate. This exercise should help an advanced candidate decide how to strengthen their writing and reflection to prepare for retaking an entry.

Exercise 15-4: Finding the Big Ideas

Your Entry	Your Score	Big Ideas to Revisit	Next steps		
			Study the big idea	Write again, with the standards embedded	Rewrite with a new lesson, different evidence

Key Words from the Standards	Finding the Evidence
The language of the standards	*Match your writing to the language of the standards*

Directions: Use this template to help you identify and consider your evidence for big ideas described in the Introduction and in the Level 4 Rubric for an entry. Reread your Standards to find key words and phrases related to these big ideas, and then analyze your Written Commentary to find your evidence.

16

Building the Professional Community

The Five Core Propositions

So, you have sent off the portfolio exercises and you have completed your assessment center tasks. **Congratulations**! You are done with the National Board Certification process for this school year. How do you feel? Can you say it was worth the work no matter what your score results? You will have plenty of time to reflect on your response to that question and time also to reflect in general about your experience as you wait for news of your score. You are now a "candidate in waiting" (as in "waiting for your score report"). This chapter will ask you to think about your next steps, and what comes after the process of National Board Certification.

Imagine you have joined a group whose challenge is to climb a mountain that is three years high, the total time a candidate has to achieve National Board Certification. Some of your colleagues took a look at the mountain and shook their heads, deciding it was not for them. You joined the group willingly, even though you knew the climb would be high and rigorous. It was an exciting opportunity to put yourself to the test. As you traveled together, the members of your group helped support one another, even though the journey was fundamentally an individual challenge and an individual learning experience.

Some climbers in your group moved quickly and will reach the peak of the mountain in the first year. Others worked hard, but will not make it to the top in their first attempt. Accustomed to success, they may be devastated at the news. Some of these will turn back, feeling that they put forth their best, and that reaching the top is simply not worth any more effort. Others will rest and recover from their disappointment. They will review their scores, re-examine the terrain, and renew their determination to reach the top in their second or third year of candidacy. Their climb will be slower, but their knowledge of the mountain will undoubtedly be more thorough.

We have met many teachers who chose to take this journey. We know teachers who have attained National Board Certification in their first year, others who persevered for a second and third year to reach success, and many who made an initial attempt, but gave up along the way. We also know candidates who despite their retakes and reflections have not attained the external distinction of accomplished teacher. Is it simply not possible for some? What have these teachers gained at the end of the journey? Will their teaching practices improve as a result of their experience?

I don't know if I am going to achieve certification, but I know that I can continue to pursue that goal. I do know this: My conversation around teaching is changed. I reflect in specific ways regarding my students and I evaluate my presentation in terms of student achievement...this has caused me to really think about how what I am teaching is meeting the needs of my students...

- Shirley Allen, NBCT New Jersey
Written as a candidate in waiting.

We truly believe that National Board Certification is attainable for any teacher who strives to meet the Standards and seeks professional improvement through reflective practice and collegial relationships. However, some candidates will embark on the journey prematurely. One does not set out to climb a mountain without knowing the terrain and conditions, and without first acquiring the needed conditioning, skills, and appropriate gear. Attitude is important, but it is not enough.

Readiness for National Board Certification is determined by acquiring an understanding of the task and then making sure you have the experience, skills, and resources to be successful. It is important to have adequate support and guidance so that you do not struggle unnecessarily.

We are also convinced that teachers who take the journey, successful or not, will be stronger as a result. Certification is a by-product of the new journey that has just begun for anyone who has been part of the National Board Certification process. The heart of this new journey lies in the understanding of the *architecture of accomplished teaching* and the opportunity for continued dialogue with fellow professionals.

Moving Forward

*The competent, caring, and qualified teacher is foremost
a developing person.*

- The Life Cycle of a Career Teacher[65]

Describe, analyze, and reflect. You will either achieve National Board Certification this year, or not. In either case, you have completed a rigorous process of self-analysis and you have learned the skills of reflective practice. You are to be commended for this outstanding achievement.

We believe that teachers' work with students will continue to improve as a result of the National Board Certification process. Whatever their skill level, the experience starts teachers on a new trajectory—a path on which their purpose is clearer, their efforts more focused, with constant reflection as the impetus for on-going teaching improvement and increased student learning.

> *I've learned that there is an NBCT process and then there is me. I have caught only a glimpse of the tip of that NBC mountain that I am attempting to scale, but now I have a clearer understanding of The Five Core Propositions and Standards that hold the mountain up and the process that I will use to climb that mountain. The funny part is that mountain is actually me and I am not scaling it, but molding and sculpting myself to become an accomplished teacher. What I've learned so far in this journey is that though the NBCT process is immense and challenging, I just need to take it one step at a time and keep reminding myself that getting certified is not the end all. It will just validate that I am on the right path to becoming an accomplished teacher.*
>
> *- Merry Blechta, precandidate Hawaii 2006*

In the ever-expanding world of knowledge, no teacher will ever learn all there is to know. Among the ranks of newly-certified NBCTs, different levels of ability are represented—from those who "got it' from the beginning and scored at 3.5 and above on nearly every entry, to those who struggled to understand and made the minimum passing score by the skin of their teeth after one or more attempts. Among a group of candidates, there may be only slight differences in scores between those who successfully achieve National Board Certification and those who do not. What is success? If reduced solely to a number of points on a scale, it seems an empty achievement. When teachers routinely use reflective thinking skills and consciously work at teaching to the Standards, instructional practices that lead to improved student learning are the true measures of success. Reflective practice within the context of a learning community is the key for teachers to maintain excellence in the course of their careers.

At the National Board facilitator training we were told about a research study that showed NBCTs who had attained Certification with high scores (in the Level 4 range) demonstrated superior classroom performance compared to teachers who had attempted, but not achieved, National Board Certification (NBPTS Validation Study: A Distinction That Matters). I felt instantly doubtful, knowing that, although I was an NBCT, I was not a member of that highest-scoring group. Then a woman in the back of the room raised her hand and said words to this effect: "I may not have earned my Certification with the highest scores, but come and take a look at me in a couple of years—I've only just begun!" Murmurs of agreement sounded from many other NBCTs in the room. I will be forever grateful that this woman voiced for all of us the power of the process. Meeting the Teaching Standards in your practice is a lifelong professional journey.

- Bess

The Message

The condition for membership in the community is that one learns, continues to learn, and supports the learning of others.

- Roland Barth[66]

What is the message to your fellow teachers and to the community in general? We believe that it is, to paraphrase Roland Barth, that accomplished teachers learn, continue to learn, and support the learning of others. Whether you successfully achieve a passing score in your present cycle of certification or not, this is the message we hope you will carry forward.

Having completed the process of National Board Certification, many eyes will be on you. As a candidate waiting for scores, this is a time for contemplation about what you have learned, what value it holds for you, and what you might say to curious colleagues who have not yet ventured forth on the same path. Are you in a better place to serve your students than you were when you started? Can you recommend the process to others? Are the National Board Standards and assessment significant contributions to the teaching profession?

When scores are released, if not sooner, you will face questions from others: Fellow teachers, potential candidates, supervisors and your family members may all ask you about the process. They may want to know why you decided to do it and what you learned. Like it or not, you will be a representative for National Board Certification with a message about what it means to the profession.

We encourage all candidates who have completed the process to plan for this role and prepare a response to the inevitable questions that will be asked. Think about what you have learned and how it will impact your teaching; think about how your portfolio work compares to other professional development experiences you have had; think about what it would look like for all teachers to complete a portfolio entry and engage in the dialogue of the Standards. Think about the power of the process, regardless of whether National Board Certification is achieved.

> *The time is right, students deserve no less, and the teaching*
> *profession can retain and renew its members, consistent with a*
> *vision of excellence across a lifetime of practice.*

> *- The Life Cycle of a Career Teacher*[67]

Delivering the Message

Delivering "the message" is an important aspect of marketing in the business world, and an important aspect of your communications with your colleagues and others. Like all good sound bytes, it should be succinct and memorable. Author Malcolm Gladwell (*The Tipping Point*, 2004) [68] describes three key elements for an effective message:

1. Identify the recipients: Target "connectors" or key people to hear your message. Think about well-regarded teachers in your school or principals who are willing to encourage their teachers to engage in the process. Talk to business representatives or legislators who may leverage funding sources about the importance of candidate support as one way to support education reform.

2. Make the message "sticky": Be sure that the message will stay with the person who hears it. Think about the audience, and provide the information that will be most meaningful to them.

3. Consider the context and timing of your message: Teachers may not be receptive to hearing about a process that involves time and hard work at the end of a faculty meeting. Parents are unlikely to read a lengthy note describing your certification experience and

Creating Your Message

Questions	Target Audience	Insert The Five Core Propositions in Your Response	Create Your Sound Byte
Consider questions such as the following:	Administrators, Other Teachers, Parents, School Board, Community members.	Which of the propositions is important for this audience to hear?	What will you say?
Why did you do this?	Other Teachers	(IV) Think systematically	*I wanted to know more about my teaching, my strengths, and areas that I needed to consider more deeply. I learned a lot about myself as a teacher.*
What did you learn from this process?	Other teachers Community Members	(V) Members of learning communities (IV) Think systematically	*I learned through the process that connecting to families and their resources improved my classroom teaching.* *The process enabled me to think deeply about my teaching, as an individual and with a group of colleagues.*
How has this changed your teaching?	Parents Community Members	(I) Knowledge of students (II) Knowledge of subject	*My teaching is stronger because I think deeply about my students as individuals.* *My knowledge of content is stronger because I delve deeply into my topics and relate them to topics of interest for these students.*
What is different about your classroom?	Administrator	(III) Manage and monitor student learning	*I have thought deeply about how my classroom climate encourages learning. I have purposefully arranged my lessons and my materials to meet the needs of varying levels of students in the classroom.*
Why should I pursue/support NB Certification?	Administrator Other Teachers	(I) Knowledge of student (IV) Think systematically	*Teachers who think and write with the core propositions in mind know more about their students and their subject* *Teacher who write and reflect on their teaching think systematically about improving student learning.*

Figure 50: Creating Your Message.
Sample answers to questions for candidates-in-waiting, new NBCTs, or new Advanced Candidates, are presented here. These answers promote understanding of the National Board for Professional Teaching Standards and the certification process as an important contribution to the teaching profession.

how it has strengthened your classroom. Think about the best time and place for each audience to hear the message. Refer to Figure

50 (Creating Your Message) and Exercise 16-1 at the end of this chapter to help you prepare responses for different audiences.

Preparing for the Score Release

As the score release date draws closer, it is important for you to anchor yourself by acknowledging the value of the process, be prepared to accept your results, and once again be prepared to talk about the importance of the experience you have had. When scores are released, you will be able to privately access your account to see your results. These will be delivered by way of a simple sentence along with your tabulated score report. It will state *"Congratulations, you have shown evidence of accomplished teaching"* or *"You have not shown evidence of accomplished teaching."* It is important to note that there is no value judgment about you as a teacher. It is a simple statement of fact about the work that was submitted.

As a candidate for National Board Certification, you have taken part in a high stakes, often public, arena to describe your teaching practices in reference to the highest Standards for the profession. When the scores are released, there may be a flurry of activity around you and other candidates in your state or district. You may or may not be successful on this particular release date, and should be prepared to respond again to the questions that will be asked: What did the experience mean to you? Why was it significant, even if you are not successful? Why is it significant if you were?

After the Scores: The Advanced Candidate

When your scores do not meet the threshold needed for National Board Certification, you will be referred to as an "advanced candidate." This title assumes that you will continue the process and resubmit portions of the assessment in the next cycle. Many people will ask "Will you continue?" and "Why?" Why would you want to keep going? How can you put forth more effort after already spending over a year of your time and energy?

All advanced candidates will be faced with these questions at a personal and public level, as they consider whether or not to resume the journey toward certification. Even when they make the decision to resubmit, advanced candidates will in some way be called on to defend their decision to re-enter the process.

If you do not achieve, it may be hard not to dwell on feelings of despair, but instead, consider how you can convey the message of accomplished teaching, even though you did not immediately reach your goal. Start by remembering why you entered the process, and emphasize your personal and professional growth, new ways of thinking about your teaching and, most of all, the impact it has had on your work with students.

According to one research study, 98% of teachers who have completed the process state that it is the "best professional development that I have ever experienced." Teachers who pursue National Board Certification show significant improvements in their teaching practices, regardless of whether they achieved certification.[69]

Although you did not meet your goal in the current cycle, remember that advanced candidates often delve even more deeply into the Standards and the architecture of their teaching. You will continue to engage in meaningful professional growth for your personal benefit as well as that of your students.

> *My principal came by and saw my classroom. He asked me what I had been doing. I told him a little bit about the process of National Board Certification that I had been involved with for over a year. He told me that he could see the difference in my teaching—keep doing it. When he noticed how my classroom practice had changed, it gave me an opportunity to talk to him about the process of certification. Even though it took me another year to achieve certification, the visit inspired him to support the process with financial support and professional development release time.*
>
> *- Michael Breslow, NBCT New Jersey*

After the Scores: The New NBCT

After the tremendous investment of time and energy, it feels wonderful to hear the good news and know that you have achieved National Board Certification. However, there can be another side to the experience of being a new NBCT, and you should be prepared to respond appropriately. Some teachers who achieve find that colleagues respond to them differently. Some report that fellow faculty members feel threatened by their new status. Others report that they are suddenly viewed as an "expert."

When the list of newly certified NBCTs is publicly released, new NBCTs in many districts may find themselves at the center of a media blitz. It is an opportune time to deliver a succinct message about the role of the National Board Teaching Standards in advancing the teaching profession. Your message as a new NBCT has a potential to develop more support in your district, school. or community and to encourage more teachers to pursue certification. Use this moment, while you are in the public eye, to mobilize leaders in your community to provide support for the certification process.

As a new NBCT, it is most fitting to communicate your pleasure in respect to having achieved a personal goal. Certification is an opportunity available to virtually every teacher, and by focusing on your growth in the process rather than your status as a new NBCT, you may encourage others to consider pursuing the same goal. Emphasize the positive aspects of the process rather than describing it in terms of the many hours that were spent writing and re-writing entries. Above all, maintain positive relationships with your fellow teachers. Collegiality among professionals, regardless of certification, encourages rich dialogue that benefits all teachers and students.

> *... I find myself recruiting other teachers who are new to the process and encouraging those who were not successful the first time around to try again. I let the advanced candidates know that there is hope the second time around. ... I want them to join me in defining accomplished teaching.*
>
> *-Christine Rodek, NBCT New Jersey*

The Learning Community

> *...because the teacher culture is relatively more stable over time, long-term teachers have more opportunities than short-term principals do to shape what people in the school community believe, say, and do.*
>
> *-Patterson and Patterson[70]*

The National Board for Professional Teaching Standards has redefined the profession, and the process you have completed has undoubtedly redefined you as a teacher. You cannot return to your classroom, close the door, and teach your students in isolation. This experience is a beginning rather than an end. If you have been a solitary practitioner in the past, your future should be different. It is important to carry the professional learning community experience forward as an integral part of your practice.

Learning communities take many forms. They may be found within the school staff, at university classes, by way of informal teacher inquiry groups, and through partnerships with the families of students. When *teachers are members of learning communities*, they are enriched by diverse perspectives on teaching and learning and are prompted to *think systematically about their practice and learn from experience*.

> *The whole process taught me how to objectively look at my teaching and find ways to make it better. Since this process began, my work has been more reflective. My standards are higher, and my outlook more positive. I have also met a group of outstanding teachers that I might not have gotten to know otherwise.*
>
> *- Colleen Collins, NBCT Hawaii*

As a result of the National Board Certification experience you have a new contribution to make to your classroom, in your school, in your community, and ultimately in the profession as a whole. Through your work on Entry 4: Documented Accomplishments: Contributions to Student Learning, you have had an opportunity to review your past work with learning communities to improve student achievement. Now, it is time to reflect on what you will do next. As a learner, partner, leader, or collaborator, your continued professional growth rests on your interactions with others in one or more of the many forums available to you at your school or beyond.

Teacher Leadership

> *If teachers wish to transform accountability from a set of policies "done to" teachers and students to a constructive influence on teaching and learning, then teachers must take the lead in the systematic documentation of their practices in teaching and curriculum, and the relationship of those practices to student achievement. A growing number of teachers who have pursued certification through the National Board for Professional Teaching standards (NBPTS) have already made such systemic observation and reflection a regular part of their professional practice*
>
> *-DarlingHammond & Sykes[71]*

School administrators have long been regarded as the leaders in the field of education and it has been a tradition for teachers to move out of the classroom and into the ranks of administrators in order to lead. However, the topic of teacher leadership has begun to appear in professional literature with increasing frequency. Across the nation, the need for school improvement is urgent and principals cannot be expected to do the job alone. The National Board Teaching Standards provide a vision of *what teachers should know and be able to do* for all educators, uniting and empowering teachers to lead the profession from within.

Leading does not necessarily mean heading up a formal organization. Teacher leaders may be found in formal roles such as department head or curriculum developer, or through their informal assistance to colleagues and their ability to influence the school culture. Your voice is especially important in discussions involving school reform, where short-term solutions are often selected over longer-term investments in teacher professional development.

Whether mentoring a new colleague or taking the lead on school reform, teachers are encouraged to use the opportunities naturally offered within a school to affect change, contribute to student learning and build resiliency in the face of challenging circumstances. Being a teacher leader means reaching beyond the walls of one's own classroom, working within a larger learning community, and impacting the fundamental culture of the school.

Your experience has left you better informed about your profession and practices. Be willing to share what you have learned. When teachers speak out together, their voices will be stronger, and they will be more readily heard as advocates for students and for better learning conditions. Collectively teachers have a huge impact on the profession by promoting opportunities that lead more of their colleagues to accomplished teaching practices.

Use the skills you have learned in the process of National Board Certification to invigorate your teaching, nurture others, and contribute to the profession. Find the teacher leader within yourself as you move forward in your work with and for students.

Reaching the Teaching Standards

At the beginning of this book, we asked you to generate a list describing the qualities of an accomplished teacher, and then connect those qualities to The Five Core Propositions. It was not difficult to do. Apart from National Board Certification, recent studies suggest that characteristics described in The Five Core Propositions contribute to the effectiveness as well as to the professional longevity of many teachers.

In separate studies of teachers recognized for excellence, two researchers identified similar dispositions. Concerned with the issue of retaining good teachers in urban public schools, Professor Sonia M. Nieto studied the question *What Keeps Teachers Going?* in conversations with exemplary teachers. Among other things, she found that the teachers believed in their ability to shape the future by impacting the lives of their students.[72] In *Why Great Teachers Stay*, Jackie S. Williams writes of the "courage, resiliency, flexibility, and hopefulness" revealed through her interviews with another group of outstanding teachers.[73]

In both studies, teachers were deeply *committed to students and their learning*. Their care and belief in students as individuals was demonstrated through high expectations for each one. They believed that their efforts made a difference in students' lives.

Williams refers to the teachers as life-long learners with a "burning need" for intellectual stimulation, who endlessly searched for new approaches to help students learn, while Nieto describes their engagement in the "intellectual work" of teaching. Both groups were characterized by their involvement in professional activities. They took classes, taught classes, mentored new teachers, actively participated in professional organizations, and engaged in reflective practice. They were members of learning communities, clearly dedicated to improving their knowledge of the *subjects they teach and how to teach those subjects to students.*

The Five Core Propositions provide you with a structure and a beacon for accomplished teaching practices that are sure to bring more focus, higher achievement, and greater satisfaction in your work with students. Great teachers keep going because they believe passionately in what they do and constantly renew their professional expertise through participation in the learning community.

Closing Thoughts

Learning communities sustain educators through the inevitable ups and downs of teaching and prompt them to reflect in new ways. They are critical for professional growth and the empowerment of teachers.

As a result of the National Board Certification experience you have a new contribution to make to your classroom, in your school, in your community, and ultimately in the profession as a whole. The journey that began with individual reflection continues with the vision for a stronger professional community, enhanced one teacher at a time.

Find your own path for teacher leadership and continued professional growth in your journey of accomplished teaching. The National Board Standards beckon you forward and light your way along the path.

We education leaders can find our way through these tough times by understanding that we are not powerless—that, indeed, we hold power to make decisions that profoundly influence, for good or ill, the lives of teachers and students in our schools.

-Carolyn M. Shields[74]

Key Tips for Candidate Support Providers

Candidates often think of the portfolio submission or the assessment center as the final part of the certification process. Actually, the process may be over in terms of work submitted, but for most candidates the span of time between completion of the assessment and the score release is an important time for personal reflection. Though the process of certification is over, candidates will face questions and comments about their experience in the process.

- CSPs can help teachers reflect productively in the "candidate-in-waiting" phase by preparing them ahead with questions that prompt them to think about the positive aspects of the process. Ask candidates what they have learned, how they have become stronger teachers, how their work in the process has affected their work with students. Refer to Figure 50 (Creating Your Message) and Exercise 16-1 in this chapter to help candidates be prepared to discuss the certification process.

- Candidates readily offer horror stories about the process, including the number of hours spent teaching and writing, the collection of artifacts, the pain and suffering of seeing themselves on video, etc. While it can be a bonding experience to share such stories within the group, it may be damaging to carry them to curious teachers contemplating the process. As a CSP, refocus the conversation on The Five Core Propositions and encourage candidates to reflect and prepare to share favorable comments with their colleagues. Spending time Creating Your Message, Exercise 16-1 will help candidates to stress the positive aspects of the process and be prepared to explain the process as a rich professional development experience. Read ahead to Chapter 17, Exercise 17-1 for an additional worksheet to use with candidates.

- One strategy that an author of this book, MaryAnn, uses is to have candidates write themselves a letter on the first day of support sessions. The question: Why have I decided to pursue National Board Certification? When the unopened letter is returned to them after the assessment is completed, it reminds them of their reasons for entering the process and shows them how far they have traveled on this particular professional journey.

Exercise 16-1: Creating Your Message

Questions Consider questions such as the following:	Target Audience Administrators, Other Teachers, Parents, School Board, Community members.	Insert The Five Core Propositions in Your Response *Which of the propositions is important for this audience to hear?*	Key Points for Your Sound Byte *What will you say?*
Why did you do this?			
What did you learn from the process?			
How has this changed your teaching?			
What is different about your classroom?			
Why should I pursue/ support NB Certification?			

Directions: Use this template to create a message for different audiences about your professional development experience during the National Board Certification Process. Your goal is to convince others that the NBPTS Standards and certification process is a valuable professional development opportunity, embedded in classroom practice and focused on improving student learning.

17

Providing Candidate Support

Featured Resource:

Guide for Ethical
Candidate Support

While the rest of this book has been written primarily for candidates, this chapter has been written especially for the candidate support provider (CSP). Whether you are new or experienced as a candidate support provider, we highly recommend that you participate in the CSP training offered by the National Board as a foundation for your work. The training will help you better understand the perspective of the NBPTS. It will also give you more insight into the certification process and portfolio requirements. To find training and resources for candidate support providers, contact the NBPTS and/or an existing support program in your area.

Providing support to candidates is both rewarding and demanding. Candidates and supporters will work together for a period of one to three years, and often develop lasting professional relationships as they travel the path toward National Board Certification together. As a CSP you must recognize that your relationship with the candidate is at least a year in duration. Therefore, it is important to consider how you can best support a candidate, and also to consider your boundaries in doing so.

The Five Core Propositions for Providing Support

You may be a reader, a group facilitator, or a CSP working individually with one or more teachers. In either case, we recommend you consider The Five Core Propositions for accomplished teaching as a guide for your work with candidates:

1. **Teachers are committed to students and their learning.**
   How well do you know your individual student-candidate(s)? Are they well prepared for the National Board Certification process? Have they had experience at analytical and reflective practice? Do they understand the time commitment involved? What are their learning preferences and needs? Are you both clear about the nature of your support to them?

2. **Teachers know the subjects they teach and how to teach those subjects to students.**
   What is the area of expertise you can offer to the candidate(s)? Are you experienced in the National Board Certification process? If not, do you need more information? Are you aware of resources available to help you and your candidate(s)? Do you understand the limitations of the support you are able to offer?

3. **Teachers are responsible for managing and monitoring student learning.**
   Have you provided the most current and accurate information to candidate(s)? Have you helped them find useful resources? Do you seek feedback from your candidates and check to make sure their needs are being addressed? Have you established effective communication systems with and among your students?
   Although candidates will bear responsibility for their performance on the NBPTS assessment, like any good teacher, facilitators should periodically check student understanding to make sure teaching is effective. Candidate support providers who facilitate groups should seek feedback from participants to manage and monitor their progress. Facilitators may also help candidates find experienced readers who can give them feedback as they draft their entries.

4. **Teachers think systematically about their practice and learn from experience.**
   As a candidate support provider, do you reflect on your work and constantly try to improve your interactions with candidates? Does your understanding of an accomplished performance on the NBPTS assessment continue to grow?

5. **Teachers are members of learning communities.**
   Do you network with other candidate support providers? Do you take part in professional networks/support systems in your area? Do you stay abreast of new information from NBPTS? Do you participate in training opportunities for candidate support providers?

Your context in working with candidates may determine the nature of your support to them, but it will still be up to you to set your boundaries for the relationship. These boundaries may be influenced by your understanding of the NBPTS *Guide for Ethical Candidate Support,* by the number of candidates with whom you choose to work, and the amount of time you have available. Most important, however, is that you clearly establish and reiterate that the responsibility for the writing and development of the entries and assessments for National Board Certification process belongs to each candidate individually.

Working with candidates can become very "sticky" without this constant reminder to both parties. There will always be candidates who want you to be responsible for their success or lack of success, and there will be those who will cause you to feel badly when you simply do not have the time or energy to read their work for them. When you read candidates' work, they will want you to reassure them that it is worthy of a passing score.

CSPs must refrain from advising candidates to make changes to an entry and must never attempt to predict how well it will score. Such actions are inappropriate to the National Board Certification process. Throughout support sessions, it is wise to reiterate that the candidate alone is responsible for the final portfolio entry.

On the other hand, candidates need encouragement throughout the National Board Certification process, which is long and hard at times, particularly just before the deadline. CSPs combine the roles of cheerleader and coach in their feedback to candidates. It is important to acknowledge candidates' growth, even if they still have a long way to go. "*Your description is clearly focused on the question*" or "*I see much more detail in your analysis section*" are helpful and encouraging, while comments such as "*This is definitely a four*" or "*This is a great response,*" send the CSP into the role of an assessor. The *worst* thing a CSP can do is to offer a comment that sounds like a score.

Setting the Stage for Group Sessions

The learning community is an important aspect of the certification process, as it is through sharing, dialogue, and reflection that teachers have opportunities to consider new perspectives and methods in their teaching. In any group there will likely be a variety of personalities, philosophies, and styles of teaching, and it is important that the climate is one of acceptance for all. When the CSP directs the discussion to the teaching standards, rather than to any particular style of teaching, candidates are encouraged to concentrate on their instructional choices, their assessments, and their use of instructional resources as they focus on improving student learning.

The learning community is framed as a dialogue among peers, and it is important to build a sense of interdependence among participants rather than encouraging dependence on you as the support provider. You have expertise to share, but the responsibility for the learning rests with each individual.

The Environment

A comfortable learning environment where candidates feel physically and psychologically at ease is an important aspect of support sessions. Groups do not always have the choice of where to work, as they may be offered an available room in a school or district. As a support provider, consider whether you can rearrange the furniture to facilitate dialogue. A large U-shaped set up may work well with a relatively small group, while a larger group might be seated at several smaller tables. This enables candidates to share their work and their writing. Think about how you want candidates to talk together, and then utilize the room to the best of your ability for flow and comfort. Let the room invite the kind of conversation that you want candidates to engage in during your support sessions.

If possible, personalize the space with candidate-made posters. Colorful descriptions of The Five Core Propositions created early in a support session series can be re-taped to the wall for subsequent sessions as graphic reminders of the group's work and "home-base" for support sessions. Lighting, room temperature, and parking are other aspects to consider if you have choice of facilities.

You may also want to consider the availability of technology as you select or prepare your space. A connection to the Internet will provide you with easy access to the NBPTS website during support sessions. Candidates may also want to use laptops during work sessions to take notes or complete writing exercises.

Refreshments

Refreshments are part of most support sessions, and sharing food can help build a sense of community. Teachers often come to sessions on the run between other commitments or after a full day of teaching, and are grateful for a bite to eat. While you might bring refreshments to the first session, encourage participants to determine how food will be provided at subsequent sessions. Teachers often create sign-up sheets and take turns bringing snacks for the group. From the beginning, encourage the group participants to take ownership of logistical tasks like this, as part of an overall sense of ownership and responsibility.

Trust and Risk

The strength of the learning community will rest in sharing and dialogue about teaching and learning. The quality of the dialogue depends on the degree of trust established among group members as they become acquainted through activities in the first few support sessions. As deeper levels of reflection are explored in subsequent sessions, self-esteem and ego are on the line. How will you create a climate of trust and support among group members? Here are few suggestions:

- Build in short "ice breakers" to help members learn more about one another and discover common interests.
- Integrate "quick write" exercises or activities with small group sharing.
- Imbed frequent "think-pair-share" moments with questions pertinent to the session topic.
- Periodically, take a "temperature check" of the group by asking each member to describe how they are feeling about the process, what progress they have made, what challenge they are currently facing, etc.
- Start or end the session with a simple open-ended question to be shared with a partner or in a small group.
  - ◆ Opening questions: Where are you right now? How are you feeling?
  - ◆ What did you do this week? What was one success that you had since we last met?
  - ◆ Closing questions: What is your next step? What one thing did you hear today that you will use this week? What did you hear tonight that you want to remember?

Between sessions, maintain communications with a quick e-mail or phone conversation to help candidates to stay connected and to address any feelings of anxiety that may develop.

Stating the Purpose

The purpose of the group is to study, internalize, and discuss evidence of the National Board Teaching Standards in authentic classroom practices. If the group is being held in the context of a course or series of classes for credit, any additional purpose is clearly established and agreements are included as part of the course syllabus and grading criteria. If not, it is important that the purpose is explicitly stated to the group members.

The members of the group may determine its purpose. Is it a group of active candidates only? Pre-candidates only? Teachers seeking professional development for re-licensing purposes? A mixture of members with different goals? Candidate-only groups will be focused on support intended to help members achieve the extrinsic benefit of National Board Certification. Members of non-candidate teacher study groups seek the intrinsic benefits of studying the Standards. When a group includes members of both types, it is particularly important that the support provider define its purpose.

While active candidates often begin the process for the extrinsic rewards of recognition and/or financial benefits, it has been our experience that they invariably make a shift during the course of the process, and intrinsic motivation takes hold. That being said, it is challenging to meet the needs of both candidates and non-candidates in a single group, as candidates keenly feel the pressure involved in completing the high stakes assessment.

Establishing Ground Rules

Ground rules for support sessions are extremely important. They will be discussed in more detail later in the chapter but, to begin the discussion here, the first and foremost expectation for productive group sessions is that participants must write in order to provide subject matter for dialogue and reflection at each group session. (See Chapter 2: Support Systems.) When teachers arrive at sessions week after week having done no reading, reflecting, or writing about the Standards, dialogue about reflective practice is significantly limited. One cannot learn to swim without putting a foot in the water and practicing some strokes. Likewise, reflective writing pieces are the "strokes" that help participants develop as accomplished practitioners.

Reflection must be based on work with students and reading about the Standards. Participants are expected to read, teach, reflect, and write; to record evidence of their teaching practices through student work samples and video; and to bring these artifacts to sessions to help foster the growth of all participants. When teachers repeatedly come to sessions unprepared, they often inhibit progress in the entire group. Without reflection and writing, their questions continue to be ambiguous rather than specific. They do not show growth between sessions, and tend to take the facilitator's time away from those who are ready to move to deeper understandings.

The Role of the Candidate Support Provider

By definition, the CSP must be knowledgeable about the National Board Certification process. Hopefully, he or she has participated in the NBPTS Candidate Support Provider training to review and personalize the NBPTS *Policy for Ethical Candidate Support* to gain a better understanding of his or her role in working with candidates. The support provider will show teachers how to use available resources and materials, how to "unpack" and respond effectively to their entry questions, and prompt them to improve analytical and reflective thinking. Often, one of the first challenges for a CSP is to help candidates make the shift from "what I am teaching" to "what my students are learning."

As a Guide

Candidate support providers need not be experts on every certificate, but can help direct candidates to appropriate resources. It is important to establish from the beginning that candidates are responsible for their own learning, and should attempt to seek answers to their questions from NBPTS before asking the CSP. Even when you are able to answer candidates' questions, if the information can be found in the NBPTS materials, refrain from answering and direct them instead to the appropriate section or resource. It is important that they become familiar with the NBPTS website, read their portfolio instructions thoroughly, and refer to these often during the course of the portfolio work. This sends to the candidate a strong message of personal ownership for the process and the product of certification. When information cannot be found from other sources, candidates should be encouraged to use the NBPTS candidate support services, described on the website.

Participants must feel that their time is well spent at support sessions, and the CSP must maintain control of the content, use of time, and direction of the dialogue to insure that they are of maximum benefit to all. Sessions are often a combination of brief presentations followed by exercises and/or sharing of reflections. As teachers begin to teach and write to their entries, drafts and videos may be shared for feedback and discussion. Any activities not directly related to portfolio development, such as ice-breakers, should be minimized. This includes conversations about school events or circumstances, and particularly to venting of frustrations about situations beyond a teacher's control.

As a Facilitator

Another aspect of the CSP's role is to insure that participants contribute equally to discussions about accomplished teaching practices, and to remind participants that there are many different approaches. It is important to hear the voices of all teachers, both the confident and the less certain. Minority opinions may prompt others to think critically about their practices and consider new perspectives.

When there are differences in views and in comfort levels regarding group sharing, dialogue is encouraged and all contributions should be honored and respected. If discussions become one sided or evaluative, the CSP might step in to refocus teachers' questions and responses. Skillful CSPs direct teachers back to the Standards to seek validation of the choices they make, and emphasize that candidates are responsible for their own choices and evidence specific to their own teaching practices.

As they encourage reflection and dialogue, CSPs deliberately prompt and sometimes challenge thinking through carefully layered questions that guide candidates to think more deeply. Their role is to balance support, provide an appropriate degree of challenge, and prompt professional vision.

Working with Candidates

The CSP will illustrate key components of the process and will help candidates develop new skills through their participation in the group sessions. It is important to be systematic and thorough in laying a firm foundation. Some of the key elements for initial sessions include:

- Reflective writing based on The Five Core Propositions.
- Organization of the entry instructions, connected to the architecture of accomplished teaching.
- Types of writing in the entry: Description, analysis, and reflection.
- Unpacking an entry question, finding the cues for a complete response.

Basic learning principles apply to adults as well as to students. New information must be "in the zone" (See Chapter 6) to be accessible to the learner. As a teaching strategy, a CSP may seek a similar activity or entry question to create a common background for candidate discussion.

As Entry 4 is the only one that is virtually the same for all candidates, it is often used to illustrate and practice the types of writing, and to help candidates focus a response on the impact on student learning. Teacher's initial drafts seldom contain evidence-laden details. This understanding usually develops over time through continuous reflection and writing.

In support sessions, dialogue helps teachers to make the bridge between new and old, and to consider applications for newly integrated information. The exercises in the text are intended to provide starting places for focused dialogue among group members. When sessions include ample time for active participation between candidates as well as with the support provider, they have opportunities to absorb and create meaning from the process.

Such dialogue is, by nature, reflective and helps train participants to both think and write in ways that will support their work as candidates. Talking about teaching and the Standards with colleagues is a precursor to developing similarly reflective discourse in the Written Commentary for each entry. The average teacher rarely finds time for such quality conversations with fellow professionals, and most candidates find it a stimulating and refreshing aspect of their support experiences.

Reading Entries

All candidate support providers should have as much information about the assessment process as possible. In areas where candidate support networks are readily available and well organized, training for readers—or the readers themselves—may be provided.

When candidates seek help from new readers, experienced support providers can assist by scheduling a session to introduce readers to the big picture of the National Board for Professional Teaching Standards, candidate requirements, and the NBPTS *Policy for Ethical Candidate Support*. The reader must remember the personal nature of each entry, respect the candidate's work as thoughtful and valid, and refrain from making judgments about his or her capabilities in the classroom.

Everything that relates to a specific candidate, including all written work and even candidate status, is confidential. All support providers are expected to respect and honor this aspect of the National Board Certification process.

In order to provide appropriate and effective feedback to the candidate on a portfolio entry, you need to understand the Standards being assessed and the specific requirements of the entry. In addition to the writing and related artifacts, the candidate should provide you with "tools" including the Level 4 Rubric descriptors and prompts from the Portfolio Instructions, as described earlier in this book.

As a CSP, you must know how you can and cannot help the candidate. If your focus is on content, and you have limited experience of the NBPTS Certification process, do not attempt to advise the candidate on process-related questions. You must confer with your candidate so that both of you agree on the nature of your support, your understanding of task requirements, and your purpose for reading entries. A CSP cannot help but be invested in the success of the candidate, but must understand his or her role and limitations. It is not the CSP's job to advise, but rather to prompt the thinking of the candidate.

Figure 51 (Ways to Read - a Tool for Readers) offers a CSP ways to read and ask questions about an entry from different perspectives. Take a minute to look at this figure with candidates. A CSP might ask a candidate to focus a way to read, so the candidate can take ownership for finding evidence of accomplished teaching in their writing.

There are additional ways to invite a reflective discussion about accomplished teaching illustrated in the research today. One alternative perspective that might be helpful when talking with candidates is described by authors Fenwick and Steffy, et al in The Three-Minute Classroom Walk-Through (2006)[75]. Figure 52, (Sample Leads for a Reflective Discussion) frames a reflective discussion in terms of the five aspects of Steffy's research. This framework provides an outline to use with candidates or other teachers to ensure a thorough and reflective discussion about various aspects of teacher choice as they relate to classroom instruction.

Ways to Read – a Tool for Readers

	What is the focus?	What tools do you need?	What are some good questions to offer candidates as you read?
Read for core propositions.	Perhaps you want to use roman numerals or a highlighter to note places in the reading where you see the propositions.	The core propositions. Five colored highlighters.	Can you tell me more about what you know about students? What were the teaching objectives that you used for this lesson? How do they relate to the teaching expectations for students? What kind of assessments did you use in the entry? Tell me about your collaboration with other teachers for this entry… How did you work to include families in your entry?
Read to see if a candidate has answered the questions.	This is similar to reading for evidence.	A copy of the entry question. A pencil or highlighter as a way to identify the answer to each part of the question.	Can you help me to find the answer to the entry question? Where in your writing do you see…
Read for evidence of the Standards.	This way to read necessitates that the candidate has spent time reading and writing to the standards. This kind of writing happens more often with an advanced candidate.	The level four rubric. A copy of the Standards.	Can you tell me where you have shown an example of this kind of methodology as explained in the Standards? Let's look at the verbs you have used to describe your teaching… What kind of teaching methods/strategies did you choose for this lesson? Why?
Read for connectivity.	It is hardest to read for this aspect.	A good understanding of the entry question. The rubric. The contextual information that the candidate has written. A copy of Exercise 12-1 to show that the writing must have few holes and fractures.	Does the candidate refer to the contextual details within the writing? How does the description in the first few pages relate to the analysis/reflection in the entry? Can you "draw a line" between the factors in the first few pages and last few pages? Can you answer what happened? Can you answer why?
Read for level of detail.	You are reading to find specific examples of practice as described by the rubric.	The rubric.	The best way to do this is one-on-one with the candidate. With the candidate, have the rubric open and available as you both scan the document. Try to turn each aspect of the rubric into a question and use a highlighter to actually pinpoint a place in the writing where evidence is written. When reading for evidence, often a facilitator might use leading questions to encourage a candidate to think more deeply about their writing. Then a facilitator might turn the rubric into a question and scribe for the candidate the answers to the question that might inspire a different, deeper level of candidate reflection.

Figure 51. Ways to Read - a Tool for Readers.
Different perspectives, tools, and questions for reading a candidate's entry are described.

Sample Leads for a Reflective Discussion

Aspects of the Discussion	Beginning and Leading the Conversation
Situation	<ul><li>Tell me about…</li><li>How would you describe…?</li><li>Tell me more about…</li></ul>
Teacher reflection on curricular or instructional technique	<ul><li>Explain the ….</li><li>Why did you….?</li><li>What happened before this?</li><li>What happened next?</li><li>Why did you make this choice for these students, at this time, in this place?</li><li>What materials…..?</li></ul>
Teacher Choice	<ul><li>What do you know about your students that led you to this instructional/curricular teaching decision? Explain…</li><li>Why did you…?</li></ul>
The decision and thinking about teaching practice in a general way [reflection]	<ul><li>Tell me more about…</li><li>How did you feel when…?</li><li>Next time…</li><li>Discuss why…</li><li>What are you planning to do next?</li></ul>
Student impact	<ul><li>What have you noticed in your students…?</li><li>What kind of assessment did you use…?</li><li>How did you gauge success…?</li><li>What did the rubric look like…?</li><li>Where are your students now?</li></ul>

Figure 52: Sample Leads for a Reflective Discussion.
Adapted from *The Three-Minute Classroom Walk-Through,* five aspects of a reflective conversation about teaching are shown with prompting questions.

Working with Advanced Candidates

Advanced candidates may need a different kind of support, including recognition of the stages of grief experienced as a result of disappointing score results. We recommend that you walk through Chapter 15 with them, including the text and exercises, to help identify the specific areas that will help them improve their work. Figure 53 (Talking with an Advanced Candidate) may provide a useful outline for your discussion. Once specific areas of need are identified, selected exercises from previous chapters may be used to help the candidate build their skills.

Tools for Feedback

At the end of Chapter 16, we have provided some tools which may be useful to candidates. These include a Reader's Response Guide cover sheet, and two different types of Response Sheets. CSPs may wish to share these with candidates as tools to create and provide for their readers.

The Entry Prompts Reader Response Sheet invites the reader to indicate whether or not each question has been clearly and completely answered. As the prompts are designed to elicit evidence of Standards from the candidate, it is critical that a direct response is given. Candidates often give responses that are related to the prompt, but fail to address the prompt directly. Sometimes the prompt is only partially answered. By providing prompts to the reader on the response sheet, the feedback is structured to answer the specific question, "Did I respond to the prompt?"

On the Scoring Criteria Reader Response Sheet the reader is asked to indicate to what degree he or she sees evidence that the criteria have been met. In this case, the reader must consider the entry as a whole to give a response to each of the criteria. The scoring criteria for Entry 4: Documented Accomplishments are shown on the sample sheet. The Scoring Criteria Reader Response Sheet might be the only response sheet given for Entry 4, which has fewer question prompts than the classroom-based entries.

One or both types of response sheets may be used, with the reader acting as a detective in the search for evidence. The use of a response sheet helps focus the task of the reader to specific aspects of the entry and helps streamline and structure the feedback process for the reader.

Questioning Strategies

Questions to prompt reflection are found in the chapter exercises throughout this book. Other resources may offer useful models for coaching candidates.

Talking with an Advanced Candidate

Beginning the Discussion:
Where are you in the grieving process? Listen for signs that indicate:

Stage	Kinds of Questions/Comments
Denial	I don't know how this happened! Maybe parts of my portfolio were missing.
Anger	You read my entries and you didn't say anything about a problem! Why did this happen to me? I worked so hard!
Bargaining	Well, if I had better students or a better classroom, if I had more support I might have done better. It really wasn't all my fault.
Depression	I must not be an accomplished teacher. I will never be able to do it. I just don't have the skills. I can't write well enough.
Acceptance	I am ready to go on. I know I can do it. I will get more help and think deeply about the entry as I re-write. I will achieve!

Continuing the Discussion:
Are you ready to read my entry critically? Read with a candidate to discover:

What I see	Next Step
I see a gap in my writing and the standards	Do I need more content preparation?
I cannot find a beginning, middle, and end to my entry	Do you need more connectivity to the standards? Do you understand how to connect your writing, set the scene, make teaching decisions, show improved student learning?
I do not see answers to all the aspects of the question.	Did you answer the question?
I do not clearly see the different choices I made in regard to the students I chose	Did you choose students who allowed you to showcase your teaching?
I did not see examples of the standards in my videotape	Did the videotape actually show what was required in the directions?

Figure 53: Talking with An Advanced Candidate
A candidate support provider may need to talk with an advanced candidate with a different kind of sensitivity. A suggested outline is offered as you work through the process with an advanced candidate.

The Coaching Model

Although professional dialogue can be prompted in many ways, one of the most effective and appropriate methods for CSPs is the Cognitive Coaching™ model developed by Art Costa and Robert Garmston.[76] Through carefully chosen questions, the support provider prompts the candidate to consider specific aspects of the work without advising or suggesting specific revisions. The candidate has the sole responsibility for decision-making, but is guided to deeper thinking through the supporter's use of strategies including paraphrasing, clarifying, and prompting for elaboration.

In paraphrasing, the CSP avoids any interpretation, but simply reflects back or summarizes what he or she sees in a video, reads in an entry, or hears from a candidate. This allows the candidate to confirm that the reader "heard" the intended message.

Clarifying questions ask for more information about the teacher's thinking. This may be used when the teacher's response seems inadequate or unclear. Clarifying questions may help the candidate realize that more detail is needed to provide evidence. They may also be used when the response "wanders" from the question, to help the candidate see that he or she has not directly addressed the entry question.

> *Every so often, I just write "So what?" It is a clue for my candidate to re-examine the paragraph or sentence for its relevancy.*
>
> *- Sue Hovey, NBPTS Program Facilitator, University of Idaho*

In prompting for elaboration, the CSP urges the teacher to reflect more deeply, consider other aspects of the situation, and add even more detail. The use of specific details and examples in an entry are important, as they help provide the evidence and authenticity sought by an assessor.

We will use a fictitious conversation between a CSP and candidate to provide examples of these three types of CSP-response questions. Notice that the conversation contains many pauses, allowing the candidate to think before responding to the CSP's questions. In this example the candidate is a *Middle Childhood Generalist*, and the subject is an entry focused on literacy development:

> **CSP:** Let's start with the analysis section of this entry. I'd like you to read aloud the first prompt in your Portfolio Instructions, and your response to the prompt.
>
> **Candidate:** (Reads from Instructions): "What are the relevant and important characteristics of each child you have selected?" (Reads from her entry):

"One of the children I have selected is Kimo. I chose him because he is at the bottom of the class and needs a lot of help."

CSP- Paraphrase Response: You selected Kimo because you feel he needs more help than other children.
(The CSP simply restates what the candidate has said or implied. The candidate considers, "Is this what I meant to say in response to this prompt?")

PAUSE

Candidate: Yes, that's right. I thought I should choose him because he needs so much help.

CSP- Clarifying Response: Do you feel you have answered the question, "What are the relevant and important characteristics" of Kimo?

PAUSE

Tell me more about Kimo. Describe some of his characteristics that made you think of featuring him in your entry.
(The CSP has brought the candidate back to the wording of the prompt. She consciously provides a multiple response option by using the word "some"; the teacher is encouraged to share more than one feature of Kimo that is important or relevant.)

Candidate: Writers' Workshop is a regular feature of my classroom. Most of the other children readily choose their own topics and write with fluency. Kimo rarely has a topic idea of his own. Even after I help him decide what to write about, he has difficulty thinking of what to say. He can express himself well verbally, but not in writing. He transferred to my class from another school in November.
(Open-ended questioning has encouraged the teacher to give specific details about this student. Now the CSP can ask many more questions derived from the entry prompts, to help the candidate think about the most important aspects of her teaching that address the prompts.)

PAUSE

CSP- Elaboration Responses: Based on what the candidate has shared, the CSP might ask any or all of the following questions to prompt deeper thinking and more detail from the candidate:

1. What are some of the reasons these particular characteristics of Kimo are important when you think about goals for him in literacy?
2. When you think about those goals, what are you thinking of as teaching choices that you might make in the area of instructional strategies and methods for Kimo?
3. Given these characteristics of Kimo, do you think that your work with him will enable you to provide the evidence called for in this portfolio entry?
4. Tell me about the second child you chose for this entry. Does this child have different characteristics and needs?
5. Will your work with these two children allow you to demonstrate a range in your teaching abilities for this entry?

The CSP asks questions that prompt the teacher to think more deeply and analytically. Each question will prompt more conversation about what the teacher knows about students, content area, and teaching methodologies. The questions relate closely to the prompts in the Portfolio Instructions. Through the conversation with the CSP, the candidates are led to think about their teaching practice and their responses to the entry prompts.

By using thoughtfully chosen questions and pauses, the CSP encourages the teacher to reflect and articulate personal thinking. An experienced facilitator may deliberately "map" the conversation about an entry from the big idea of the lesson through the small parts that are needed to construct it. The teacher is led to think about the "big idea" — the goals for the lesson—to analyzing decisions about selected strategies, student groupings, materials, assessment, and next steps for students.

Clearly, the CSP must have a good understanding of the entry requirements in order to effectively prompt the candidate. The CSP's job is to guide a professional dialogue that helps the candidate make his or her own decisions. CSPs should not attempt to provide answers as, in doing so, they reduce the candidate's personal responsibility for the work.

Cognitive Coaching is just one model that may help increase professional dialogue among educators who seek to improve student learning. By targeting thought processes as the focus of behavioral change, it encourages teachers to be self-monitoring, self-managing, and self-modifying reflective practitioners.

What if the Candidate's Work Lacks Substance?

As a reader and CSP for candidates, you are charged with the difficult task of giving feedback without overtly judging the quality of the work. As you gain experience reading for many different candidates, you will inevitably see entries that you feel are significantly lacking in evidence of accomplished teaching. What should you do? Should you tell a candidate they are not ready for National Board Certification? Should you help the candidate "fix" the entry? How much help should you give?

The purpose for using questioning strategies in a personal conversation with the candidate, as described above, is to help candidates make their own decisions. This is especially important when the work seems well below the entry requirements. There may be a variety of reasons for a poorly written entry: Is it due to lack of focus? Lack of writing ability? Lack of evidence? Lack of teaching ability?

Even for many capable teachers, the skills required for a well-written entry are new. Never before have they been asked to write about what they do and why they do it. Learning how to provide evidence requires focus and organization, as well as detail and precision in writing. Teachers often assume that the reasons behind their teaching decisions are obvious and feel irritated when told they must explicitly describe their thinking processes. They are often unaccustomed to "thinking about their thinking," and need time to develop conscious reflection skills.

A reader or CSP should never tell candidate they are not ready for National Board Certification, as it simply is not appropriate to do so. Only the candidate should make this decision. By using the questioning strategies described in the previous section, the CSP may be able to determine what kind of help the candidate needs, and can guide the candidate to self-understanding.

If detail or evidence is missing in the work, the CSP consciously structures a question that requires the candidate to discover what has been left out, as in our sample conversation: *"Do you feel you have answered the question, 'What are the relevant and important characteristics of Kimo?'"*

Other questions encourage the candidate to elaborate, give rationales, and open up the professional decision-making process: *"Tell me more about Kimo. What are some of the characteristics about Kimo that have made you think of featuring him in your entry?"* (Listen to candidate response, then ask) *"Do you think some of the things you've just told me about Kimo have influenced your teaching decisions for him? Tell me more about that...."*

Teachers are often able to verbally articulate needed evidence that is lacking in their initial written drafts and can learn to put their thoughts in writing through assistance from their CSP assistance and participation in candidate groups. Based on the example above, when the teacher can talk about "Kimo," his personal qualities, learning challenges, and the responses to them, the teacher may simply need to learn new thinking and writing skills.

When the teacher cannot describe "Kimo's" specific characteristics and is not able to explain teaching decisions in regards to "Kimo," other needs are indicated. Faced with an inability to adequately respond to the entry prompts and CSP questions, the candidate is encouraged to re-evaluate readiness for the process.

This teacher can be referred back to the Standards for the entry, asked to compare each Standard to the Written Commentary, and highlight where the evidence has been provided. It is the responsibility of the candidate to identify the evidence in the work. Candidates who are unable to do so cannot expect to be successful.

Even in this case, teachers may learn how to think about their work as they participate in candidate groups and hear other teachers describe their students and think aloud about their teaching decisions. Groups provide less capable candidates with models and motivation for needed professional growth. When teachers realize they are not ready for National Board Certification, they may decide to quit the process altogether or to postpone it and continue participating as pre-candidates.

So, how much help should you give? Candidate support providers may differ in their responses to this question. Some may feel that only minimal help should be given, as accomplished teachers must "prove" that they are deserving of National Board Certification. However, there is growing consensus in the field that National Board Certification is, first and foremost, a professional development experience. For this reason, many CSPs are willing to coach candidates through the process of growth for three years when called upon to do so. Advanced candidates, by definition, need to develop their thinking and writing abilities in relationship to the task requirements, and may benefit tremendously from the candidate support relationship.

Advanced candidates deserve special consideration by candidate support providers. They are already heavily invested in the National Board Certification process, and have experienced the disappointment of falling short of success. Often the difference between candidates who successfully certify and those who do not is literally a matter of a few points. We encourage you to help all candidates reflect on the intrinsic value of the certification process from the beginning of the support experience. In doing so, a positive professional climate is established, and the teacher is more able to adjust and move forward as an advanced candidate.

Candidate support providers do not "fix" entries by suggesting specific revisions or telling a teacher to change a lesson. They *do* help candidates understand what is needed by prompting deeper thinking and helping them develop needed skills. Teachers are expected to grow and improve their practices as part of the National Board Certification process. They are respected as professionals who are solely responsible for the content of their written entries and performance on the assessment center exercises. Candidate support providers are expected to honor and support each teacher's professional development journey, no matter where they are on the path. This is the key to National Board Certification. You are not the keeper of the key, but the link that helps each candidate unlock his own personal story of accomplished teaching.

It may help you, as a support provider, to think of National Board Certification as a process in which candidates sort and choose from their repertoires of teaching skills and behaviors to find those that represent the essentials of accomplished teaching. Candidates must distill years of practice and identify and articulate Standards-based practices in their portfolio responses.

Discussion Points for Candidates and Support Providers

Establishing the ground rules of the CSP/reader-candidate relationship is extremely important in order to honor the intent of the National Board Certification process, and to clarify responsibilities and expectations from both sides. Candidates and their CSPs must thoroughly discuss the nature of their relationship including time, communications, and responsibilities of each party.

Time

Time will be an issue for candidates throughout the first year of National Board Certification due to the demands of the process. CSPs must define the amount of time and availability they have for a single candidate. This is especially important for those working with more than one candidate.

Candidates are often timely with entry submission to readers as they begin the process, and, for the most part, CSPs are able to stay paced with them. As the submission deadline approaches, candidates working down to the wire want CSPs to read more entries and give feedback more quickly. The CSP may become exhausted trying to keep up with candidate requests. Discussion points about time for CSPs and candidates include the following:

1. **Quantity**: The candidate will complete four written commentaries, and will most likely produce multiple drafts for each one. What volume of material will the CSP read for a given candidate? First drafts only? Multiple drafts of one entry? Multiple drafts of each entry? Many CSPs limit the number of candidates for whom they will read and/or limit the number of drafts they will read due to time constraints.

As part of a quantity-control effort, the CSP might request that the candidate complete certain exercises (as found in earlier chapters), or might have someone else pre-read the entry for a specific purpose. A teacher-colleague might be asked to read for clarity and alignment of goals, instruction, analysis, and reflection before the process CSP reads for evidence of Standards.

2. **Feedback**: After giving the reader an entry, how soon can the candidate expect feedback? How will the feedback be given? Is the reader providing feedback on content, process, or both? Candidates will want feedback as soon as possible when they are engaged with an entry.

3. **Schedule**: The candidate might prepare a master calendar and share that with the CSP, with dates for anticipated completion of drafts. This encourages the candidate to stick to a schedule and pace himself through the work, and allows the CSP to anticipate when help might be needed most.

4. **Availability**: The CSP may wish to define specific days and times of availability for candidates, rather than being "on-call." Some CSPs establish "office hours" for candidates during which they are available to receive calls. Candidates must remember that experienced CSPs may be providing support for up to 20 candidates, and it is wise to have a back-up reader in case one person is not available.

Communications

In an ideal picture of the candidate-CSP relationship, the two parties meet regularly for extended dialogue over the candidate's work. In reality, few candidates will enjoy this degree of attention. CSPs are often busy professionals with a variety of commitments, and must consciously define the nature of and schedule for their support.

An initial face-to-face meeting helps set the tone for the relationship between candidate and CSP, but thereafter other formats, such as phone, fax, and e-mail may provide more flexible options for both parties. CSPs and candidates may have different comfort levels with each style of communication, and there are advantages and disadvantages to each.

Some CSPs really want to "see" candidates and provide multi-dimensional feedback. The face-to-face meeting offers a candidate a chance to hear a message, see an expression, and sense a body position and tone while reacting to constructive criticism. Face-to-face and phone conferences allow CSPs to use the questioning strategies that help develop candidate thinking processes; however, they require both parties to commit to a common meeting time and suitable location.

Those with busy schedules may prefer to communicate by fax or e-mail as they are less time-restrictive. Although fax and e-mail are less personal, the candidate is provided with written feedback that can be revisited while teaching and writing. Such methods may be the only option for those engaged in long-distance support relationships. Fax and e-mail can also be combined with phone or face-to-face conversations. See Figure 2 (Selecting the Right Kind of Support for You), in Chapter 2: Support Systems. Find what works for you!

Responsibilities of Each Party

In the candidate-CSP relationship, both parties have a responsibility to keep agreements regarding the nature of support and the CSP's time availability. See the suggested Guiding Principles, Figure 3 in Chapter 2: Support Systems.

The CSP has a responsibility to limit support to what is appropriate given regarding their area of expertise. CSPs help candidates develop skills and perspectives, but do not direct candidates to any specific action on an entry. The candidate must begin early, and write often. The writing is the vehicle for growth, and without it candidate supporters cannot help. In a group support situation, it is especially frustrating to the facilitator when candidates come to the session unprepared.

Likewise, candidates who wait until the last minute to begin writing do a disservice to themselves as well as to their readers. A poorly written entry is a chore to read. By writing early and often, candidates develop their understanding and skills well ahead of their deadlines, and can approach remaining entries more easily. Candidates typically spend a great deal of time on the first entry, as they build understanding and skills for the process. The candidate also has a responsibility to provide as much information to the reader as is possible and necessary for effective feedback.

Once an entry has been submitted, that entry becomes the property of NBPTS. CSPs and former candidates must be mindful about how entry pieces are shared or otherwise used for training purposes.

Mentor programs need [to build] relationships and foundational skills. "Getting it" takes a little prompting (mentor relationship), a little skill (foundational support), and then candidates come to it themselves.

-Kathy Prisbell, NBCT/Candidate Support Provider, New Jersey

As Support Sessions Come to a Close

Most candidate support providers feel a sense of investment in the candidates they have accompanied through the process, and await the results of scoring with excitement and anticipation. They hope that their work has been fruitful in terms of helping candidates to tell their own stories effectively and to achieve National Board Certification.

At the same time, most are well aware that the likelihood of every candidate achieving certification on their first attempt is slim, and they must be prepared to support and encourage those who move into advanced candidacy. It is important to remind candidates before scores are released that completion of the process itself is a notable achievement, and they are different as teachers because of the process.

In the previous chapter, we talked to candidates about reflecting on the value of the certification process, and preparing a suitable message in response to questions that will be asked before and after scores are released. We have included an exercise at the end of this chapter to help you work with candidates as they reflect on their experience. The opportunity to craft a message can be a powerful way for a candidate to summarize the value of the process of certification. It also personalizes and promotes a positive attitude about a high and rigorous process of certification.

We encourage you to use Exercise 17-1: Reflecting On Your Message to help candidates prepare for their future status, either as a new NBCT or an advanced candidate. If the process itself has value for teachers, the message should be similar in both cases. Connecting to the deeper outcomes of the experience may help advanced candidates move forward, and emphasizes the significance of the National Board Teaching Standards for the profession as a whole. You might also refer to Figure 50 (Creating Your Message) in Chapter 16: Building the Professional Community to lead candidates through these reflective questions as your support sessions come to a close.

Once scores are released and advanced candidates are identified, continue to provide support to those who are faced with decisions about re-submitting entries or exercises. Refer these candidates to Chapter 14: Scoring and Chapter 15: Advanced Candidacy for assistance, and help them weigh the issues in making choices about which sections to resubmit. As they re-enter the process, provide tools to help them analyze their performance on the entry that did not do well, or direct them to resources that may help them prepare to retake an exercise. Be there as a support and remind them of the value intrinsic to the process.

Your Growth as a Candidate Support Provider

As a candidate support provider, you serve as a guide for candidates who are finding their way through a complex process. You too are changed as a result of the individuals you encounter in the process and the challenges that are posed to you. As your support sessions come to a close, reflect on your own growth through the process. What worked well? What could be improved? What would you do differently if you taught these lessons again? Do these questions sound familiar? As you know by now, the journey of accomplished teaching is never over.

Key Points for Candidate Support Providers

- To read and give feedback, you will need large blocks of uninterrupted time. If you find an entry is a chore to read, STOP—try to pinpoint a key problem (such as lack of clear goals, lack of architecture) and return it to the candidate for revision. Do not tax yourself by trying to give extensive feedback on an entry that has fundamental problems. Previous chapters in this book, including Chapter 9: Reflective Practice, may help candidates understand how to improve an entry.

- Consider bias as a factor when you read. If you encounter poor technical writing in candidate work, remember the National Board does not take away points for grammar and spelling errors.

- When conferencing with a candidate, read the entry ahead of time so that you can give thoughtful feedback. When you meet with a candidate, it is helpful to have video equipment and a quiet place to talk. The use of markers, sticky notes, and colored pens are also helpful as you conference with candidates.

- Your work as a candidate support provider is about reflection and growth, for the candidate and for you. Stay open-minded to candidates and what you can learn from them. Sharing is a two-way street!

- Be sure that you are familiar with the NBPTS *Guide for Ethical Candidate Support*, so that you understand the limitations of your support. You must NEVER share entries or videos submitted by former candidates including your own entries. All submitted entries are the property of NBPTS.

- There are many ways to read for a candidate. Be sure to ask the candidate how they want to have you read, and concentrate on this one aspect as you read through an entry. In this way, the candidates will take responsibility for the entire entry, and begin to see your reading as specific and narrow, not holistic. Refer to Chapter 9: Reflective Practice and Ways to Read in this chapter for focal points and suggestions on reading entries.

- Many candidate support providers limit their reading to a certain number of times per entry. This is a decision that readers must make, based on their time commitments and their preferences. Consider limiting the number of times that you read a particular entry. Reading multiple times may suggest to a candidate that you are a part of the writing experience for the entry, and this is not what you want. As a CSP, you want to be sure to let the candidates retain ownership for each entry piece.

Exercise 17-1: Reflecting on Your Message

Messages Based on The Five Core Propositions

Key Aspects of The Five Core Propositions	Who will I be speaking to?	What will I say?

Messages Based on Research

Key aspects of the research	Who will I be speaking to?	What will I say?

Directions: Use the templates above to develop succinct messages that will help you respond to questions about the National Board Certification process. Your goal is convince others that the NBPTS Standards and certification process are valuable contributions to the teaching profession.

REFERENCES

[1] Morrow, J.G. (1999) *The best thing about my teacher*. Nashville, TN:Broadman & Holman.

[2] Berg, Jill Harrison. Improving the Quality of Teaching Through National Board Certification, Theory and Practice. Norwood: Christopher-Gordon Publishers, Inc., 2003.

[3] Wormeli, Rick. Meet Me in The Middle: Becoming an Accomplished Middle-Level Teacher. Portland: Stenhouse Publications, 2001.

[4] Danielson, Charlotte Teacher Leadership.Alexandria: ASCD, 2006.

[5]"Recruitment." www.nbpts.org. National Board Certification. 2006 <http://www.nbpts.org/for_nbcts/recruitment/cfm>."

[6]"Research." www.nbpts.org. National Board Certification. 2006 <http://www.nbpts.org/resources/research.cfm>.

[7]Schmoker, Mike, Results Now.Alexandria:ASCD, 2006.

[8]Heibert, J. and Stigler J.W. (2004fall) A World of Difference Classrooms abroad provide lesson teaching math and science *Journal of Staff Development, 25(4)* 10-15.

[9] O'Neil, John. "Credentials Count." NEA Today (January 2003). 08 May 2004 <http://www.nea.org/neatoday/0301/scoop.html>.

[10]"Archived: A Nation at Risk." April 1983. ED.gov. National Commission on Excellence in Education. 08 May 2004. <http://www.ed.gov/pubs/NatAtRisk/risk.html>.

[11] Carnegie Foundation Task Force on Teaching as a Profession. (1986). A Nation Prepared: Teachers for the 21st Century. The Report of the Task Force on Teaching as a Profession, Carnegie Foundation for the Advancement of Teaching.

[12]"Press Release: Number of National Board Teachers® Tops 55,000® ." January 9, 2007 ". www.nbpts.org. National Board for Professional Teaching Standards.2007. < >.

[13] "Why America Needs National Board Certified Teachers." August 2002. www.nbpts.org. National Board for Profession Teaching Standards. 08 May 2004. <http://www.nbpts.org/pdf/why.pdf>.

[14] "NBRC:NCATE,INTASC,NBPTS standards." nbrc.stanford.edu. NBRC:National Board Resource Center. 08 May 2004. <http://nbrc.stanford.edu/align/standards.html>.

[15] Ibid – "Higher Education Initiatives"

[16] What Matters Most: Teaching for America's Future. 1st ed. New York: The National Commission on Teaching and America's Future, 1996.

[17] Grossman, "Teaching: From A Nation at Risk to a Profession at Risk." Harvard Education Letter Research Online (2003). 11 June 2004. www.edletter.org

[18] Lussier, David. "Letter to the Editor." Education Week 02 April 2002, .

[19] About Graduate Credit." 17 May 2004. www.nbpts.org. National Board for Professional Teaching Standards. 18 May 2004 <http://www.nbpts.org/highered/ace.cfm >.

[20] Steffy, Betty E., Michael P. Wolfe, Suzanne H. Pasch, and Billie J. Enz. Life Cycle of a Career Teacher. Thousand Oaks: Corwin Press, 2000.

[21] Ibid - Steffy

[22] "NBPTS Guide to National Board Certification." www.nbpts.org. National Board for Professional Teaching Standards.2006. <http://www.nbpts.org/candidates/guide/>.

[23] "Making Good Choices." NBPTS Facilitators Institute I Guide ( ): p.1.

[24] Ibid - Making Good Choices.

[25] "Portfolio Instructions." www.nbpts.org. National Board for Professional Teaching Standards. 2006 <http://www.nbpts.org/candidates/portfolios.cfm>.

[26] Heibert, James, Ronald Gallimore, and James Stigler. "The New Heros of Teaching." Education Week ( ): .

[27] "Certificate Knowledge Center." 04 2004. www.nbpts.org. National Board for Professional Teaching Standards. 2006 <http://www.nbpts.org/candidates/ckc.cfm>.

[28] Ibid – "Making Good Choices"

[29] Apleman, Maja. "Working with Teachers." <u>Thought and Practice:the Journal of the Graduate School of Bank Street College of Education</u> 3 ( ): pp74-84.

[30] National University, La Jolla CA
<http://www.nu.edu/Academics/Schools/SOE/TeacherEducation/degrees/710-716.html>

[31] Ibid – "Making Good Choices"

[32] Portfolio Instructions." <u>www.nbpts.org</u>. National Board for Professional Teaching Standards. 2006
<http://www.nbpts.org/candidates/portfolios.cfm>.

[33] Shelley Sherman, "Responsiveness in Teaching: Responsibility in its most Particular Sense" The Educational Forum. West Lafayette: winter 2004. vol 68, Iss.2; pg 115- 124.

[34] Tripp, David. <u>Critical Incidents in Teaching Developing Professional Judgement</u>: Routledge Falmer, 1994.

[35] Stipek, Deborah and Kathy Seal <u>Motivated Minds: Raising Children to Love Learning</u>, Henry Holt and Company, LLC, New York, 2001.

[36] Ibid – Stipek

[37] Levine, Mel, <u>A Mind at a Time</u> Simon and Schuster:New York, NY 2002.

[38] Moran, Seana Mindy Kornhaber, Howard Gardner. <u>Orchestrating Multiple Intelligences</u>, Educational Leadership, Sept. 2006, Vol 64 No.1 ASCD pg 27.

[39] Owens, Cathy. (2005, July). *Take One! An evidence centered approach to accomplished teaching.* Session presented at the biannual conference of the National Board for Professional Teaching Standards, Washington, D. C.

[40] Carol Ann Tomlinson and Jane Jarvis, <u>Teaching Beyond the Book, Educational Leadership</u>, Sept. 2006, Vol 64 No.1 ASCD pg 17.

[41] Vygotsky, L. S. (1978). Mind and society: The development of higher mental processes. Cambridge, MA: Harvard University Press.

[42] Rodgers, Carol R. "Communities of Reflection, Communities of Support" published in *Research on Professional Development Schools: the Teacher Education Yearbook, VIII.*

[43] Gordon Morrow, Judy <u>The Best Things About My Teacher, Notes of Appreciation From Students.</u> Nashville, TN:Broadman Holman.

[44]"Standards."2006. <u>www.nbpts.org</u>. National Board for Professional Teaching Standards. 2006 <http://www.nbpts.org/standards/stds.cfm>.

[45]"Early Adolescence / Science Portfolio Instructions."2006. <u>www.nbpts.org</u>. National Board for Professional Teaching Standards. 18 2006 <http://www.nbpts.org/candidates/guide/04port/04_ea_sci.html>.

[46]Corcoran , C.A. & Leahy, R.(2003). Growing Professionally Through Reflective Practice.Kappa Delta Pi. 30-33.

[47] Steffy, Betty E., Michael P. Wolfe, Suzanne H. Pasch, and Billie J. Enz, <u>Life Cycle of a Career Teacher</u>. Thousand Oaks: Corwin Press, 2000.

[48] Ibid – Corcoran and Leahy.

[49] Ibid – Steffy.

[50] Taggart, Germaine and Alfred Wilson, <u>Promoting Reflective Thinking in Teaching: 44 Action Strategies</u>. Thousand Oaks: Corwin Press 1998.

[51] Middle Childhood Generalist Portfolio Instructions."2006. <u>www.nbpts.org</u>. National Board for Professional Teaching Standards. 2006 <http://www.nbpts.org/candidates/guide/04port/04_ea_ela.html >.

[52]Lussier, David. "Letter to the Editor." <u>Education Week</u> 02 April 2002.

[53] Henriques, Marlene. "Candidate Support." National Board for Professional Teaching Standards - 2003 National Conference. Hyatt Conference Center at Reston Town Center, Washington, DC. 15 November 2003.

[54] Ibid - "Portfolio Instructions" – *Middle Childhood Generalist*, Entry 2, 2006-07.

[55] *Idaho Advice.* Used with permission from Sue Hovey, NBPTS Program Facilitator, University of Idaho.

[56] Armstrong, Thomas, <u>The Best Schools</u>, ASCD: Alexandria, VA, 2006.

[57] Ibid – "Portfolio Instructions"

[58] Ibid – Corcoran and Leahy.

[59] Scoring Guides." www.nbpts/org. National Board for Professional Teaching Standards. 18 May 2004 <http://www.nbpts.org/candidates/scoringguides.cfm>.

[60] "Portfolio Instructions" – *AYA Social Studies - History* Certificate, 2006.

[61] "Candidate Resource Center: About the Scoring Handbook." Nov 2003. www.nbpts.org. National Board for Professional Teaching Standards. 18 May 2004 <http://www.nbpts.org/candidates/scoringhandbook.cfm>.

[62] Ibid Candidate Resource Center: About the Scoring Handbook <http://www.nbpts.org/candidates/scoringhandbook.cfm>.

[63] Greene, Bob *From Failure to Famous* Readers' Digest <http://www.joesabah.com/dseibert/008.htm retrieved 3-04-07>

[64] Elizabeth Kubler-Ross and David Kessler Macmillan Library References USA Inc Simon and Schuster 2005 On Grief and Grieving: Finding the Meaning of Grief through the Five Stages of Loss.

[65] Steffy, Betty E., Michael P. Wolfe, Suzanne H. Pasch, and Billie J. Enz. Life Cycle of a Career Teacher. Thousand Oaks: Corwin Press, 2000.

[66] Barth, Roland, "The Culture Builder." Educational Leadership, 59.(1) : 5 – 11.

[67] Ibid – Steffy.

[68] Gladwell, Malcolm, The Tipping Point Little, Brown and Company: USA 2002.

[69] Ibid – Lussier.

[70] Patterson, Jackie and Jerry Patterson, "Sharing the Lead." Educational Leadership, 61 (7): 74 – 78.

[71] Darling-Hammond & Sykes, 1990 as referenced in Accountability for Learning Douglas Reeves ASCD 2004 p.50.

[72] Nieto, Sonia M., What Keeps Teachers Going?. Columbia University: Teachers College Press, 2003.

[73] Williams, Jackie S., "Why Great Teachers Stay," <u>Educational Leadership</u>, 60 (1) :71-74.

[74] Shields, Carolyn M. , "Creating a Community of Differences.," <u>Educational Leadership</u>, 61 (7) : 41.

[75] Fenwick English, Betty Steffy, Larry Frase, William Poston, <u>The Three Minute Classroom Walk-Through Changing School Supervisory Practice One Teacher At a Time</u> Corwin Press: Thousand Oaks, CA 2004.

[76] Costa, Arthur and Robert Garmston, <u>Cognitive Coaching a Foundation for Renaissance Schools</u>. Norwood, MA: Christopher-Gordon Publishers, 1994.

INDEX

Writing About Your Entry 4
Artifact (Exercise 10-6), 175,
182
Written Commentary, 114. *see
also* writing
    alignment to learning goals,
      187–189
    common pitfalls in, 190–193
    composing, 76–77

Y

Your Contextual Information
Sheet (Exercise 6-1), 91, 94,
107

Your Growth as a Candidate
Support Provider, 322
Your Instructional Context
(Exercise 6-2), 94–96, 108

Z

zone of proximal development,
103